Contemporary Customary Land Issues in Africa

Contemporary Customary Land Issues in Africa:

Navigating the Contours of Change

Edited by

Horman Chitonge

and Bridget Bwalya Umar

Cambridge Scholars Publishing

Contemporary Customary Land Issues in Africa:
Navigating the Contours of Change

Edited by Horman Chitonge and Bridget Bwalya Umar

This book first published 2018

Cambridge Scholars Publishing

Lady Stephenson Library, Newcastle upon Tyne, NE6 2PA, UK

British Library Cataloguing in Publication Data
A catalogue record for this book is available from the British Library

ISBN (10): 1-5275-1100-6
ISBN (13): 978-1-5275-1100-2

CONTENTS

Part III: Land, Mining, and Rural Livelihoods

Part IV: Comparative Case Studies of Land-Tenure Reforms and Livelihoods in Africa

List of Tables

List of Figures

ACRONYMS

AC	Advisory Council
ACET	African Centre for Economic Transformation
AfDB	African Development Bank
AGRA	Alliance for Green Revolution in Africa
ANC	African National Congress
AU	African Union
BSACo	British South African Company
CAS	Centre for African Studies
CDC	Chongwe District Council
CDE	Centre for Development and Enterprise
CHDM	Chris Hani District Municipality
CLS	Customary Land Secretariat
CSO	Central Statistical Office
CSOT	Community Share Ownership Trust
CSR	Corporate Social Responsibility
DAFF	Department of Agriculture, Forestry, and Fisheries
DBSA	Development Bank of Southern Africa
DfID	Department for International Development
DLA	Department of Land Affairs
EAZ	Economic Association of Zambia
ECA	Economic Commission for Africa
EU	European Union
FDI	Foreign Direct Investment
FGD	Focus Group Discussion
FMD	Foot and Mouth Disease
FSRP	Food Security Research Project
FTLRP	Fast Track Land Reform Programme
GDP	Gross Domestic Product
GRZ	Government of the Republic of Zambia
IFC	International Finance Corporation
IFI	International Financial Institution
IFPRI	International Food Policy Research Institute
ILD	Institute for Liberty and Democracy
ILO	International Labour Organisation
IMF	International Monetary Fund
KRS	Kusanga Research Station

KZN	KwaZulu-Natal
LAP	Land Administration Project
LLDP	Lilongwe Land Development Programme
LRRP	Land Reform and Resettlement Programme
LURLAP	Land Use and Rural Livelihood in Africa Project
MACO	Ministry of Agriculture and Cooperatives
MMD	Movement for Multiparty Democracy
MTNR	Ministry of Natural Resources and Tourism
NECSA	National Energy Corporation of South Africa
NGO	Nongovernmental Organisation
NORM	Naturally Occurring Radioactive Metals
NPC	National Planning Commission
PCLET	Parliamentary Committee on Land, Environment, and Tourism
PE	Political Ecology
PGM	Platinum Group Metals
PLAAS	Institute for Poverty, Land, and Agrarian Studies
PPA	Participatory Poverty Assessments
SADC	Southern African Development Community
SAP	Structural Adjustment Programme
SNNP	South Nations Nationalities People
SSA	Sub-Saharan Africa
UCT	University of Cape Town
UNDP	United Nations Development Programme
UNIP	United National Independence Party
UNZA	University of Zambia
USAID	United States Agency for International Development
VC	Village Council
VDC	Village Development Committee
WRD	World Development Report
ZACF	Zambia Agricultural Consultative Forum
ZANACO	Zambia National Commercial Bank
ZANU PF	Zimbabwe African National Union, Patriotic Front
ZAWA	Zambia Wildlife Authority
ZDA	Zambia Development Agency
ZEMA	Zambia Environmental Management Agency
ZESA	Zimbabwe Electricity Supply Authority
ZLA	Zambia Land Alliance
ZNA	Zambia National Archives

CHAPTER ONE

CONTEMPORARY CUSTOMARY-LAND ISSUES IN AFRICA: AN INTRODUCTION

HORMAN CHITONGE AND
BRIDGET BWALYA UMAR

Land-tenure and agrarian-transformation debates in Africa are once more taking centre stage in policy discussions across the continent. The African Union (AU) Framework and Guidelines on Land Policy in Africa (AU/AfDB/ECA 2010) identifies several reasons for the growing attention given to land-tenure issues in Africa. These include the growing population, global climate change, urbanisation, steadily rising food prices globally, and the growing demand for cleaner energy from biofuels. The document also mentions increased investment in land-intensive economic activities. These and other related factors are reported to have induced a "new scramble for Africa" leading to "accelerated exploitation of resources...together with the establishment of industries and processing infrastructure," all of which require land (AU/AfDB/ECA 2010, 11). In this new scramble for Africa, tenure relations and rural livelihoods are increasingly under scrutiny as the demand for land grows, leading to the redefinition of land rights and relations and to contestation over rights, particularly in rural areas. In this context, this book examines evolving tenure relations and local politics concerning customary land and how these are contributing to changing land-tenure practices and rural livelihoods in many parts of the continent. Drawing from the Zambian experience, the book's chapters focus particularly on the dynamics induced by the policy and practice of alienating customary land to leasehold tenure. The book also presents a comparative analysis of the current land-tenure reforms in Ethiopia, Malawi, and Ghana and of land use and rural livelihoods in Zambia and South Africa. A chapter on Zimbabwe's Fast Track Land Reform Programme

(FTLRP) also discusses an interesting interplay between artisanal mining and farming in terms of a two-way flow of investment from mining to farming and vice versa.

The starting point for any discussion of changes in customary-land tenure in Africa today is the fact that land still holds a special position in many African communities, especially in rural areas. Not only is land a factor of production and an important source of livelihood for the majority of rural households, it is also a cultural and spiritual resource that plays a prominent role in uniting past, present, and future generations. The AU Framework and Guidelines on Land Policy in Africa (AU/AfDB/ECA 2010, 8) document captures this well when it argues:

> to the vast majority of societies in Africa land is regarded not simply as an economic or environmental resource, but as a social, cultural and ontological resource. Land remains an important factor in the construction of social identity, the organisation of religious life and the production and reproduction of culture. The link across generations is ultimately defined by the complement of land resources which families, lineages and communities share and control.[1]

Viewed from this angle, land is a central component of the African worldview and ontology, a fundamental resource around which life in its entirety—particularly in rural areas—revolves. This embedded nature of land relations in most of Africa's rural communities has often been a source of confusion and misunderstanding, especially among non-Africans (Makunike 2009), who, during colonial rule, projected "their own (European) models of land tenure onto African societies" (Bassett 1993, 5). Over the years, the approach of interpreting land-tenure relations in Africa through the lens of Western property-rights and ownership concepts has continued to hinder and sometimes frustrate efforts to grasp the essence of tenure relations and arrangements that are specific to the continent (Okoth-Ogendo 1989).

While the land question in Africa originates in the colonial occupation and the subsequent introduction of a European conception of ownership and property regimes, we are currently seeing a new form of contestation not just about the meaning of customary tenure but also about its relevance and ability to survive in the context of changing African societies. One clear example of this is the growing practice of converting customary land to leasehold tenure in many African countries, driven by what some analysts refer to as the "rediscovery of the agriculture sector by different investors" (both foreign and local), leading to a rising tide of "interest in land acquisition in developing countries" (see Deininger et al. 2011b, xxv).

In many African countries, including Zambia, most of the land being acquired for investment is held under customary tenure. Before investment in the land begins, the acquired land is usually converted to leasehold tenure as a way of securing the investment. This has led to the resurgence of the land and agrarian question(s) in Africa (Moyo 2008), raising questions not just about the future of customary land but also about rural livelihoods. This is especially true in a context in which job creation and opportunities in most African countries have fallen far below expectations, which means that most economies cannot absorb the rapidly growing labour force, especially in urban areas (see AfDB 2013).

The other related question resurfacing in the context of the growing demand for arable land is how to improve production and productivity, particularly on land held by semisubsistence farmers, who often access and use customary land. This question relates to longstanding concerns about land helping to improve food security and reduce rural poverty. A quick glance at the literature reveals that this issue surfaced in the 1980s, in the midst of what was then called the "African food crisis" (Berry 1984), and ignited debates, which largely attributed the crisis to the constraints that customary tenure imposed on land productivity and investment. The policy responses recommended at the time revolved around state-led land titling and other customary-land formalisation programmes, which were seen as the only way to attract investment and, consequently, stimulate productivity growth in the agriculture sector. For instance, the World Bank is reported to have provided loans to fund a series of "land titling and cadastral projects in Sub-Saharan Africa on the assumption that title will confer the necessary security to stimulate agricultural investments and thus increase productivity" (Bassett 1993, 4). While the policy to promote state-led and donor-sponsored land titling has since fallen off the land-reform radar,[2] with the World Bank adjusting its position on land titling during the course of the 1990s (see Deininger and Binswanger 1999), we are now seeing a new drive towards market-led land titling that targets customary land. Chiefs and local and foreign investors, supported by a government policy of attracting investment into rural areas, are the key drivers of this new trend towards privatisation of customary land (Cotula et al. 2009).

Yet, the experience of past land titling programmes has shown that titling customary land will not automatically lead to more investment and productivity in rural areas. A fundamental truth is that other factors influence rural residents' ability to turn land into a highly productive asset: "The notion that tenure reform is the panacea to Africa's agrarian ills is an old idea that ignores critical social dynamics that strongly influence how productive resources are acquired, utilized, contested and immobilized" (Bassett 1993, 4).

In pursuing market-led land titling, African governments strongly believe that markets will accomplish what the government-led titling programmes of the 1970s and 1980s failed to do, with the state simply creating an environment in which the land market can be activated and nurtured. But some governments, as several chapters on Zambia in this book illustrate, are ambivalent in their approach to the customary-land issue. This is evident in their adoption of policies that promote the titling of customary land through conversion into leasehold, on the one hand, while legally and publicly recognising the status of customary land and the institutions of traditional authorities, on the other. Aware of the growing ambivalence on land policy in the continent, many civil society groups and researchers have cautioned against a wholesale endorsement of the policy and practice of alienating customary land, arguing that such an approach compromises access to land for future generations in many communities, given the critical role that land access plays in rural livelihoods across Africa.

While few analysts dispute the view that access to land can play a critical role in the fight against rural poverty (see AGRA 2013), unanswered questions remain about how to improve productivity among households with access to land. Similarly, questions remain about whether the emergence of "vernacular" or informal markets on customary land would help to increase productivity and improve the well-being of those who have access to such land. In a context in which monetary transactions (informal as well as formal) on customary land are reportedly growing (Chimhowu and Woodhouse 2005; Holden and Otsuka 2014), questions arise about whether customary-land tenure will evolve into a different set of land relations and what these relations might be.

A related part of this debate is the claim that land-tenure relations in Africa are increasingly becoming exclusive and individualised, such that the idealised notion of communal land ownership is no longer tenable in many communities (see Bassett 1993; Cotula et al. 2009; Migot-Adholla and Bruce 1994; see also chapter 5 of this book). This view has attracted significant attention, as reflected by the idea that "vernacular" land markets in different parts of Africa are strengthening the individual's claim to land, a belief that has strongly influenced the land-tenure scholarship in Africa (Chimhowu and Woodhouse 2005). The reported growing refinement of individual and collective claims to and interest in land is said to be inducing struggle as some groups seek to affirm and protect their interests by reconstructing and redefining land relationships and rights (Lund

2006). This situation has brought the local politics of land, which is a theme largely ignored in the land-tenure scholarship, to the centre of the land question in Africa today.

This book contributes to these debates by examining contemporary customary-land relations and rural livelihoods. Chapters in this book focus on three key issues:

1. the nature of local land politics in the context of growing demand for customary land;
2. rural-livelihood and land-use dynamics in conditions of changing tenure arrangements characterised by increasing pressure due to demographic factors and urbanisation;
3. the relationship between land and other economic activities such as large- and small-scale (artisanal) mining and smallholder agriculture.

Although some chapters in the book examine land-tenure reforms and agrarian transformation based on case studies from countries other than Zambia, most of the chapters draw from empirical case studies conducted in Zambia under the Land Use and Rural Livelihood in Africa Project (LURLAP). To enrich the discussion of these complex issues of tenure, livelihood, and governance of land, the book provides a comparative analysis among different countries and contexts, highlighting the similarities as well as the differences.

In examining the three key issues mentioned above, the chapters in the book reflect on numerous questions. For instance, are land markets emerging in customary areas? What are the responses of the people on customary land to the reported increase of monetary transactions in land? Does the emergence of land markets on customary land threaten the tenure security of the poor in these communities? In some cases, the growth of land markets implies that the power of traditional authorities, in general, is diminishing; are the traditional authorities contesting this depletion of their power base? What local politics does the conversion of customary land engender? In cases where conversions have taken place, are there indications of shifting livelihood strategies and forms of land use in these communities? For instance, how does an increase in mining activity influence other land-based activities, such as farming? These are important questions. Although they are not new, this book discusses them in relation to the current situation characterised by rising demand for land due to population growth, climate change, a rising demand for cleaner energy, sustained economic growth, rising food prices, and urbanisation.

This book is a product of a collaborative research study (LURLAP, noted above).[3] The collaboration was inspired by several factors, including the need to conduct comparative studies among countries in the region to understand similarities and differences regarding land use, rural livelihoods, and agrarian change. So far, two country case studies in South Africa and Zambia have been conducted. Research for the South African case study was conducted in 2010 and 2011 in the Chris Hani District municipality in Eastern Cape Province, while research for the Zambian case study was conducted in two districts, Chongwe and Chibombo, in 2013 and 2014.

For the Zambian case study, Chongwe and Chibombo are both located on the outskirts of the capital city, Lusaka, and were chosen specifically because of this proximity. The media have reported that these two districts have experienced increased pressure from both foreign and Zambian investors (mainly from Lusaka city) who seek to acquire customary land for various types of investment. This is why the two districts are often referred to as "pressure points" concerning the conversion of customary land to leasehold tenure.

The two districts were also chosen because, although both are near the city of Lusaka, they have distinct features that are interesting to examine. In terms of customary-land conversion, the most interesting difference is that in Chongwe District, Chieftainess Nkomesha does not permit conversion of customary land to leasehold tenure, while Chieftainess Mungule in Chibombo District actually encourages such conversion to leasehold tenure. It is interesting that in both chiefdoms, local residents are actively involved in the "selling" of customary land, although the dynamics are different, as highlighted in several chapters below.

Land Debates in Zambia

As in other parts of Africa, land issues are increasingly becoming a significant part of national debates and politics in Zambia. To understand the current land debates in Zambia, it is necessary to provide a brief historical account of land policies and practices. Land debates in other countries are analysed in Part III of the book, which focuses on the comparative case studies.

Scholars agree that the present land-tenure system and legal framework are products of the country's colonial legacy. During the colonial period, which officially lasted from 1924–64,[4] the British colonial authorities established a land-tenure system that essentially provided separate categories of landholding for two racial groups: indigenous Africans and European settlers. The most fertile land, categorised as Crown land, was reserved for European settlers, while the less fertile land, subdivided into reserve and trust land, was specifically left for indigenous Africans (Chileshe 2005). In 1975, a little more than a decade after independence, the United National Independence Party (UNIP) government, led by Dr. Kenneth Kaunda, introduced radical land reforms but retained the dual land-tenure system introduced by the colonial government. Major changes in land tenure were introduced through the Land (Conversion of Titles) Act of 1975. This provided for the vesting of all land in the president and converted all freehold titles into leasehold titles of up to ninety-nine years. Thus, land in Zambia is currently held in two ways: through time-bound leasehold titles granted by the president on state land; and through occupation under customary tenure on customary land administered by traditional authorities, allocated largely on the basis of membership in a community.

This dualism in land tenure has been a source of contestation since independence. Those who are critical of customary-land tenure have questioned its effectiveness in promoting agriculture and sustainable livelihoods among the country's growing population (Chinene 1993). Such critics have called for the formalisation of customary land, arguing that this would provide smallholder farmers with land security and enable them to use it as collateral for loans and investment (Chinene 1993). As in many African countries, the dominant view, especially during the 1980s and early 1990s, has been that the customary-land tenure system is inconsistent with the operations of modern market economies and that unclear property rights in customary tenure create inefficiencies in both the allocation and use of land resources.

In Zambia, this view gained prominence in the early 1990s when the Movement for Multiparty Democracy (MMD) came to power. The MMD government tried to correct the alleged ills of customary tenure by promulgating the Lands Act No. 29 of 1995 (henceforth the 1995 Lands Act), amid strong opposition from many parts of society. The 1995 Lands Act, among other things, provides for the conversion of customary land to leasehold tenure. Supporters of this policy maintain that the recognition of property rights in customary land would lead to the emergence of a land market, reduce tenure uncertainty and insecurity, and make it possible for such land to be used as collateral. The Zambian government adopted this view and has been pursuing a strategy of "opening up" the countryside to investment by promoting conversion of customary land to leasehold tenure (Chitonge 2015).

Aware of how the policy and practice of privatising customary-land rights affects their power base (land), some chiefs have strongly opposed this policy and practice (see more details in chapter 2).[5] Chiefs opposed to the policy argue that conversion threatens their powers over traditional land; by allowing their subjects (and outsiders) to acquire individual leasehold rights on customary land, they are losing control not just of land but also of rural communities more generally. Given the increasing demand for land, there are worries that "almost all land could become state land. Chiefs' palaces may find themselves on state land," as a key informant argued (LURLAP Interviews 2014). The chiefs' fears about loss of land are compounded by the law's lack of provision for the possibility of converting land on leasehold tenure back to customary tenure upon expiry of the lease. According to M'membe (2005, 40), "if land has been converted from customary to statutory [leasehold] tenure, it cannot be taken back to its original tenure again," although this view is contested by Ministry of Lands officials, who maintain that what changes at conversion is the *tenure* (from customary to leasehold), not the *category* of land, which still remains the same (*customary land*).

So far, there has not been a single case in which land under leasehold tenure has reverted to customary tenure. All we have seen is customary land being converted to leasehold in a one-way-traffic manner. Many analysts and civil society groups observe that even when the title deed issued on what used to be customary land is cancelled, the land does not revert back to customary tenure: it remains under leasehold tenure administered by the Commissioner of Lands (see Zambia Land Alliance 2008; Kabilika 2010; Tagliarino 2014). Thus, the argument about the category remaining the same even when the tenure changes has little practical significance given that tenure prescribes the terms and conditions under which land is held and administered (see Bruce 1986). At this stage, it is not clear what the category-tenure debate is intended to achieve. What is clear, however, is that neither the law (the 1995 Lands Act) nor the current draft constitution provides for the reversal of land tenure from leasehold back to customary tenure.

The category-tenure debate has introduced ambiguity into the conceptualisation of land tenure. This has led to intense debates, especially at a moment when the contest for the administration of different types of land seems to have deepened. The main point of contention is whether customary land, once converted, becomes state land or remains customary land held under leasehold tenure. For instance, while a key informant from the House of Chiefs[6] maintains that land conversions have been one-sided from customary to leasehold tenure and not vice versa, Ministry of Lands' officials argue that the land category does not change. This is how they are able to insist that customary land still constitutes 94 percent of all land in

Zambia. But one legal expert interviewed for the LURLAP study argued that the law is very clear on this: conversion *is* one-sided, and there is no provision in the 1995 Lands Act that allows customary land held under leasehold tenure to be converted back to customary land under any circumstance. This is the same view expressed by Tagliarino (2014), who argues that when an investor obtains a leasehold title over customary land, the land reverts to the state once the lease expires and is thereafter under statutory tenure. He further notes that the 1995 Lands Act is silent on whether converted land remains customary land under the authority of traditional leaders, and points out that in practice, "converted land is treated as state land governed by the Land Commissioner. [But] it is also unclear whether the grant of a leasehold title to converted land necessarily extinguishes all customary rights previously attached to the land" (Tagliarino 2014, 4). The Zambia Land Alliance (ZLA) similarly observes that if customary land is leased and for some reason the lease expires or is cancelled, the leased land no longer falls under the jurisdiction of the chief. It would seem, therefore, that once customary land is converted to leasehold, all customary rights to that land are extinguished, and so is the chief's authority over that land.

The House of Chiefs proposed that the current legislation on conversion be repealed. They have argued that chiefs should be allowed to grant their subjects signed documents authenticating individual ownership of land so that leasehold tenure can be held on customary land without converting it to statutory tenure, which is the practice in many other African countries, including Ghana, Tanzania, and Mozambique.

Those who share M'membe's (2005) view that the state is actually consolidating statutory land at the expense of customary land (see also Chitonge 2015) estimate that customary land now represents only around 70 percent of the nation's total land mass. USAID (2010) suggested that about 10 percent of customary land has been converted to state land since the enactment of the 1995 Lands Act. However, no official records exist to indicate how much customary land has been converted to leasehold so far. Estimates accounting for protected areas such as game parks, forest reserves, and national parks, which are administered by state agencies even if they fall under customary areas (and are therefore not under the administration of traditional authorities), assert the proportion of land effectively under customary authorities (customary land) at 34 percent as of 2014 (Chitonge 2015).

As population growth fuels the demand for land, this land debate is most likely to intensify not just in Zambia but also in other African countries. While the debate over the category of converted customary land is far from resolved, the law (1995 Lands Act) was clearly intended to create "one-way traffic" (from customary to leasehold), with the deliberate purpose of doing away with customary tenure. Given the MMD government's commitment to free-market ideology, there can be no doubt about what the 1995 Lands Act was intended to achieve. As M'membe (2005) contends, the whole idea of converting customary land to leasehold, provided for in Section 8 (1) of the 1995 Lands Act, was aimed at getting rid of customary land. As more land is converted from customary to leasehold tenure and reserved for the exclusive use of those who enact the conversions, it is likely that little customary land will remain in the foreseeable future (Tembo 2014).

Reports in both the print and electronic media show that many sectors of society are concerned about the "sale" of customary land, a practice that is especially prevalent in peri-urban areas such as Chongwe and Chibombo Districts. In 2014, the then-Republican vice president, Dr. Guy Scott, noted that the chiefs, who were supposed to be the custodians of customary land, were the ones disadvantaging their subjects by selling land. He held that, according to Zambian law, the chiefs did not own the land but were merely trustees on behalf of their subjects and that they should, therefore, not sell it (*Lusaka Times* 2014). It has been observed that in areas where customary land has been "sold" and converted for tourism, local people have lost full access to common-pool resources on which they depend for their livelihoods (*Southern Guardian* 2005, cited in Mudenda 2006).

Other analysts and commentators have, however, alluded to the positive aspects of such conversions. USAID (2010), for instance, suggested that in some cases conversions have resulted in much-needed investment in rural areas and the creation of opportunities for local employment, contract farming, secondary businesses, the development of infrastructure and social services, and the transfer of know-how. These debates are discussed in greater detail in the chapters in this volume.

The Micropolitics of Customary Land

The book begins with two chapters that outline the micropolitics of customary land in Zambia, drawing from case studies in Chongwe and Chibombo Districts. Chapter 2, by Horman Chitonge, presents a micro-level view of the politics around land tenure, focusing on land relations at the village and chiefdom levels. The chapter discusses in detail the broader theoretical and historical context of land politics in Africa, and Zambia in particular, highlighting that because of the crucial role that land plays in people's lives, especially in rural areas, land relations are by nature political. The author employs the concept of embeddedness to analyse the micropolitics of customary land. He argues that to understand local land politics, it is essential to examine closely the local structures of power and institutions through which land relations are constructed, given meaning, and reproduced. This chapter also discusses the local processes involved in acquiring customary land, focusing on the procedures that precede the act of converting land from customary to leasehold tenure.

In chapter 3, Orleans Mfune focuses on ongoing debates about the relevance of customary-land tenure in Zambia. As the country seeks to navigate the winds of change, debates about the relevance of customary tenure have featured strongly in public and scholarly discussions. Drawing on insights from political ecology, the author shows that these arguments are not situated in a vacuum but are supported by narratives about customary-tenure systems that now hold sway among Zambia's political and economic elites. The author interrogates these narratives in the light of empirical data from various sources, including archival data, interviews, and focus-group discussions. The chapter further illustrates that despite two decades of reform aimed at tilting customary tenure towards private tenure, customary land remains the only land on which the poor continue to depend.

Land Markets on Customary Land?

Chapters 4 and 5 explore the theme of land markets and examine whether the reported sale of customary land points to the emergence of a land market. In chapter 4, Gear Kajoba explores the land-tenure dynamics in Chongwe and Chibombo Districts in the broader Zambian context of an emerging market economy. Kajoba defines an emerging market as one that makes a transition from a state-controlled to a free-market economy, and observes that Zambia began its transformation from a socialist/commandist economy to a liberalised market economy in 1991. Kajoba argues that residents and some traditional authorities perceive the formalisation of land rights, in the form of converting customary land to leasehold tenure, as a way of securing local rights to land and as a means of improving livelihoods. In this context, conversions of customary land to leasehold are prompted by the perceived threat of future land loss resulting from the continuing expansion of the city of Lusaka, with some community members "selling" part of their land to local and foreign investors. However, the author observes that although the sale of customary land has created opportunities, it has reduced the landholdings available for present and future residents.

In chapter 5, David Kafwamba examines and critiques the narrative that customary-tenure systems are static and do not provide for individualised land rights. Kafwamba argues that the dominant literature views customary-land tenure systems as monolithic, conservative, and incapable of adapting to change. The chapter shows how customary-tenure systems have historically responded to influences such as colonialism and the development of land markets. The author argues that, although traditional authorities in the study areas acknowledge that customary-land titling results in a loss of their own authority, they nevertheless assert that land titling ensures that the expansion of Lusaka city does not displace their subjects in the future. The chapter also shows how, in one chiefdom where the traditional leader has refused to give permission to convert customary land to leasehold tenure, a clandestine land market has emerged in which locals secretly exercise their right to sell land.

Land, Rural-Livelihood Dynamics, and Mining

Chapters 6, 7, and 8 discuss the connections among rural livelihoods, land use, and artisanal mining, drawing on experiences from Zambia and Zimbabwe.

Chapter 6, by Orleans Mfune and David Kafwamba, examines policy changes in Zambia over time and the ways in which they have affected livelihoods. One of the chapter's key arguments is that these policy changes have induced shifts in the land-use forms and livelihood strategies pursued by local people. To illustrate this, the chapter traces the livelihood patterns of local people, noting that most people formerly relied on hunting and growing drought-resistant crops such as sorghum and millet. But a colonial policy that favoured the growing of maize has caused local people to abandon their traditional crops, and they now rely almost exclusively on maize, which is less resistant to drought.

The chapter concludes by noting that the postcolonial government has largely maintained colonial policies, by continuing to favour the production of maize through a system of production and marketing subsidies. This chapter, while focusing on land and agricultural policy changes, complements chapter 10, which presents empirical data on the dominant forms of land-use and livelihood strategies pursued by people residing on customary land in South Africa and Zambia.

In chapter 7, Grasian Mkodzongi examines the influence of small- and large-scale mining activities on the livelihoods of rural dwellers in Zimbabwe in the context of the Fast Track Land Reform Programme (FTLRP). The chapter shows that FTLRP beneficiaries (both A1 and A2) are using income from mining activities to boost investments in land-based activities, mainly agriculture. The author argues that a crucial link between the FTLRP and the growth of mining activities is the opening up of large chunks of formerly white-owned farmland to a large population that was previously confined to communal land. These people now have access to farmland through the FTLRP. Some of the FTLRP beneficiaries have discovered mineral deposits on their land or in nearby areas, deposits that they extract through artisanal mining techniques. They use income or wages from such mining activities to invest in land, particularly crop and livestock farming. The chapter contends that diversification has *not* led to the replacement of farming as a source of livelihood, given that income from mining is used predominantly to invest in land. In this sense, the chapter makes an argument similar to that in chapter 10, that although rural residents have diversified their sources of income, they still use land as their basis for launching other livelihood strategies.

In chapter 8, Moonde Kabinga looks at the social and economic implications of large-scale land acquisition for mining in customary areas in Zambia. The chapter discusses the implications of alienating customary land for mining activities in the context of the political and economic priority given to copper mining in Zambia. The chapter notes that most of the land acquired for mining activities in Zambia is customary land, and in most cases local people occupy the land on which new mining operations are initiated, which often leads to the people's displacement or relocation. This chapter also observes that despite negative impacts of mining on local communities, the government of Zambia has worked hard to lure foreign investment into the mining sector, to take advantage of the relatively higher prices of copper and related metals on the global market, especially in the period prior to the current decline of commodity prices.

The analysis of different mining experiences in various parts of Zambia reveals that local communities whose land is alienated for mining activities do not benefit from these investments; on the contrary, they endure the pain of being displaced, losing their land and livelihoods, and are forced to suffer the negative environmental impact of mining.

Land Use and Rural Livelihoods in Comparative Perspective

In chapter 9, Bridget Bwalya Umar discusses whether formalisation of customary-land rights leads to improved productivity, increased investment in land, and the encouragement of conservational approaches to land use. Drawing from the customary-land formalisation programmes in Ethiopia, Ghana, and Malawi, the author concludes that the case studies reviewed offer no evidence that formalisation of land rights results in increased productivity or investment. However, the chapter shows that the adoption of land-conservation practices is associated with land users who feel that they have stronger land-tenure security.

The author observes that in all three case studies, the policy of formalising land rights actually induces land-tenure insecurity among local people, contrary to what the official policy is intended to achieve. In Ethiopia, people on state land feel more insecure (even though they may have formal registration or title) as a result of having been previously evicted from their land regardless of whether they possessed a formal document. In Malawi, the policy of privatising customary land has been implemented since the 1970s, but this has not produced any of the benefits anticipated by policymakers, i.e., greater tenure security, the growth of a robust land market, and flexible land-ownership forms. In Ghana, although formalisation has scored some success, the programme faces many challenges, including the high cost of formalising land rights, a factor that has tended to exclude the poor.

In chapter 10, Horman Chitonge presents a comparative analysis of the land-use and livelihood strategies of households living on customary land in South Africa and Zambia. The chapter discusses these topics in two different contexts: the former homelands in South Africa and the rural areas under traditional authorities in Zambia. Analysis of the data from the South African and Zambian case studies shows interesting similarities and differences in land-use and livelihood strategies, despite the two countries' historical and socioeconomic differences. Levels of wage employment in rural areas are reported to be very low in both countries, with only 3 percent of respondents reporting wage employment as their main source of livelihood. The author concludes that while households in the study areas combine several strategies, both farm and non-farm, the role of land remains central, especially given that both economies are struggling to create *real* employment opportunities that provide viable livelihood alternatives to farming as well as to absorb the growing labour force in both urban and rural areas.

All these chapters, discussing the local land politics of Zambia, the clandestine market in customary land, and the interconnections of land and mining in Zimbabwe, reveal that the land question seems to be imposing itself once more on the national agenda across the continent. The growing significance of land debates is not accidental; particular factors are causing the "land question" to emerge as one of *the* most important topics. For this reason, it is important to understand the current dynamics, particularly with regard to customary land.

Notes

[1] See chapter 2 for further discussion of the multifaceted dimension of land in Africa.

[2] Most of the land titling programmes implemented in Africa during the 1980s and 1990s failed. Three factors cited to account for this failure include poor understanding of local land rights, a lack of broad-based information campaigns, and the use of high-cost approaches (see Deininger et al. 2011a, 312).

[3] LURLAP is a regional comparative research project with cases studies in South Africa, Mozambique, Botswana, Tanzania, and Zimbabwe. The Zambian case study involved researchers from the University of Cape Town (UCT) and the University of Zambia (UNZA). At UCT, students and staff from the Centre for African Studies (CAS) completed a survey, while at UNZA, students and staff from the Department of Geography and Environmental Studies completed it.

[4] From 1889 to 1924, Zambia was a Northern Rhodesia protectorate ruled by the British South African Company on behalf of the British government. The British colonial government officially took over the governing of the protectorate only in 1924.

[5] However, it must be noted that some chiefs have embraced this practice, often "selling" customary land at the expense of their own people (Minister of Lands 2013).

[6] The House of Chiefs is a statutory body provided for by Statutory Instrument 41 of 1998. It is made up of three elected representatives, who are all gazetted chiefs, from each of the ten provinces of Zambia. It advises the state on customary land matters.

References

Adams, M. 2003. "Land tenure policy and practice in Zambia: Issues relating to the development of the agricultural sector." Accessed January 2. http://fsg.afre.msu.edu/zambia/resources/Land1.pdf.

African Development Bank. 2013. *Annual Development Effectiveness Review 2013: Towards Sustainable Growth for Africa*. Accessed October 23, 2013. www.afdb.org.

African Union, African Development Bank, and the Economic Commission for Africa. 2010. *Framework and Guidelines on Land Policy in Africa*. Addis Ababa: AU-AfDB-ECA.

Alliance for a Green Revolution in Africa. 2013. *Africa Agriculture Status Report: Focusing on Staple Crops*. Nairobi: AGRA.

Bassett, T. 1993. "Introduction: The land question and agricultural transformation in sub-Saharan Africa." In *Land in African Agrarian Systems*, edited by T. Bassett and T. J. Crummey, 5–18. Wisconsin: University of Wisconsin Press.

Berry, S. 1984. "The food crisis and agrarian change in Africa: A review essay." *African Studies Review* 27 (2): 59–112.

Bruce, J. 1986. *Land Tenure Issues in Project Design and Strategies for Agricultural Development in sub-Saharan Africa*. Madison: Land Tenure Center, University of Wisconsin.

Butler, J., R. Rotberg, and J. Adams. 1978. *The Black Homelands of South Africa: The Political and Economic Development of Boputhaswana and KwaZulu*. Berkeley: University of California Press.

Centre for Development and Enterprise. 2005. *Land Reform in South Africa: A 21st Century Perspective*. Research Report No. 14. Johannesburg: CDE.

Chileshe, R. A. 2005. *Land tenure and rural livelihoods in Zambia: Case studies of Kamena and St Joseph*. PhD diss., University of Western Cape.

Chimhowu, A., and P. Woodhouse. 2005. "Vernacular land markets and the changing face of customary land tenure in Africa. *Forum for Development Studies* 32 (2): 385–414.

Chinene, V. R. N. 1993. *Land: Need for Reform—its Impact and Implication*. Paper presented at the National Conference on Agriculture Towards a Bread Basket, Pamodzi Hotel, Lusaka, March 1–2.

Chitonge, H. 2015. "Customary land at a crossroads: Contest for the control of customary land in Zambia." *SADC Law Journal* 4 (1): 45–67.

Chitonge, H., and L. Ntsebeza. 2012. "Land reform and rural livelihood in South Africa: Does access to land matter?" *Review of Agrarian Studies* 2 (1): 89–111.

Claassens, A. 2014. "Law, land and custom, 1913–2014. What is at stake today?" In *Land Divided, Land Restored: Land Reform in South Africa for the 21st Century*, edited by S. Walker and B. Cousins, 68–94. Johannesburg: Jacana Media.

Cotula, L., S. Vermeulen, R. Leonard, and J. Keeley. 2009. *Land Grab or Development Opportunity? Agricultural Investment and International Land Deals in Africa*. London/Rome: IIED/FAO/IFAD.

Deininger, K., and H. Binswanger. 1999. "The evolution of the World Bank's land policy: Principles, experiences and future challenges." *The World Bank Research Observer* 14 (2): 247–76.

Deininger, K., D. A. Ali, and T. Alemu. 2011a. "Impacts of land certification on tenure security, investment, and land market participation: Evidence from Ethiopia." *Land Economics* 87 (2): 312–34.

Deininger, K., D. Byerle, J. Lindsay, A. Norton, H. Selod, and M. Sticker. 2011b. *Rising Global Interest in Farmland: Can it Yield Sustainable and Equitable Benefits?* New York: World Bank. www.worldbank.org.

Department of Agriculture, Food, and Fisheries. 2010. *Abstract of Agricultural Statistics*. Pretoria: DAFF.

Department of Land Affairs. 1997. *White Paper on Land Reform in South Africa*. Pretoria: Department of Land Affairs.

—. 2001. *Land Redistribution for Agricultural Development*. Pretoria: DLA. Accessed November 18, 2008. www.dla.gov.za.

Government Republic of Zambia. 1995. *Lands Act*, No. 29. Lusaka: Government Printers.

Hichaambwa, M., and S. T. Jayne. 2014. *Poverty Reduction Potential of Increasing Smallholder Access to Land*. Working Paper No. 83. Lusaka: Indaba Agricultural Policy Research Institute.

Holden, S., and K. Otsuka. 2014. "The roles of land tenure reforms and land markets in the context of population growth and land use intensification in Africa." *Food Policy* 48: 88–97.

Lund, C. 2006. "Twilight institutions: Public authority and local politics in Africa." *Development and Change* 37 (4): 685–705.

Lusaka Times. 2014. "Government to issue circular on traditional land conservation." *Lusaka Times,* August 23. Accessed August 14, 2015. http://www.lusakatimes.com/2014/08/23/government-issue-circular-traditional-land-conservation.

Makunike, C. 2009. "Large-scale agricultural investment in Africa: Points to ponder." In *Land Grab: The Race for The World's Farmland*, edited by M. Kugelman and S. L. Levenstein, 85–93. Washington DC: Woodrow Wilson International Center for Scholars.

May, J. 2000. "The structure and composition of rural poverty and livelihoods in South Africa." In *At the Crossroads: Land and Agrarian Reform in South Africa into the 20th Century*, edited by B. Cousins, 21–34. Cape Town: Programme for Land and Agrarian Studies.

Migot-Adholla, E., and J. W. Bruce. 1994. "Introduction: Are indigenous African tenure systems insecure?" In *Searching for Land Tenure Security in Africa*, edited by J. W. Bruce and E. Migot-Adholla, 1–14. Washington DC: World Bank.

Minister of Lands. 2013. "Policy statement by Hon. Harry Kalaba, MP, Minister of Lands, Natural Resources and Environment, on the protection and administration of customary land in Zambia." December 13. Lusaka.

M'membe, F. 2005. *The Zambian Land Tenure System and the Process of Land Alienation: The Need for Land Reform in Zambia*. BA thesis, University of Zambia, School of Law, Lusaka.

Moyo, S. 2008. *African Land Questions, Agrarian Transition and the State: Contradictions of the Neo-Liberal Land Reforms*. Dakar: CODESRIA.

Mudenda, M. M. 2006. "The challenges of customary tenure in Zambia. Shaping the change." XXIII FIG Congress, Munich, Germany, October 8–13.

Nkwinti, G. 2010. "Speech by the minister of rural development and land reform." Budget vote for 2010/11. Accessed March 24, 2010. http://ww2.ruraldevelopment.gov.za/DLAinternet//content/document_library/Ministry/Ministry_Minister_Speeches/Speech2.pdf.

Ntsebeza, L. 1998. *Land Tenure Reform, Traditional Authorities and Rural Local Government in Post-Apartheid South Africa: Cases Studies From the Eastern Cape*. Programme for Land and Agrarian Studies (PLAS), Research Report No. 3. Cape Town: University of the Western Cape.

Okoth-Ogendo, H. 1989. "Some theory in the study of tenure relations in African agriculture." *Journal of the International African Institute* 59 (1): 6–17.

Parliamentary Committee on Lands, Environment and Tourism. 2013. *Report by the PCLET, Second Session of the Eleventh National Assembly*. Lusaka: National Assembly of Zambia.

Tagliarino, N. 2014. "Conversions of customary lands to leasehold titles: Zambia. Focus on land in Africa." Accessed September 16, 2015.

http://www.focusonland.com/fola/en/countries/brief-conversions-of-customary-lands-to-2leasehold-titles/.

Tembo, E. 2014. "Alienating land in customary areas in Zambia." *Lusaka Times*, August 1. Accessed September 16, 2015. www.lusakatimes.com/2014/08/01/alienating-land-customary-areas-zambia.

USAID. 2010. "Property rights and resource governance. USAID country profile: Zambia." USAID. https://www.land-links.org/wp-content/uploads/2016/09/USAID_Land_Tenure_Zambia_Profile.pdf.

Walker, S., and B. Cousins, eds. 2014. "Introduction." In *Land Divided, Land Restored: Land Reform in South Africa for the 21st Century*, 1–23. Johannesburg: Jacana Media.

Zambia Land Alliance. 2008. "Land policy options for development and poverty reduction: Civil society views for pro-poor land policies and laws in Zambia." Lusaka: Civil Society Consultative Forum.

Part I:

The Politics of Customary Land in Zambia

Chapter Two

The Micropolitics of Customary-Land Conversions in Zambia: Emerging Trends and Practices

Horman Chitonge

Introduction

In recent years, the media and academic literature have given greater attention to the conversion of customary-land tenure to leasehold tenure in Zambia.[1] Most of this growing literature emphasises that the practice negatively impacts local people's livelihoods and, at the same time, undermines the authority and future of traditional leaders (see Brown 2005; FSRP 2010; Kabilika 2010; Ng'ombe and Keivani 2013; Sitko 2010; ZLA 2008). For instance, a policy statement issued by the Minister of Lands at the end of 2013 states, "my office is overwhelmed with cases of Zambians who are complaining of being displaced from their ancestral and family lands in preference for investors and the urban elite at the expense of vulnerable communities" (Minister of Lands 2013, 4).

The local media have been actively reporting the practice of alienating customary land for quite some time. For example, a newspaper article during the mid-1990s raised the following concerns:

> In Zambia...land is being dished out to foreigners and investors without considering the long-term consequences such actions will have on the people .... Zambia has entered a phase where land grabbing is escalating at an alarming rate ... In Chief Kabamba's area, for instance, Serenje District Council has already given out 4,800 hectares of land to a South African investor on the grounds that ... this will bring development to the district ... People from outside the province are coming to stake claims to land in the name of development and local people cannot fight Lusaka businessmen or South African investors (cited in Roth et al. 1995, 30).

The literature also reveals that the practice of converting customary land benefits a small group of urban elites (mainly from Lusaka and other large towns), foreign investors, and local elites, including some village heads, chiefs, subchiefs, and some well-resourced emerging local farmers (see Sitko and Jayne 2014), who are taking advantage of the opportunity to convert customary land to leasehold tenure.

While most stories and studies focus on the negative effects of converting customary land to leasehold tenure for the benefit of outsiders, they often overlook the "intricate local politics" around customary-land administration, allocation, control, access, and use. So far, there has been little attention given to the contestations arising from the definition and redefinition of tenure and access rights at the local level (see Lund 1998). Stories often portray local communities as homogenous groupings bound by strong kinship ties and loyalty to the chief or village headperson, thereby foreclosing the possibility of contest over land. In the past, when land was abundant, contests might have been rare; but given that demand for land is growing in many communities, contestations over land are becoming common, and this is slowly changing the politics of access to and control over land at the local level.

This chapter focuses on local land politics captured through a case study conducted in three chiefdoms in central Zambia. Through a detailed analysis of the institutional structures, processes, and the actors involved in the conversion of customary land to leasehold tenure, the chapter shows that contestations over land are becoming common and are often shaped by the different interest groups that influence the administration, allocation, and norms regulating access to land and other resources. These different interest groups often compete for control over land at the local level, giving rise to what I refer to as the "micropolitics of land."[2] By focusing on local land politics, the chapter does not suggest that issues surrounding land are not influenced by macropolitics (i.e., nationally and globally); rather, it serves to highlight the often-ignored local dynamics concerning customary land. The literature on land politics in Africa has often focused on the struggle for control of customary land between the state (usually central government) and traditional authorities (see Boone 2007; Herbst 2000), with little attention given to local contestations and struggles (see Lund 2006).

Analysis of the data gathered from the three chiefdoms suggests that the practice of converting customary land is generating complex power relations in rural areas, leading to various contests over land. Understanding the emerging contestations requires paying attention to intricate local land politics. In this regard, the chapter uses Karl Polanyi's concept of embeddedness to explore the nature of micro land relations and politics.

The chapter is organised in seven sections. The next section discusses the broader theoretical and historical context of land politics in Africa generally and Zambia in particular. The third section outlines the organisational structure of local communities, to highlight the institutional setting in which micro land politics are embedded. The fourth section discusses the local processes involved in acquiring customary land, to illustrate how local institutional structures shape the micropolitics of land. The fifth section discusses micro land politics, focusing on how different actors articulate their interest in land and the emerging contest over it. The sixth section discusses emerging trends and practices, stressing the ambivalence of national land policies and legislation. The final section sums up the discussion.

The Theoretical and Historical Context of the Micropolitics of Land

The Concept of Embeddedness

The concept of embeddedness is widely attributed to Karl Polanyi (1944), who used the term to illustrate that markets are deeply rooted in social and political relations in societies. In using the concept, Polanyi was contesting the idea of "self-regulating markets" as something independent of and separate from social relations. Polanyi's argument was that instead of viewing the market as ruler over human beings, society, and nature, the market should be seen as an intricate part of the social fabric that humans create as they interact with nature and with one another (Polanyi 1944). In this sense, the concept of embeddedness locates institutions and power within and as part of social relations. Various analysts have employed the concept to examine social dynamics, social relations, and institutions in society. Granovetter (1985, 482), for instance, uses the concept of embeddedness to examine social relations and the institutions that shape them, arguing that both "behaviour and institutions … are so constrained by the ongoing social relations that to construe them as independent is a grievous misunderstanding."

In the context of land-tenure debates, Pauline Peters uses the concept of embeddedness to argue that notions of the *commons* and *communal*, which are often used in discussions of land-tenure relations in Africa, fail to capture the intricacies of land relations. Instead, she proposes that the most appropriate concept is that of embeddedness, which better highlights the complexity of land relations in Africa (Peters 1987). Drawing from this understanding, Bassett (1993, 5) has argued that few dispute the idea that "land access, control, and management strategies are embedded in social, political, and economic structures that vary and change over time." Analysts have applied this view of embeddedness widely to the analysis of land relations in Africa, using different expressions such as the "web of interest" (Meinzen-Dick and Mwangi 2008) and "rootedness" (Chauveau and Colin 2010; Bassett 1993). In this paper, the term is used to mean that land relations are intricately intertwined with the complex social, political, economic, cultural, and religious texture of the community. Thus, if land relations are interwoven in the local social structures, power relations, and practices, then to understand local land politics, it is essential to examine closely the local power structures through which these relations are defined, redefined, controlled, and contested. As Bassett has previously observed, "the process of acquiring and defending rights in land is inherently a political process based on power relations among members of the social group" (Bassett 1993, 18). From this perspective, the rules and norms that regulate access to and use of land (see Bruce 1986) lie at the centre of local politics, to the extent that land allocation and distribution influence power relations. But before we discuss the local structures through which land is governed, a brief comment on the importance of land in local communities is befitting.

Land as a Vital Resource

Land is an extremely important resource in any community. As the Draft Land Policy (2006, 2) in Zambia rightly points out,

> Land is the most fundamental resource in any society because it is the basis of human survival. Land is the space upon which all human activities take place and provides continued existence of all life forms and minerals. Land performs basic and fundamental functions that support human and other terrestrial systems such as to produce food, fibre, fuel, water or other biotic materials for human use; provide biological habitats for plants, animals and micro-organisms; regulate the storage and flow of surface and ground water; provide physical space for settlements, industry and recreation.

Additionally, in Africa, land has several other dimensions, such that land connects the past, present, and future generations; hence the transgenerational dimension of land (see Okoth-Ogendo 1989). In this sense, land in Africa is not just a means of production or a source of economic and political power; land permeates the entire human existence, providing a critical link between the material and the spiritual worlds, the past and the present (Akuffo 2009). This multidimensional nature of land in Africa makes land relations complex, so that in "order to fully understand the social processes through which power over land is vested" one needs to "go beyond [the] man-land issues, which the doctrine of ownership implies, to encompass man-man relations, which create and determine power in land-based societies" (Okoth-Ogendo 1989, 9). For instance, in Africa land is not perceived as property belonging to a particular person (not even the king or chief), as is the case in other places, but rather as a "web of relationships" structured by cultural and traditional norms and practices (see Agbosu 2000; Gluckman 1969).

Furthermore, the multidimensional nature of land relations places them at the centre of social and political formations in society. Land forms the basic foundation of polities—be they states, nations, kingdoms, chiefdoms, villages, or a mere settlement—and defines and confines these formations (Bentsi-Enchill 1965). There cannot be a polity without land; any form of polity is inherently rooted in and defined by a particular piece of land. As Uchendu (1970, 478) has rightly observed, land "is not only the physical dimension of a community but the spatial aspect of the polity." As the spatial confines of a community, land plays a central role in defining relations between not just polities but also members within a particular polity. Consequently, control over this vital resource becomes an important element in defining social and power relations among people at the local level. Historically, in many societies the ability to lay claim to and control land has been a source of power, privilege, status, and wealth (Bentsi-Enchill 1965). In feudal societies in particular, land was

> the most important economic resource. It was the basic means of production. Hence its ownership and control carried with it the exercise of economic and political power over men. Thus, the feudal oligarchy, which claimed ownership over the bulk of the lands, regulated socially people's relations to the land as the basic means of production. (Agbosu 2000, 3)

Traditionally, land has also been a source of status and influence. It has been reported, for instance, that in Uganda "[the] majority of land purchasers buy for social and political advantages, since owners of land have the right to sit on local councils, the first step on the political ladder" (Platteau 1996, 52).

British colonial advisors were well aware of the power that comes with control over land and warned against alienating customary land through individual freehold titles, a practice they saw as posing a threat to the policy of indirect rule:

> The authority of chiefs, sub-chiefs and heads of clans and families is bound up with the land. The grant, therefore, to individuals of absolute rights of

> ownership would tend to disrupt the native policy, and so, too, would the indiscriminate sale of tribal land by chiefs. The control of alienation of land has in consequence been one of the planks of the British system of Indirect Rule (Meek 1946, 10).

As rightly noted in this quotation, the loss of control over land entails loss of control over people in customary areas.

Land Relations in Africa

Understanding the intricate nature of land relations in Africa is difficult, especially for non-Africans, who often interpret them through the simplistic and more familiar Western lens of absolute ownership of property (Bassett 1993; Bentsi-Enchill 1965). Such understandings are "loaded with the values of Western materialism" (Okoth-Ogendo 1989, 7), leading to what has been termed the "ownership trap" (Okoth-Ogendo 1989, 11). For example, scholars have observed that the colonialists' preoccupation with the notion of "private property" failed to "entertain the notion of multiple rights in land," resulting in serious distortion in their understanding of customary-land tenure in Africa (Mamdani 1996, 139; Meinzen-Dick and Mwangi 2008). The "ethnocentric" approach adopted by the colonialists to understand land tenure in Africa, and the "attendant political agendas," has led to a clouded understanding of customary-land tenure relations (Bassett 1993, 5). The tendency among "colonial apologists to project their own (European) models and concepts of land tenure onto African societies has hindered our understanding of development and change in this area" (Bassett 1993, 5). Consequently, land and tenure relations are conceptualised in a disembedded manner; that is to say, they are delinked from the social relations and structures of the community in which they are situated, with land becoming a mere property or commodity mediated by a contract that sets out and defines expendable and absolute rights. Customary land in Africa, despite the onslaught of colonial and neocolonial forces, "remains deeply embedded in the social and cultural systems of tribes, clans, and other traditional groups, despite the competing machinery of the modern state" (Blocher 2006, 182). To understand these relations requires an examination of the way local communities are structured and how they function (Bassett 1993; Chauveau and Colin 2010).

Local Institutional Structures

This section discusses the institutional and administrative structures in which land-tenure relations are embedded. Understanding the institutional structures of local communities is important because land-tenure arrangements and other rules governing access to natural resources derive from the social norms, relations, and practices that are embedded in and practiced through institutional structures (Meinzen-Dick and Mwangi 2008; Toumlin 2008). In most African countries, traditional institutions are still the most accessible governance structures for most people in rural areas, especially when it comes to land issues (Herbst 2000). Thus, an analysis of local institutions and how they function can enrich our understanding of land-tenure arrangements. However, as noted above, the institutional setup and administrative structures and practices vary according to local cultural and traditional norms. Some chiefdoms have well-developed and clear institutional structures through which decisions are made; while in other chiefdoms the structures are not so clear. Despite the differences in the institutions and structural composition of local communities, common elements exist in many communities, such as the traditional leaders (chiefs, subchiefs, village heads) and the traditional institutions and structures of governance.

The Chief/Chieftainess

In all three chiefdoms (Bunda-Bunda, Mungule, and Nkomesha) where the LURLAP study was conducted, clear institutional structures regulate and guide the day-to-day lives of local people, including land administration, allocation, and use. At the top of the institutional hierarchy is the chief/chieftainess, who is the head of the chiefdom and assumes office through a hereditary system based on family lineage (see Figure 2.1). The chief's tenure of office is for life, although in some instances when chiefs become too old to discharge their expected duties effectively, they retire and a successor is appointed from the royal family.[3] While the chief may not have direct involvement in the day-to-day administration of land in the chiefdom, he or she is the final authority regarding converting customary land to leasehold as currently practiced in Zambia.

To make this conversion, local residents or outsiders are required, by law, to obtain permission from the local chief in whose chiefdom the piece of land earmarked for conversion is located. The Lands Act No. 29 of 1995 (the 1995 Lands Act) is clear about the powers of local chiefs concerning alienation of customary land. Article 8 (1) of the 1995 Lands Act, which provides for the conversion of customary land, states that "after the commencement of this Act, any person who holds land under customary tenure may convert it into a leasehold tenure not exceeding ninety-nine years on application, in the manner prescribed." However, "the conversion of rights from a customary tenure to a leasehold tenure shall have effect only after the approval of the chief and the local authorities in whose area the land to be converted is situated" (Article 8 (2)). In this sense, chiefs have discretionary powers over the conversion of customary land as long as they are free to issue (or to refuse) such permission. If the chief refuses to grant permission to convert customary land, there is nothing one can do. Thus, chiefs wield significant power in terms of having the final say on land-administration matters in customary areas.

Advisory Council

In the administration of the chiefdom, the chief is assisted by the advisory council (AC), sometimes called the council of elders (*indunas*). This council comprises senior village heads, who are appointed by the chief. In Mungule chiefdom, for instance, the AC consists of four senior village heads, while in Nkomesha and Bunda-Bunda the AC has more than seven members. However, in all three chiefdoms the role of the AC is to advise the chief on any matter related to the administration of the chiefdom, including land matters. The AC meets once every month, but the chief can convene a meeting whenever an urgent matter needs to be discussed. For instance, if a land dispute between members of the community cannot be resolved at the village level, the chief will often convene the council to try to resolve the matter. While the AC makes recommendations to the chief, the chief often makes the final decision; the chief is therefore not bound to follow the AC's recommendations.

Committees

To facilitate the administrative process, most chiefdoms have established committees, which deal with specific matters such as cultural, disciplinary, and social development, including fundraising. In Mungule chiefdom, the cultural committee is tasked with, among other things, organising the annual cultural ceremony of the Lenje people, known as *Kulamba Kubwalo*. The committee collects mandatory contributions from local residents and business entities to support the ceremony. Local residents indicated that contribution towards *Kulamba Kubwalo* is a non-negotiable duty of every community member. Other than the cultural committee, the disciplinary committee is a common structure mentioned by residents, and its functions are self-explanatory.

Zonal Structures

In Nkomesha and Bunda-Bunda chiefdoms, villages are grouped into zones, and each zone has a committee with a chairperson and committee members. Within this hierarchy, the village heads report to the zone chairperson, who in turn reports to the chief. Thus, zones form the intermediate structures between the village and the higher administrative structures in chiefdoms where these structures exist. Members of the zone committees are village heads, who are elected to the committees by the people. The zonal structures and village committees are the only bodies whose members are elected directly by local people; membership in the other structures is hereditary or via appointment by the chief. Although zonal structures make rules and can settle disputes, their powers are largely advisory, either to the chief or the village heads.

Village Councils

At the lower end of the administrative structures in the study areas are the village councils, which are led by village heads. There are two types of structures at the village level: the village council and the village committee. The village council (sometimes referred to as the council of elders) comprises close family members of the village head, and the council's duty is to advise the village head on matters related to the administration of the village. One of the village council's most important functions is to elect the village head (from among close family members) whenever there is a vacancy. The village council also has the power to remove the village head if there are serious irregularities or a failure to discharge duties. Ordinary community members do not take part in the selection process or in the removal of the village head, although complaints from community members can lead to removal.

The village committee (VC), which is sometimes known as the village-development committee (VDC), consists of ordinary village members who are elected by the local community for a specific term of office. The function of the VC is to coordinate development works in the village, such as the maintenance of bridges, roads, and water facilities. Members of the VC mobilise the community to perform duties when the need arises, for example, to contribute labour to build community facilities such as boreholes or to carry out road maintenance. Members of the VC, especially the village secretary, assist the village head in other day-to-day administrative tasks such as keeping and updating the village register, taking notes at village meetings, convening village meetings, or reporting to the chief or zone chairperson on any matter of importance, including any misconduct by the village head. The VC is also supposed to play a part in the land-allocation process, and committee members are expected to approve new land allocations in the village. But in most villages, the village heads allocate land without consulting the village committee members. As one respondent explained, "Usually the village head is only supposed to allocate land after consulting the village committee, but nowadays you find that these headmen are allocating land without the approval of the committee" (LURLAP Interviews 2014).

Village Head

The most common administrative structure in a traditional African village is the village head. Either a man or a woman can occupy this post. Village heads form a crucial part of the administrative hierarchy within traditional structures because they are the ones in direct contact with local residents, and they are responsible for the day-to-day administration of the village. The village heads are not paid for their services to the community, and most of them highlighted this as a challenge during interviews. The village heads are responsible for allocating land to new community members or any resident who may need additional land. Village heads know every piece of land in the village and which land is vacant or idle. Thus, they are strategically placed in the customary-land tenure system. As one respondent put it, "The process of acquiring land starts with the headman and that is where the key is. Without him, you cannot get land. If you can't meet the headman's demand it is not easy to get land" (LURLAP Interviews 2014).

Similar to the appointment of chiefs, the position of village head is inherited through a family-lineage system; the community does not elect village heads in the three chiefdoms where this study was conducted. The process of becoming a village head differs according to local traditional practices but also circumstances. In rare cases, the chief may appoint someone to establish a new village within the chiefdom. In precolonial times, many villages were established through the first-settler principle, whereby the first person to settle in an area automatically became its head (Channock 1985). In such cases, when the first village head dies, his family (village council) convenes a meeting and chooses a successor from within the family. As mentioned earlier, although people do not elect the village head, community residents can reject a village head if that person is not performing according to expectations. A village head from one of the villages in the Mungule area confirmed this: "The people in the community have power to say they do not want the person chosen as the village head, and if that happens the family [village council] has to sit down again and choose someone else" (LURLAP Interviews 2014).

This seems to be a well-established practice in all three chiefdoms in the study, although it was not clear how often people passed a vote of no confidence in a village head or how often this leads to the person's removal from office. Some participants in the focus-group discussions (FGDs) noted that the decision to remove the village head is taken only in rare cases when someone has completely failed to discharge duties or when there are continuous complaints from community members (LURLAP FGD 2014).

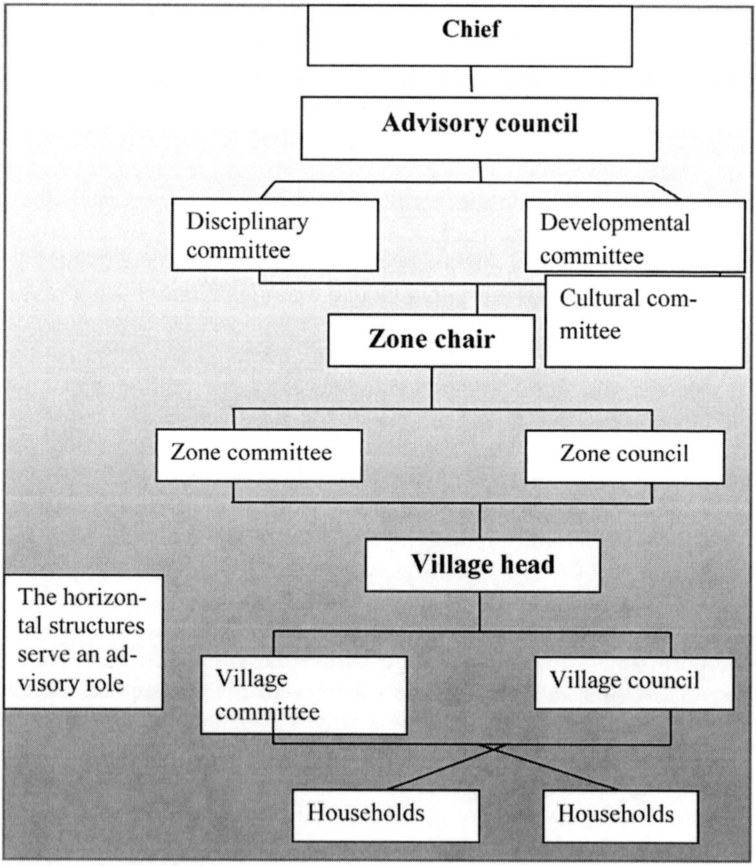

Figure 2.1. Administrative structure in a traditional Zambian village
Source: Compiled by author

Interviews with local residents made clear that the village head plays a central role, not just in the community's land-allocation process but also in the entire governance system of the village.

As Figure 2.1 shows, the administrative structure described above is hierarchical, although there are horizontal structures such as the village and zonal committees.

The institutional structure shown above provides the background to the micropolitics of land in customary areas and the conversion of customary land to leasehold tenure. Before we discuss the intricate politics of customary-land conversions, it is important to explore the land-acquisition process within the administrative structures outlined above.

The Process of Acquiring Customary Land

There are several ways to acquire land under customary tenure, depending on the circumstances of the person acquiring the land. Acquisition of customary-land rights is key to the process of converting customary land to leasehold tenure, since only persons with existing rights to customary land are allowed to convert. Furthermore, the process of acquiring rights to customary land is crucial to understanding the micropolitics of land, given that rights and interest in land are contested, constructed, consolidated, and defended through the land-allocation process at the village level (see Bassett 1993; Okoth-Ogendo 1989).

A non-resident (outsider) who wants to acquire customary land can approach a local resident who has land to spare, and the two can negotiate the terms of allocation. If they agree, then both parties go to the village head so that the newcomer can be introduced and have his/her name recorded in the village register. Once someone's name is entered in the village register, it means that the person is formally accepted as a community member. If the person is allocated land, even if he or she does not reside in the community, that person is assumed, by means of the land acquired, to be a community member. Outsiders, whether they acquire land directly from the village head or from a local resident, must be registered in the village book to confirm their community membership. By virtue of this membership, the right or interest in customary land is created. In recent practice, this process has reversed; outsiders now acquire land first and then use the acquired land to gain membership in the community.

In certain instances, an outsider can go directly to the village head to ask for land, and if land is available in the village he or she can be given land and the name recorded in the register. It is, however, uncommon for ordinary community members to go directly to the chief to ask for land.

Only high-ranking politicians, businesspersons, or investors go directly to the chief. When ordinary members need more land, the first point of contact is the village head, or they can simply negotiate with someone in the community who has more land. In most negotiations, the local resident, village head, or chief receives money (plus other gifts) as a "token" of appreciation for the land, and this is essentially what is referred to as the "selling" or "buying" of customary land.

As noted earlier, the village head is expected to consult the village committee before he or she allocates land to an outsider or newcomer. One respondent explains the procedure:

> The person asking for land will go to the headman and explain everything. The headman will then tell him or her to see him on another day, because he has to discuss the issue with the committee [village committee]. If land is available, the person will be allocated his or her own plot and the rules of the village will be explained to the person (LURLAP Interviews 2014).

Another respondent confirmed this:

> You have to apply and forward your papers to the village head who then introduces the applicant to the village committee. After that then the committee will sit to discuss if there is any available land they can allocate to the applicant (LURLAP Interviews 2014).

Thus, according to traditional practice, the village head is supposed to allocate land only after consultation with the village committee. However, because of the relatively large amounts of money that land seekers offer for customary land, some village heads are allocating land to outsiders without consulting the village committee. In one case, a woman reported that part of her land was "given away" by the village head when she was sick: "When I was sick, the headman gave part of my land to his sister, and when I asked him why he had given my land away, he told me that I am neither the headman nor the chief. So now, our case is with the zone chairman" (LURLAP Interviews 2014).

In another incident, a woman complained about the village head selling part of her land: "We used to have 53 hectares before the death of my father, but after his death and now that I am a widow my land is being depleted by the headman who keeps selling my land without even consulting me" (LURLAP Interviews 2014). Incidents of village heads selling land already allocated to someone else have become common, especially in the Mungule area, where "selling" customary land is reported to have become rampant.

For wealthy investors, the process of acquiring land is slightly different. In most cases, investors go directly to and negotiate with the chief, not the village head. The chief then summons the village head to find out if land is available. For foreign investors wanting to acquire large portions of land, representatives of the Zambia Development Agency (ZDA), a statutory body created by the Zambian government to attract and promote investment in Zambia, negotiate with the chief on behalf of investors. Although some of these large investors live on the land they acquire (especially the Chinese), they do not go through the village head and their names are not recorded in the village register. The local community tends not to regard such newcomers as part of the local community.

The Process of Converting Customary Land to Leasehold Tenure

As indicated above, once a person has secured rights or an interest in customary land, that person can then begin the process of converting the land to leasehold tenure (see 1995 Lands Act). To do so, the person must, again, approach the village head and declare the intention to convert. The duty of the village head is, first, to verify that the land earmarked for conversion belongs to the person intending to convert it. Second, after this verification, the village head will then introduce the person to the chief. The word of the village head is crucial in determining whether the chief will grant permission. If the village head expresses doubt about the tenure status of the land in question, then the chief may not grant permission to convert. So, from the beginning of the process of acquiring customary land, the role of the village head is central.

It is important to note that customary land "bought" or acquired by an outsider remains under customary tenure until the "buyer" converts it to leasehold tenure. This has been a source of confusion regarding what is bought and sold, especially if one views the "selling" in Western terms of a full-blown property transaction. But as noted, customary land in Africa is not simply a property that can be bought and sold like any other property. In this sense, what the outsider "buys" is not, strictly speaking, land but the right to be declared a right holder (or resident) with existing interest in the land. Even people who are not community residents can do this as long as the person "selling" customary land confirms that he or she has granted ("sold") part of the land to the outsider in question and the whole process is officially endorsed by the village head.

Conditions for Conversion

In theory and in law, people who wish to convert customary land to leasehold tenure are required to have had existing rights to customary land for a period of not less than five years. These rights can be acquired through various means, such as "buying" from a local resident who has land to "sell" but also through inheritance, residency, continued use of the land, first settlement, or through allocation from the village head or chief. But in practice, outsiders who "buy" or are allocated customary land by the village head often begin the process of converting it to leasehold tenure immediately; the five-year requirement is rarely enforced. For local Zambians who acquire customary land, the practice has been to build some structure on the acquired land, such as a house or cottage, or to grow crops on the land, to confirm usage and interest. The non-Zambians who acquire customary land (investors) often initiate the conversion process as soon as the chief grants permission and the local council approves it; the five-year requirement does not seem to apply in this case. This chapter does not deal with the process of converting customary land beyond the permission of the chief (for details of the conversion process after one has secured the chief's permission, see Abanda et al. 2011).

While anyone with existing rights in customary land can embark on the conversion process, many local residents interviewed for this study indicated that although they would like to obtain a title for their land, they are not converting it mainly due to lack of financial resources. The conversion process is complicated and expensive for most of the poor rural residents (see Abanda et al. 2011).

During our interviews, we discovered several costs involved, including "tokens" of appreciation for the village head and the chief. As one respondent explained, "Most of us know about the possibility of getting a title deed for our land, but the problem is with the preparation of the money for getting the title. It is costly" (LURLAP Interviews 2014). Another respondent confirmed this: "Getting a title is becoming a common thing because all of us have the desire to convert, it is just that finances are a problem. In fact, the chief and the headman encourage us to protect our land by getting titles" (LURLAP Interviews 2014).

Traditionally, a person who is being introduced to the chief cannot go empty-handed; the person is expected to prepare some gift to present.[4] One respondent explains this requirement: "The greatest challenge, or reason, is money, because you need to go with the *induna* (village head) to the chief and definitely you cannot go empty-handed. In short, the whole process involves money in the form of a token of appreciation" (LURLAP Interviews 2014).

But with rising demand for land, what used to be considered a "token" of appreciation, often a gift in kind, is now conventionally interpreted to mean payment in cash, although there is no predefined amount. Residents interviewed stated that some village heads now ask for large sums of money before allocating land, especially to people from Lusaka who have the money to pay (see Chitonge et al. 2017). Residents further revealed that some village heads ask for significant amounts of money for introducing a person wanting to convert land to the chief (LURLAP Interviews 2014). In addition to giving the "token" of appreciation to the village head and to the chief, a person wanting to convert land must also pay for the services of a planner, a surveyor, and officials representing the local government authorities (council), to survey, map, and verify the land prior to the papers being submitted to the deeds office for the issuance of a title deed. For ordinary people living in rural areas, this is way beyond what they can afford.

The Micropolitics of Customary Land

The institutional structure, the process of converting customary land, and the various actors involved form the context in which the micropolitics of customary land should be situated. The administrative structure and the actors discussed above show that the politics of customary-land tenure is intricately embedded in the relations of the community's sociopolitical fabric, which is the place where production and property rights interact to define and shape power and land relations. For this reason, land relations cannot be appropriately understood if they are disembedded from the webs of relationships and social interactions that define and shape them (Benjaminsen and Lund 2000). When customary-land tenure relations are conceptualised as embedded in social relations, it becomes clear that the "perception of what constitutes property at any point in a people's history is invariably the product of the total milieu in which they live, rather than any particular aspect of it" (Okoth-Ogendo 1989, 7). In this instance, allocation, use, and control of customary land involve processes that are deeply ingrained in and shaped by local power relations and validated by local institutions, norms, and practices (which change over time). The power relations in this case are mapped onto or mediated through the institutional structures and flow through a hierarchical structure from the individual, via the village head, to the chief. In other words, the institutional structures reflect how power relations regulate interactions concerning land (Lund 2006). What looks like an innocent process of the village head allocating land to someone who has asked for it actually involves much more.

The rules governing the land-allocation process and the practice of entering names in the village register, for instance, do not just appear out of nowhere. They are constructed, shaped, and reshaped, often through a process of tacit struggle over resources and power as the different interests in the community contest for control and meaning. Earlier literature on traditional African societies tended to depict rural communities as homogenous groupings defined by loyalty and deference and held compactly in place by strong kinship ties. For instance, Meek (1946) argued that rural folk in Africa do not contest the power of traditional leaders; they always recognise and submit to their authority. As a result of this understanding, Meek recommended that the British colonial authorities preserve the practice of customary tenure under traditional authorities as the only way of maintaining control over the countryside (Meek 1946). Similarly, a recent study of customary-land dynamics in Ghana stated that while struggles over land in peri-urban communities do exist, state and local communities do not challenge the chiefs who are selling traditional land for their own benefit because both the residents and the politicians dare not challenge traditional leaders (Ubink and Quan 2008).

In the literature on customary-land tenure in Africa, the contests between state and traditional authorities have been highlighted, with no attention given to village-level land politics, giving the impression that only state and traditional leaders have land disputes. For instance, Herbst (2000) maintains that one of the greatest challenges for African states today is their inability to project power over their entire territory, and this manifests in the administration of land in rural areas, where chiefs act as sovereigns. In the case of land politics, this notion of the chiefs' absolute power over land is rooted in the idea of chiefs being "residual owners" of the land (Gluckman 1944). But this is a distorted understanding of land relations in African communities: "Chiefs are mere administrators and not owners vested with exclusive dispositive rights. It is the *stool*, the symbolic representative of the social group or community, in which ownership is vested" (Agbosu 2000, 21).

Contests Over Land

When the "real" owner of land is a social group or community, contest over land is inevitable when some members of the group feel that their interests are overlooked. In this sense, local land relations are constantly defined by active tensions as various social groups and interests compete for control. Although there might not be open conflict over land, differences of interest between the chief and local residents, or village heads, always create and sustain active tensions that can erupt into an open contestation when the balance of forces (equilibrium) is disrupted. Contestation over land becomes more pronounced when demand for land grows and land shortages emerge.

Active tensions in Nkomesha chiefdom are palpable between some local residents and the chief, who has consistently refused to grant permission to convert customary land to leasehold. Although the tensions have not yet erupted into an open contestation, some local residents who want to convert customary land have conveyed a sense of frustration and despair about the chief's current moratorium. When asked in a focus-group discussion if they were interested in acquiring titles to their land, most residents made it clear that the only reason they do not have titles for their land is because "there is a blockade from the chieftainess' office. This issue of not giving us title deeds is tying our ability to develop because we are not free. If only our chief could help us in this. We still need help on the issue of title deeds, we need help on how to get title deeds" (LURLAP FGD 2014). Another example of active tension emerging is the issue of the "selling" of customary land. Although residents are aware that "selling" land in Nkomesha chiefdom is prohibited, some of them actually "sell" it clandestinely, as one respondent indicates:

> All I can say is that it is true this activity of selling land is common even when we know that it is wrong because her royal highness does not allow it. The manner in which the land is sold is illegal because land is sold without the knowledge of the chief (LURLAP Interviews 2014).

In the study area, we found two conflicting interests in the debate about conversion at the village level. On one side, the chieftainess Nkomesha does not allow residents to "sell" customary land, arguing that she is protecting the interests of traditional land and culture by doing so. On the other hand, some local residents, especially those with small businesses, view selling and converting part of their land as a way of getting themselves out of poverty. When asked about the benefits of selling customary land to outsiders, residents argued, "What makes us sell our land to people from Lusaka is that we want to improve our living standards by using the money to build better houses. We sell land in order to build better structures, to make our homes beautiful" (LURLAP FGD 2014). One woman in the group proudly declared, "I sold land to someone who built me a good house" (LURLAP FGD 2014).

This apparent conflict of interest over conversion in Nkomesha chiefdom is likely to increase as the pressure on customary land grows. This might give rise to more open forms of contestation and a reinterpretation of the rules governing land tenure, thereby creating an "open moment," which occurs

> when social rules and structures are suddenly challenged and the prerogatives and legitimacy of politico-legal institutions cease to be taken for granted. In such circumstances the stakes rise considerably … because such an "open moment" offers a double-edged possibility of reassertion or erosion of power (Lund 1998, 2).

Open contestation can be about the meaning and interpretation of the rules that govern social interactions. In the case of land, Bassett observes that "land rights are rooted not only in changing economic and political structures but also in the interpretation and transformation of meanings" (Bassett 1993, 14). A good example is the interpretation of what is actually sold when a village head receives money in exchange for customary land.

In the current context in which demand for customary land is growing steadily, the stakes are rising. Contestation and conflicts of interest are therefore expected to become more pronounced. Consequently, the micropolitics of land in customary areas can only become more sharply defined, especially in areas situated near major towns and developed infrastructure. We have seen this begin to manifest in some local residents' dissatisfaction with the policy prohibiting them from obtaining title deeds for their land.

A different study that looked at the effects of customary-land conversion in peri-urban areas in North-Western Province in Zambia also found evidence of heightened tensions, mainly between traditional leaders (the chief) and the local people, "with the former being accused of indiscriminately selling land to private investors while his subjects had no land; the chief was said to be dealing directly with private investors when allocating land without consulting his subjects" (Ng'ombe et al. 2014, 1997).

Contestation occurs not just between the chief and the local people but also at the village level, where village heads pursue interests that conflict with those of other residents. One example is the issue of village heads asking for money from local residents who want to "sell" customary land. Local residents interviewed for this study accused village heads of abusing their position by asking residents to pay a "token of appreciation" for introducing to the chief the person seeking permission to convert customary land. In addition, some village heads are reportedly asking for money to enter people's names in the village register:

> We make payment to ensure that our names are registered in the village register. But this is something that is just happening today. You can imag-

> ine even the money from the sale of the land is split in half and shared with the headman. At whatever price you sell the land, there must be a share for the headman to permit the person who buys land to establish themselves in the village (LURLAP Interviews 2014).

On the other hand, the village heads argued that since they are not paid for the service they render to the community, asking community members to pay a "token" is the only way they can be compensated for the time they spend dealing with community issues such as allocating land or resolving disputes. Local residents, however, see the tokens as a form of extortion. Such conflictual relations, and the perception of abuse perpetuated by customary institutions and structures, often lead to open contests as opposing groups seek to assert or dislodge each other's interests and power. When the tension is "normalised" or "naturalised" through the making of concessions, alliances, or simply reinterpreting the power of one group over the other, the situation settles back into a dynamic equilibrium.

Competition over resources and meanings is essentially what constitutes politics. Lund (2006) has suggested that politics at the local level resembles politics at the national level, where the state is an arena of constant contestation over valuable resources, including both power and meaning. Since land is a critical resource whose distribution will always be controversial (Chauveau and Colin 2010), its allocation, control, and administration will always be contested. This all serves to make access to land a deeply political issue (see Bassett 1993), all the more so because its distribution and administration are rooted in and regulated by sociopolitical institutions and practices (Boone 2007) at both the local and the national levels.

Emerging Trends

Media stories about customary-land tenure tend to position the traditional leadership on one side of the equation (often portrayed as using or abusing their positions to further their own interests) and local, ordinary residents on the other side (often portrayed as victims of greedy traditional leaders). However, a closer analysis of the local dynamics demonstrates this to be a simplistic view. The size of land owned/accessed influences how residents position themselves in the local contest for power, resources, status, and control. In this study, interviews with local residents revealed that not every community member is pushing for the chiefs to allow conversion of land or is happy that it is now possible to obtain titles on customary land. In one focus-group discussion, some residents pointed out that "customary land is better because … even people without money are getting [it], but if the land is under the state it means that everyone will have to buy land, and those without money will not have land" (LURLAP FGD 2014).

It later became apparent during fieldwork that residents who are pushing for or are happy with conversions in Nkomesha chiefdom are those with large plots who intend to sell parts of them. Residents with only small plots of land and who have nothing to "sell" worry that the practice of conversion will eventually force them to sell even the little land that they have when those with "big money" from the city come seeking to buy land.

When asked why some residents have larger plots whereas others have smaller ones, local residents indicated that those who were born in the area and got their land at a time when land was abundant tend to have larger plots: "Those of us who were born here, have large portions of land. Those who came from other places to settle here are the ones who got small portions due to subdivisions and the increasing population" (LURLAP Interviews 2014). The autochthones have been subdividing and selling off portions of their land to outsiders from Lusaka and other towns.

However, not only those who settled in the area long ago have larger plots; those from other parts of the country who settled in the area before the land shortages emerged also have larger plots. One respondent observed, "I came in 1984 and accessed 4.5 hectares of land, but I am subdividing it among my children so the portions are much smaller. In those days you could be allocated up to 12 hectares" (LURLAP Interviews 2014). Today, because of acute land shortages, it has become difficult to acquire large parcels of land in one location, even for those from Lusaka with abundant money.

Of interest here is that those with larger plots are lobbying the chief in Nkomesha chiefdom to allow conversion so that they can sell part of their land. For those who have small plots and little or no money, being allowed to convert customary land does not make much difference since they do not have the resources to successfully convert even the small plots of land they have. Those with small plots often argue that land should remain under customary tenure, controlled by the chiefs and village heads, so that they can have access to land without having to buy it. Thus, even local residents have different points of view and interests such that those with resources favour conversion, to consolidate and protect their property and investments, while those with smaller pieces of land actually see conversion as a threat to the security of their land. This active tension within these communities can lead to open contestation when, for instance, growing demand for land or a policy change at the national level disturbs the existing equilibrium.

The State in the Micropolitics of Land

The contestation at the local level is not just between local actors; the state enters the contest, forming alliances with whichever group matches its interests. As elsewhere in the continent, the state occasionally changes its position over customary land, depending on which interests dominant state actors are pursuing (Baldwin 2011). At times, the state forms alliances with customary authorities in the administration of customary land; at other times, it adopts policies and laws that seek to disempower or reduce customary authorities' control over land (Nuesiri 2014). The relationship between the state and customary authorities has mainly functioned along the rational-choice paradigm, with the state either forming alliances with or contesting the powers of traditional authorities depending on what is at stake.

The state in Zambia reveals this ambivalence at several levels. For instance, while the 1995 Lands Act (Section 8 (2)) recognises customary authorities' mandate to administer customary land, the same Act, by allowing conversion of customary land to leasehold, effectively undermines customary-land tenure and its associated institutions. Similarly, while Section 7 (1) of the 1995 Lands Act recognises customary land and defends the idea of vesting authority over it in traditional leaders, the same Act, by vesting all land in the head of state (the republican president), creates ambivalence over customary land. If all land in Zambia is vested in the president, a second investiture of the same land to customary authorities only leads to ambivalence and confusion.

This ambivalence, however, is by no means an error or a deficiency of vision by those involved in the drafting of legislation and land policies; it reflects the ambiguous way the state has positioned itself with regard to customary land administration (Boone 2007). This ambiguity exists not necessarily because the state lacks the capacity to administer customary land, as Herbst (2000) argues, but rather because of the embeddedness of land-tenure issues: the state tries to avoid direct confrontation with traditional authorities (Ubink and Quan 2008), on the one hand, and to prevent the chiefs from becoming too powerful, on the other (Baldwin 2011).

But the chiefs are not mere onlookers in all of this; by appealing to tradition and culture, they are finding ways to contest the state, to respond to processes such as conversion, which they see as undermining their authority. For instance, in an effort to mobilise his fellow chiefs against the state's proposal to deny traditional authorities the role of administering customary land, one prominent chief wrote to all 286 counterparts in Zambia, asking them to sign a petition against the draft customary-land bill (see Kanyanta 2014).

It is interesting that in contestations, both the state and the chiefs claim that they are protecting the interests of poor people in rural communities. This is how each side validates or legitimises its claims and, indirectly, its own interests in land. Local people have thus far aligned themselves with the traditional authorities, arguing that the state ignores their interests and needs. It is not clear whether the politicians will venture into the communities to make their case among the people; it is also not clear whether they will forge alliances with some of the rural elites who are aggrieved by the current tenure arrangements. There is every reason to believe that as the demand for land grows, the micro land politics in customary areas will become sharper.

Conclusion

Land, in general, is at the centre of any polity and its social expression (politics). This is understandable given the critical nature of land, especially in rural Africa, where most people directly rely on land for their livelihoods. In the Zambian context, where conversion of customary land to leasehold is promoted, the local politics of land is becoming sharper as intricate relations and rights are constructed and reconstructed. While the media have tended to portray customary land as an apolitical arena free from contestation because of the strong customary norms and rules governing its administration and use, land as a source of livelihood, status, power, and wealth cannot be apolitical given that land relations are at the heart of local politics. To appreciate the embedded nature of land relations requires a nuanced analysis of the structures, institutions, and main actors involved in land.

This chapter has discussed the institutional structures, actors, and the emerging practices around customary-land conversion, based on case studies in three chiefdoms in Zambia. By analysing the structural arrangements through which customary land is administered, used, shared, controlled, and transacted, this chapter has shed light on the nature of the micropolitics surrounding such allocation, use, and control. In the context of the practice of converting customary land, which the state in Zambia currently promotes, the micropolitics of land are becoming more pronounced as different community groups seek to assert and protect their own interests. For instance, some chiefs encourage conversion in their respective chiefdoms even though they know full well that only a few local people have the resources and know-how to successfully achieve it. While local elites seeking to take advantage of the opportunity to convert customary land support this position, poorer members of the communities do not, arguing that it will compromise their future access to land.

In chiefdoms where the chief does not allow conversion, the local elites are silently contesting the policy and are secretly "selling" customary land, without the chief's knowledge. In this sense, they are challenging the local chief's powers and seek to reconfigure their position. Although the chief has managed to maintain the position of not allowing conversions, strong undercurrents are building, supported by a state that sees the conversion of customary land as the only way to open up the countryside to investment and development. As the pressure for land builds from a growing population and economy, the politics of land will become more keenly contested, with different actors asserting and defending their interests and positions in more nuanced and open ways than before.

Notes

[1] When customary land is converted to leasehold tenure through a title deed, it permanently remains state land; it does not revert back to customary status. Zambian land policy defines customary land tenure as "a form of landholding which is generally communal … and is based on the cultural and traditional belief of each tribe"; while "leasehold tenure is generally referred to as state land from what was called Crown land in the colonial era" (Republic of Zambia, Draft Land Policy 2006, 12).

[2] This chapter focuses on the micropolitics at the village and chiefdom levels. The chapter does not discuss the "inter and intrahousehold politics" of land (see Bassett 1993 for details).

[3] It is interesting that for both Nkomesha and Mungule, the chiefdoms are headed by women, and the reason for this is that the Lenje (Mungule's chiefdom) and the Soli (Nkomesha and Bunda-Bunda) follow a matrilineal system under which the succession to chieftaincy is traced on the mother's side.

[4] Traditionally, these gifts were often paid in kind in the form of a chicken, a goat, or a bag of maize, etc. But now the common practice is to translate the token in monetary terms. While there is no fixed amount of what the token should be, residents indicated that some village heads are asking for significant amounts of money. In Ghana, where a similar practice has been reported, it is called "drink money" (see Ubink and Quan 2008).

References

Abanda, H., A. Ngombe, J. Tah, and R. Keivani. 2011. "An ontology-driven decision support system for land delivery in Zambia." *Expert Systems with Applications* 38: 10896–905.

Agbosu, L. 2000. *Land Law in Ghana: Contradiction Between Anglo-American and Customary Conceptions of Tenure Practices*. Working Paper No. 33. Madison: Land Tenure Center, University of Wisconsin.

Akuffo, K. 2009. *The Conception of Land Ownership in African Customary Law and its Implications for Development*. ACTS Conference Report.

Baldwin, K. 2011. *When Politicians Cede Control of Resources: Land Chiefs and Coalition Building in Africa*. Afrobarometer Working Paper No. 130. Cape Town: University of Cape Town.

Bassett, T. 1993. "Introduction: The land question and agricultural transformation in sub-Saharan Africa." In *Land in African Agrarian Systems*, edited by T. Bassett and T. J. Crummey, 5–18. Madison: University of Wisconsin Press.

Benjaminsen, A., and C. Lund, eds. 2000. "Politics, power and production: Understanding natural resources management in the west African Sahel." In *Politics, Power and Production: Understanding Natural Resources Management in the West African Sahel*, 6–21. Uppsala: Nordic Africa Institute.

Bentsi-Enchill, K. 1965. "Do African systems of land tenure require a special terminology?" *Journal of African Law* 9 (2): 114–39.

Blocher, J. 2006. "Building on custom: Land tenure policy and economic development in Ghana." *Yale Human Rights and Development Law Journal* 9: 166–81.

Boone, C. 2007. "Property and constitutional order: Land tenure reform and the future of the African state." *African Affairs* 106: 557–86.

Brown, T. 2005. "Contestation, confusion and corruption: Market-based land reform in Zambia." In *Competing Jurisdictions: Settling Land Claims in Africa*, edited by S. Evers, M. Spierenburg, and H. Wells, 79–102. Boston: Brill.

Bruce, J. 1986. *Land Tenure Issues in Project Design and Strategies for Agriculture Development in Sub-Saharan Africa*. Land Tenure Centre Paper No. 128. Madison: University of Wisconsin.

Chanock, M. 1985. *Law, Custom and Social Order: The Colonial Experience in Malawi and Zambia*. Cambridge: Cambridge University Press.

Cheauveau, J. P., and J. P. Colin. 2010. "Customary transfers and land sales in Cote d'Ivoire: Revisiting the embeddedness issue." *Africa* 80 (Special Issue 1): 81–103.

Chitonge, H., O. Mfune, D. Kafwamba, and G. Kajoba. 2017. "Hybrid Land Markets: Monetarised Customary Land Transactions in Zambia." *Canadian Journal of African Studies* 51.1: 123–43.

Food Security Research Project. 2010. "The status of customary land and how it affects the rights of indigenous local communities." Submission to the Committee on Agriculture and Land Study. Lusaka: FSRP.

Gluckman, M. 1944. "Studies in African land tenure." *African Studies* 3: 14–21.

—. 1969. "Property rights and status in African traditional law." In *Ideas and Procedures in African Traditional Law*, edited by M. Gluckman, 252–73. London: Oxford University Press.

Granovetter, M. 1985. "Economic action and social structure: The problem of embeddedness." *American Journal of Sociology* 91 (3): 481–510.

Herbst, J. 2000. *States and Power in Africa: Comparative Lessons in Authority and Control*. Princeton: Princeton University Press.

Kabilika, E. 2010. "The status of customary land and how it affects the rights of indigenous local communities." Lusaka: Caritas Zambia.

Kanyanta, C. 2014. "The institution of chiefs is on slippery ground – Chitimukulu." *Lusaka Times*, July 3.

Land Use and Rural Livelihood in Africa Project. 2014. Focus Group Discussions.

—. 2014. Interviews.

Lund, C. 1998. "Struggles for land and political power: On the politicisation of land tenure and disputes in Niger." *Journal of Legal Pluralism* 40: 1–22.

—. 2006. "Twilight institutions: Public authority and local politics in Africa." *Development and Change* 37 (4): 685–705.

Mamdani, M. 1996. *Citizen and Subject: Contemporary Africa and the Legacy of Late Colonialism*. Princeton: Princeton University Press.

Meek, C. K. 1946. *Land Law and Custom in the Colonies*. London: Oxford University Press.

Meinzen-Dick, R., and E. Mwangi. 2008. "Cutting the web of interests: Pitfalls of formalising property rights." *Land Use Policy* 26: 36–43.

Minister of Lands. 2013. "Policy statement by Hon. Harry Kalaba, MP, Minister of Lands, Natural Resources and Environment, on the protection and administration of customary land in Zambia." December 13. Lusaka.

Ng'ombe, A., and R. Keivani. 2013. "Customary land reform to facilitate private investment in Zambia: Achievements, potentials and limitations." *Urban Forum* 24: 33–48.

Ng'ombe, A., R. Kievani, M. Mattingly, and M. Stubbs. 2014. "Impact of privatisation of customary land rights in Zambia: A comparative study of rural and peri-urban locations." *International Journal of Urban and Regional Research* 38 (6): 1985–2007.

Nuesiri, E. 2014. *Re-Emergence of Customary Authorities and its Relation with Local Democratic Government*. Dakar: CODESRIA.

Okoth-Ogendo, H. 1989. "Some theory in the study of tenure relations in African agriculture." *Journal of the International African Institute* 59 (1): 6–17.

Peters, P. 1987. "Embedded systems and rooted models." In *The Question of the Commons: The Culture and Ideologies of Communal Resources*, edited by B. McKay and J. Acheson, 171–94. Tucson: University of Arizona Press.

Platteau, J. P. 1996. "The evolutionary theory of land rights as applied to sub-Saharan Africa: A critical assessment." *Development and Change* 27 (1): 29–86.

Polanyi, K. 1944. *The Great Transformation: The Political and Economic Origins of our Times*. Boston: Beacon Press.

Republic of Zambia. 2006. *Draft Land Administration and Management Policy*. Lusaka: Ministry of Lands.

Roth, M., A. M. Khan, and M. C. Zulu. 1995. "Legal framework and administration of land policy in Zambia." In *Land Tenure, Land Markets, and Institutional Transformation in Zambia*, edited by M. Roth. LTC Research Report No. 124. Madison: Land Tenure Center, University of Wisconsin.

Shipton, P., and M. Goheen. 1992. "Understanding African land-holding: Power and meaning." *Journal of the International African Institute* 62 (3): 307–25.

Simutanyi, N. 2008. *Copper Mining in Zambia: The Developmental Legacy of Privatisation*. Institute for Security Studies Paper No. 165. Johannesburg: Institute for Security Studies.

Sitko, N. 2010. "Fractured governance and local frictions: The exclusionary nature of a clandestine land market in southern Zambia." *Africa* 80 (1): 36–54.

Sitko, N., J. Chamberlin, and M. Hichaambwa. 2014. "Does smallholder land titling facilitate agricultural growth? An analysis of the determinants and effects of smallholder land titling in Zambia." *World Development* 64: 791–802.

Sitko, N., and T. S. Jayne. 2014. "Structural dynamism or elite land capture? A case study of emergent farm growth in Zambia." *Food Policy* 48: 194–202.

Toulmin, C. 2008. "Securing land and property rights in sub-Saharan Africa: The role of local institutions." *Land Use Policy* 26: 10–19.

Ubink, J., and J. Quan. 2008. "How to combine tradition and modernity? Regulating customary land management in Ghana." *Land Use Policy* 25: 198–213.

Uchendu, V. 1970. "Impact of changing agricultural technology on African land tenure." *Journal of Developing Areas* 4 (4): 477–86.

Zambia Land Alliance. 2008. *Land Policy Options for Development and Poverty Reduction: Civil Society Views for Pro-Poor Land Policies and Laws in Zambia*. Lusaka: Civil Society Consultative Forum.

CHAPTER THREE

"A TITLE FOR EVERY VILLAGER": IS CUSTOMARY TENURE NO LONGER RELEVANT FOR ZAMBIA'S ECONOMY?

ORLEANS MFUNE

Introduction

The existence of dual land-tenure systems that favour both private and customary tenure is one of the most enduring features of land in southern Africa. Nonetheless, the majority of rural dwellers in most parts of southern Africa have historically relied on customary tenure as the primary route to obtaining rights and obligations over land. Today, however, with the adoption of market-based economic policies and the quest for foreign direct investment (FDI) sweeping across Africa, customary tenure has again come under intense scrutiny. Customary tenure, in which land is communally owned and managed by tribal groups, is perceived as an important contributor to current rural underdevelopment and as irrelevant to market-based economies (Deininger and Binswanger 1999; Riddel 2000). In this regard, customary-land tenure tends to be marginalised in favour of private tenure or statutory control (Metcalfe and Kepe 2008). Similarly, in Zambia, writers link customary tenure with rural backwardness (Chileshe 2005; EAZ 2007), and within the political and economic elite many question how customary tenure fits into Zambia's modern economy, which has embraced neoliberalism. These, of course, are not new arguments. Writing in 1994, Gyasi noted a school of thought that viewed communal tenure as nebulous, inherently conservative, incapable of adapting fast enough to change, and therefore a drag on development.

Although empirical evidence rarely supports such views, they have nonetheless persisted among the elite in Zambia and have now gained sufficient political backing to drive new reforms that seek either to completely dissolve customary-tenure systems or radically reform them in favour of private tenure. In 2014, for example, intense debates emerged in the media and among political actors over a clause in a draft constitution that was seen as taking away the rights of tribal leaders to administer customary land (Zambia Draft Constitution 2014). Although the final amended constitution passed by parliament in 2016 retained customary tenure, the constitutional debate nonetheless exposed the views of some of Zambia's political and economic elites on customary land.

This drive towards a unitary system favouring private tenure is what some anti-privatisation advocacy groups in Zambia have called the "title for every villager" agenda. This refers to the fact that such reforms will likely affect rural landholding systems, forcing villagers to seek titles in order to assert their rights to lands they have accessed, used, and controlled for several generations. Indeed, the intense debates that emerged over this agenda show the persistent views of customary tenure as either harmful or irrelevant to development. This chapter argues that these ideas have not emerged in a vacuum; instead, they are based on powerful narratives that decision-makers have often drawn upon to shape public policy and achieve their goals. The purpose of this chapter is to unravel these narratives and to explore whether they are congruent with the reality on the ground. In this regard, the paper seeks to show the extent to which customary-land tenure remains relevant to rural development in Zambia.

The empirical data on which the chapter is based derive from various sources. These include archival data (mainly declassified government documents dating from the colonial era) from the National Archives of Zambia. Furthermore, the study used field data collected through interviews and focus-group discussions with households in Chibombo and Chongwe Districts of central Zambia. Interviews were held with traditional leaders, customary landholders, and district officials in the two study districts. The bulk of the data was mainly collected in the context of the LURLAP research project (see chapter 1 for more on the LURLAP project).

Theoretical Approach

The chapter draws on insights from political ecology (PE), which has gained ascendancy in natural-resource scholarship as a critical approach for analysing questions surrounding the use, access, and administration of land resources. To political ecologists, land is central to the livelihoods of the rural poor such that land-tenure questions have implications for access to, use, and management of other natural resources. For this reason, political ecologists have engaged with land-based issues (Blaikie 1985; Blaikie and Brookfield 1987). While different strands of political ecology exist, a major, common, and attractive feature of the discipline is its focus on narratives that tend to shape land-resource policies in developing countries. Often, these narratives have been co-created through a combination of science and socially mediated interests (Simon 2004). Political ecologists have shown how powerful actors (such as the state) have drawn on such narratives to influence the adoption of policies that serve their own interests at the expense of the rural poor. In addition to this focus on narratives, political ecologists tend to pay attention to history in their attempt to understand problems surrounding the issue of land resources (Bryant and Bailey 1997; Vaccaro and Beltran 2010). A historical perspective recognises that many land-resource problems treated in a highly simplified way are, in fact, highly complex and rooted in history. For example, many dimensions of the African land problem reflect the legacy of colonialism in Africa, as highlighted in chapter one. To understand such problems, it is crucial to examine them in the light of this history.

Using insights from PE, this chapter questions dominant neoliberal arguments about the insecurity and irrelevance of customary tenure in Zambia. It also questions ideas that view the privatisation of customary land as a cure for the backwardness of rural Zambia (i.e., ideas that preach the "good" of privatisation). While questioning these ideas, this work is also mindful of new conventional wisdom that represents customary tenure as untainted (see Amanor-Wilks 2009) and therefore in need of no reform. As Benjaminsen (2011) points out, when we examine questions regarding a resource such as land, it is important to be critical of populist narratives, not simply dominant narratives (see also Forsyth 2003). This is necessary to avoid recreating uncritical anti-neoliberal narratives (Benjaminsen 2011).

The chapter examines these issues in the context of two categories of property regime: private and common. Private property refers to a situation in which the right to use, exclude from, manage, or alienate land is restricted to the private landowner. Proponents argue that in contrast to common ownership, owners of private land can lease or rent it out and receive benefits from its use (Benjamin 2012). Landowners can also sell a portion of it for profit, if they so wish. Private property, argue its proponents, has great potential for increasing and securing the wealth and income streams of landowners.

Some argue that in contrast to private property, some property rights, such as the right to exclude or sell, do not fully apply to common property, in which shared use is seen as the norm (Benjamin 2012). Under common-property regimes, resources such as land are controlled by an identifiable group of people in a system where ownership is collective rather than individual (Beitl 2012; Mfune 2014). According to Riddel (2000), two types of common property can be identified in developing countries. The first is a resource base, such as grassland, woodland, or fisheries, that all recognised members of the group use. In some scholarly circles, such a resource has been conflated with open-access systems that lack structured ownership (e.g., Hardin 1968). However, it is currently understood that such a resource base constitutes the private property of a group, where membership is identifiable and resource use is often regulated (Meinzen-Dick and Mwangi 2009; Mfune 2014; Ostrom 1990).

The second type of common property identified by Riddel (2000) is where individual households hold land in long-term secure usufruct, although it is still viewed as part of a larger common property. Most communal land is held under this category and includes farmland, orchards, and residential land.

While communal tenure and private tenure have coexisted in many countries, the literature on tenure reform evidences a widespread movement towards land-tenure systems that are compatible with the principles and practices of a liberalised economy (Metcalfe and Kepe 2008). In this regard, in many countries tenure reforms are tilting towards private tenure because of its compatibility with modern market-based economies. Moreover, as Riddel (2000) points out, much conventional wisdom in development theory holds that communal tenure systems are a constraint on modernisation, and as the economy develops, traditional land-tenure arrangements gradually give way to private, individualised tenure with more clearly defined rights.

Setting the Context: The Drive Towards Private Tenure in Zambia

In Zambia's fifty-year history of independence, the last two decades have been the most important in terms of the quest to institute reforms aimed at tilting land tenure towards neoliberal policies. While the need for reforms has never been contentious, the types of reforms have raised many questions. In 1991, when the Movement for Multiparty Democracy (MMD) came to power, embracing liberal ideology became a priority and was applied to every sector of society, including land. It was argued that just like state land, customary land is equally crucial for private-sector development and the attraction of direct foreign investment. However, the tenure arrangements governing this land were said to inhibit such goals. Thus, the MMD, widely considered to be the architect of neoliberal policies in Zambia, argued for the need to bring all the country's lands under private tenure, noting that land-privatisation policies "would attach economic value to land, encourage real estate business and promote the regular issuance of title deeds in both urban and rural areas" (MMD 1991, 7). It is evident from this argument that from the outset, the MMD's policy on land was to dissolve customary tenure (see also chapter 1).

With this belief in the power of private rather than customary tenure to contribute to both rural and urban development, the MMD government embarked on land-tenure reforms solely aimed at phasing out customary tenure and establishing a unitary tenure system under which leasehold tenure would be the only route to access land. Occurring at the height of structural adjustment programmes (SAPs), this quest to phase out customary tenure was supported by the World Bank and the International Monetary Fund (IMF), both of which viewed the privatisation of customary land as consistent with the kind of neoliberal policies they were introducing to the country. However, as a result of pressure from civil society, traditional leaders, and other actors, the MMD government did not completely achieve its goal. Instead, the 1995 Lands Act retained customary tenure as a mode of landholding but allowed for conversion of customary land when traditional leaders gave permission. The 1995 Lands Act was thus a compromise, and for a while it appeared to have satisfied both the pro-privatisation camp and those who resisted complete privatisation and advocated to retain customary tenure.

It is important to note, however, that although the debate over whether to retain customary tenure appeared to have concluded with the adoption of the 1995 Lands Act, when the country sought to write a new constitution fifteen years later, the question of customary-land tenure's relevance reemerged. In 2014, for example, Zambian media headlines focused for months on whether customary land should continue to be under the control of chiefs and their subjects. Furthermore, some of the tabloids even ran opinion polls on the matter, asking their readers to vote on this. This continued questioning of customary tenure's relevance by the media and members of the public emphasises the need for scholarly engagement with the views underpinning this debate.

Narratives Linking Customary Land to Rural Backwardness

Two main arguments link customary tenure to rural backwardness in Zambia. First, a classic argument states that landholders under customary tenure lack the necessary "security of tenure" associated with private landholding. Some argue that as a result of insecurity of tenure, local actors lack the incentives to make long-term investments (Chileshe 1998;

MMD 1991). This argument, however, is not without precedent. Many authors have previously asserted the "insecure" nature of customary tenure, pointing out that adequate incentives for investment can occur only through the titling and registration of land (see also Cotula et al. 2004). Influential texts such as Hernando de Soto's *The Mystery of Capital* (2000) further strengthened such arguments. Although this remains a heavily contested argument, it has found a firm footing among Zambia's political and economic elite.

Second, some consistently argue that customary land is characterised by inefficient use and a lack of institutional controls to arrest land overuse and degradation. The Economic Association of Zambia (EAZ 2007, 54), for example, notes that "customary tenure is characterized by inefficient and wasteful utilization because most of the land is under communal activities such as grazing." The assumption in this argument is that customary land is intrinsically wasteful. Again, this argument, like the first one, is not really new. It is well illustrated in Hardin's metaphor of a communally controlled pastureland, where the free-rider problem results in the degradation of the commons (Hardin 1968). Environmental degradation in this regard is viewed as a disease resulting from a "sharing of the commons," under which there are no institutional controls or structured ownership arrangements. Thus, it is argued that common-property regimes have inherent qualities that lead to abuse and overexploitation of communal lands (see also Birgegard 1993).

Examining the Narratives: Macro and Microempirical Evidence

To critically examine the two claims above, we need to look at the nature of customary tenure, and in this chapter we draw on empirical evidence from Chongwe and Chibombo Districts, where the LURLAP study was conducted. Here, land under customary tenure includes farmland, grazing land, football fields, bushlands, forests, and residential land. The interviews and focus-group discussions carried out in the study sites make clear that villagers use and manage these land parcels differently. Lands such as river-line areas, grazing sites, and woodlands are communally controlled. On the other hand, individual families control some parcels of land, such as residential sites; for other parcels, exclusive control depends on the time of year and what the land is used for. Residential lands and farmlands once allocated to families are assumed to be "owned" and "controlled" by that family (Focus Group Discussions 2010). Ownership, however, is not exclusive in a Western sense. For example, while farmlands are controlled by individual families, during the postharvest season other members of the village have the right to use such parcels for dry-season livestock foraging, mice hunting, and the harvest of wild vegetables that grow during the dry season (i.e., secondary rights exist). Where community interests dominate, however, control is retained at the corporate level, with village committees providing the administrative functions required to manage such lands communally (In-depth Interviews 2010). These flexible tenure arrangements are crucial for mitigating seasonal fluctuations in resource availability, such as the scarcity of water and grazing resources (see also Mfune 2014). The results of our study show that these lands are not characterised by an absence of structured ownership and institutional controls as Hardin's narrative seems to suggest. Ownership and rights to land are just structured differently from those in Western systems.

Furthermore, while conventional wisdom holds that communal tenure is inevitably wasteful or can be characterised by resource overuse, this study found no evidence to suggest that this is always the case. Rather, this study's results show that local actors take measures to prevent environmental degradation on customary lands. For example, in the Shisholeka village of Nkomesha chiefdom, 120 households use local institutional and governance arrangements to protect communal woodland and other resources of collective importance (see Mfune 2014). Similarly, results at the household level show that local actors undertake a range of measures to protect their resource base. For example, the study found that in both Nkomesha and Bunda-Bunda chiefdoms, households still allow portions of their land to lie fallow as a way of replenishing the soil. In addition, in Nkomesha area, the study identified at least four families who have withdrawn parts of their agricultural land from cultivation over the past ten to fifteen years to allow natural vegetation to regenerate. According to these farmers, this allows them to increase access to livestock fodder, thatch grass, and sometimes even firewood (In-depth Interviews 2010). Such local practices should be understood as important agroecological practices that farmers adopt to improve the productivity of their land and their livelihood asset base.

These results simply confirm what others have previously argued, that arguments linking common-pool resource-management systems with the wasteful use or extensive degradation of land are often overgeneralised (Birgegard 1993; Ostrom 1990). Thus, although Hardin's narrative is still used to point out the "bad" aspects of communal tenure, other empirical studies have already shown how this thinking contradicts evidence on the ground (Bryant and Bailey 1997; Ruddle et al. 1992). Furthermore, some have noted that Hardin (1968), in his framing of common-property systems as inevitably degrading, was conflating common property with open-access resource regimes (Bollier 2013; Ostrom 1990).

In terms of whether landholders under customary tenure undertake long-term investment in their land, the LURLAP study found that it is important to distinguish between a parcel of land over which all group members can claim ownership and one over which ownership and control have devolved to an individual household because it is economically rational to do so. Although lands controlled by individual households are not formally registered (as there is no registry for customary land in Zambia), boundaries are often distinguished by special features such as a stream, special trees, tree stumps, rocks, hedges, termite mounds, and so forth. These boundaries are often respected based on custom and tradition and play a crucial role in the mediation of boundary conflicts.

The study found that with regard to lands that individual households control, landholders are willing to invest and improve the lands regardless of the tenure arrangements. Moreover, in all the study sites it was found that some individual households were running highly productive farms and modern houses (for rent). In fact, in Chongwe District a large part of the township was built on customary land without titles. On this land there are some modern houses, a private school, and a range of business premises (LURLAP Field Data 2014). This indicates that people have, in fact, invested in customary land without seeing a need for a title as a prerequisite for doing so.

The Relevance of Customary Land in the Livelihoods of the Poor

The agriculture sector in Zambia contributes about 16 percent of the country's GDP (Central Statistics Office 2010). In this regard, Zambia's agricultural-sector performance is important not only for the livelihoods of farmers but for the national economy as well. Over the past few years (e.g., the 2009–10 and 2013–14 seasons), Zambia has been known to achieve bumper harvests in the staple crop, maize, with surpluses being exported to countries in the region (e.g., Malawi, the Democratic Republic of Congo, and Zimbabwe) (see Burke et al. 2010; *Lusaka Times* 2014). Between 2009 and 2010, Zambia's crop harvest grew by 48 percent, the largest recorded in that decade. An interesting aspect of this bumper harvest is that 93 percent was produced by small-scale farmers using customary land, the rest by commercial farmers. Small-scale farmers not only grow food crops, they also cultivate cash crops such as tobacco and cotton. The LURLAP study showed that in both Chongwe and Mungule, small-scale farmers rely largely on customary land for their agricultural and livestock production. Nearly all respondents who identified themselves as farmers depend on customary land for both subsistence and cash-crop production. Similarly, at the national level, studies show that despite the land-privatisation drive that started in the mid-1990s, customary land still remains the dominant source of land for small-scale farmers.

Furthermore, an important feature of this record harvest is that when the Food Security Research Project (FSRP) analysed factors contributing to it, the landholding system (customary or private) was not key. In fact, the analysis showed that 61 percent of the yield growth was attributable to good weather, 32 percent to increased access to fertiliser, 5 percent to hybrid maize variety, and only 2 percent to other factors (Burke et al. 2010). Thus, while a discourse surrounding the productiveness of private tenure continues to be preached, no real evidence has emerged of such a system having contributed to food production during the twenty years of tenure reforms.

What is most clear, however, is that customary land is the type most accessible to the poor. This is important because for most developing countries, employment opportunities (especially in rural areas) outside the agricultural sector remain few (see also Chitonge and Umar in this volume). Moreover, despite the modernisation and industrialisation drives initiated in the 1960s and 1970s, the industrial sector lacks the capacity to absorb excess labour that may be released from agriculture. The reality in Zambia is that opportunities outside the agricultural sector remain slim, and even where opportunities become available, the wages are often below subsistence level. Access to land, therefore, remains critical to the sustenance of the majority poor. The situation is similar in other African countries. Devas and Korboe (2000), for example, point out that in an era of increasing commercialisation, the customary-land allocation system in Ghana increases opportunities for the poor to obtain land, and the system actually provides a greater degree of equity in land ownership and use than many other countries achieve.

Customary lands and their flexible tenure arrangements are therefore crucial for the survival strategies of rural actors. Removing some of the land currently under customary tenure, such as pasturelands, lands with water points, and communal woodlands, may not only reduce rural people's capacity to cope with changes in their environment; it may also have distributive consequences. In our LURLAP study sites, interviews with the Zambia Lands Tribunal indicate that some disputes arising from land privatisation in the Mungule area include fraudulent sale of communal spaces such as sacred graves, rangelands, and river frontages. The conversion of previously communal spaces is already disrupting communal livelihoods in that area.

Customary land is important not only for poor farmers and the rural poor but also for many of the urban poor whose livelihoods straddle urban and rural areas. As other studies have already shown, many urban dwellers in Africa still maintain ties with their rural relatives and construct their livelihoods by drawing on both urban and agricultural resources (Braun 2007; Kruger 1998; Lesetedi 2003). The livelihoods of these urban poor are multispatial, and customary-land tenure systems allow them to maintain ties with rural areas and diversify their livelihoods (Lesetedi 2003) as a way of coping with uncertainty. The importance of easily accessible land to urban dwellers is exemplified by the urban–rural migrations that occurred in Copperbelt Province when Zambia's mining industry, and the entire economy, took a downturn. During such hard times, some urbanites tended to relocate to rural areas and engage in agricultural production (see Potts 2005, 2009). In one of our study sites (Munyeta), it was discovered that nearly 10 percent of all farmers were, in fact, returnees who had migrated from urban areas and fallen back on agriculture after leaving waged employment.

Major Factors that Account for Rural Backwardness in Zambia

Our examination of the dominant narratives shows that arguments linking customary tenure and rural backwardness are often oversimplified. Establishing a link between the two is not easy, and thus far empirical evidence supporting this view is thin and spurious. Often, arguments supporting such a link tend to gloss over the deep-rooted and complex problems that surround rural development. These include historical factors, urban bias in regional development strategies, and structural macroeconomic forces that disadvantage the rural population. Indeed, this chapter contends that although customary tenure is implicated in the discourse of rural underdevelopment, the most important elements affecting rural welfare are, in fact, independent of customary tenure. A focus on customary tenure serves only to mask these other issues. In the next sections, we examine some of the most important factors that account for rural backwardness.

The Coloniality of Rural Backwardness in Zambia

A noticeable tendency in this discourse has perhaps been to ignore the roots of rural backwardness in Zambia and how these remain deep-seated.

Historical data show that the development gap between rural and urban areas has its roots in deliberate colonial policies that marginalised indigenous rural communities (often referred to as "natives") in favour of an urban population that was predominantly European (considered British citizens). During the colonial era, although customary-tenure systems were reluctantly tolerated, they were largely seen as irrelevant to colonial economic objectives that tied land and its resources to Western metropolitan economies. The category of land designated as "Crown land" (where leasehold and freehold were possible) was primarily created to serve the "settlers" and not the natives. In part, the affluence of communities on Crown land developed through the channelling of national resources to these areas at the expense of native communities. Communities in Crown areas were the prime beneficiaries of infrastructure projects such as roads, rail links, market infrastructure, and other socioeconomic services, giving landholders an edge over their counterparts on customary land. In this regard, the concentration of both political and economic power in a small European urban elite, and the consequent marginalisation of rural indigenous populations, lies at the heart of some of the rural–urban inequalities that persist today. In the context of agriculture, it is important to note that Crown lands, which were also the most productive, were selected on the basis of careful surveys, ensuring that white populations obtained premium land, while indigenous populations were concentrated in less productive lands (see Mvunga 1980).

Nonetheless, despite the unequal distribution of resources between Crown lands and customary areas, district notebooks (archival data) show that in some areas customary actors remained highly productive and were able to offer stiff competition to white farmers (ZNA 2010). Furthermore, archival documents reveal this as a widespread phenomenon in the country. In some cases, African farmers even rented spaces in Crown lands (albeit illegally) to expand their agricultural activities, against a backdrop of limited space or poor environmental conditions in customary areas arising from overcrowding due to forced settlements. Indeed, in 1934 the district commissioner of Lusaka lamented,

> There is no doubt that the business of native farming is growing and that it is attracting the worst types of natives who desire to get away as much as possible from the control of their chiefs and the BOMA. Very many natives of the Lusaka district, who should be living in the reserves, are living and paying rent to farmers quite close to their native reserve boundaries … Many of these natives who pay rent regularly are the worst tax defaulters (District commissioner, Lusaka, 20 June 1934, file 439/3/34).

Similarly, the district commissioner of Fort Jameson (now Chipata) acknowledged the productivity of native farmers and sought to curtail their activities on the basis of their potential effect on the environment. He noted, "Over-production is a serious matter in view of the shortage of arable land in the reserves and as soon as the danger from locusts is ended, *acreage* should be *reduced*" (Fort Jameson District commissioner, cited in Phiri 1980, 164).

This so-called "over-production" was taking place on customary lands. The contribution of these native farmers to the colonial economy is, however, not well acknowledged in the literature. This is primarily because before 1964, data collection on agriculture concentrated on large-scale farmers. The contribution of small-scale farmers to the country's GDP, on the other hand, was never considered important (Central Statistical Office 2010). But colonial efforts to undermine this agricultural growth went beyond measures to reduce acreage. According to Kean and Wood (1992), the colonial administration also established the Maize Control Board as part of an effort to secure a market for those European farmers whose survival was threatened by African competition in the urban food markets of the 1930s. Through this instrument, the state was able to control maize prices in a way that favoured the settler farmers. Additionally, an export ban on maize and discriminatory pricing systems were used to undermine the growth of African agriculture.

According to Malekano (2009), although indigenous Zambians were able to grow enough produce to serve both the export market and local consumption during the colonial period, market prices never favoured them. In addition, in 1928 indigenous Zambian farmers were ordered to stop exporting their produce and concentrate on producing for the domestic market, in particular the mines, which were seen as the backbone of the economy. In this regard, African farmers were disadvantaged on two fronts: they were denied access to the more lucrative export markets and forced to operate in local markets where prices did not favour them. The colonial state's efforts to stifle peoples' livelihoods explain why, at independence, Zambia had only a few semicommercial African farmers, compared to other countries in the region (Malekano 2009).

Indeed, in 1964 it was clear that the post-independence government had inherited a country tarnished with deep regional inequalities. Marked differences in terms of socioeconomic development existed between areas along the line of the rail (where Crown land was dominant) and the rural regions (on mostly customary land). Within the agriculture sector, a highly dualistic structure under which European farmers dominated the most marketable crops reflected inequalities, and there was little development of small-scale, semi-commercialised, African agriculture (Kean and Wood 1992; Malekano 2009).

However, in postcolonial Zambia, the settler-native dichotomy was replaced by the urban-rural and commercial-smallholder farmer dichotomies. Crown lands (now state lands) became the sites of urban centres and commercial farming, while rural smallholders continued to occupy customary land. There was to be no transfer of fertile state lands to the customary-land category to enable smallholders to have access to productive lands. Instead, the 1995 Lands Act would begin the process of transferring customary land to state land. From this we can see that although the native-citizen dichotomy no longer exists, the colonial spatial patterns of landholding remain virtually unchanged. Moreover, unlike some countries, such as Botswana, where customary land has been increasing, in Zambia customary land is now gradually diminishing as conversions to state land increase. Indeed, with this emphasis on conversion of customary land to leasehold tenure, the question that continues to be ignored is whether smallholders can also obtain space on state land in areas with fertile soils. It seems hypocritical for the state and other powerful actors to argue that customary tenure is wasteful but then to target customary land for so-called FDI, while large swathes of fertile state land remain unutilised. In Chongwe, for example, twenty commercial farmers own well in excess of 40,000 hectares of state land (with some of the land not being utilised) (Chongwe District Council 2005), yet the majority of people subsist on farms averaging less than five hectares. At the national level, more than 75 percent of the country's farmers operate on farms of this small size, with 50 percent of these relying on farm sizes of less than a single hectare (Zambia Agriculture Research Institute 2008).

Urban Bias and Rural Development

An important factor often ignored in narratives linking customary land to rural backwardness is the urban bias inherent in regional development. In Zambia, the two decades following independence saw a heavy focus on industrialisation as part of a bid to modernise the country and the economy. The downside of this industrialisation project was heavy concentration of investment in urban areas at the expense of rural ones. Even today, much investment continues to be concentrated in urban areas. Rural ones, meanwhile, are characterised by inadequate economic infrastructure and lack of markets and access to municipal services. Moreover, Zambia inherited a local governance system that ignores customary areas in its planning and service-delivery functions. This colonial system was created to serve the interests of the small, elite white populations of the urban centres, but it has persisted to this day. Consequently, the modern-day local government system delivers municipal services only as far as township or municipal boundaries (on state land) and not to rural customary areas. Thus, our study sites in Chongwe and Chibombo Districts, for example, fall outside municipal boundaries and lie outside formal planning systems. These rural areas also lack provision of modern water-reticulation systems, sewerage services, and other basic amenities. This neglect is surprising given that rural dwellers pay the local taxes and levies that municipal authorities often demand. As a result, rural people—even in this day and age—are subsidising urban services. It is clear, then, that to stimulate rural development, Zambia's local governance system requires fundamental reform.

Agricultural Policies and Customary Land

Although as noted above, smallholder farmers are largely responsible for Zambia's bumper harvest in the staple crop, maize, comparison of smallholders (subsisting on customary land) and commercial farmers reveals great disparities in their levels of productivity (Golden Valley Research Trust 2008). Commercial farmers undoubtedly reap higher yields from their land than smallholders do, but can we attribute this to land tenure? Far from it. Many factors that condition farmers' productivity levels are independent of tenure issues. These factors include access to inputs, mechanised farming implements, technical extension services, and credit (Adams et al. 1999). Commercial farmers have access to loans, using their land as collateral, while farmers depending on customary land do not. In my view, however, this problem is not inherent to customary tenure; rather, it is embedded in the failure of successive governments to carry out reforms that would strengthen the position of customary-tenure holders and afford them the same legal rights that leaseholders have. Evidence from other countries such as Ghana and Botswana demonstrates that privatisation is not required to strengthen the rights of customary landholders.

Furthermore, the current agriculture-financing mechanisms in Zambia, even if smallholder farmers' lands were to be titled, do not favour smallholders. The financing mechanisms are heavily tilted towards commercial farmers. For example, some commercial banks require that loan applicants have not less than 100 hectares of land, a record of financial transactions over a certain period of years, and a minimum specified turnover during these years (Zambia National Commercial Bank, ZANACO 2014). When one considers that more than 50 percent of Zambia's smallholder farmers subsist on average farm sizes of less than a single hectare, it is clear that access to credit for smallholders will be problematic regardless of whether they are farming on private or customary land.

Adams et al. (1999) effectively critique the fallacy that land reform (alone) in favour of private tenure will inevitably translate to rural agricultural gains. They note that land reform can have positive impacts on production and investment only if reform is accompanied by access to inputs, credit, extension services, and markets, and when governments take initiatives to stimulate investment. But in Zambia, access to inputs, credit, and extension services have been highly problematic ever since the adoption of neoliberal policies that heralded a reduction in input subsidies to farmers and the collapse of rural credit institutions (Lewis et al. 2010).

In the study area, most respondents noted that apart from limited access to fertiliser and other inputs via the state's subsidy programme, the Farmer Input Support Programme (FISP), they had no access to credit services either to support crop production or livestock development (LURLAP Interviews 2014). The situation in Chongwe and Mungule is no different from that in other parts of the country, where rural dwellers also struggle to access inputs and credit. In locations such as Eastern Province, where cash crops such as cotton and tobacco are grown, private cotton and tobacco companies have filled the vacuum left by state credit institutions. These agroprocessing enterprises run outgrower credit schemes and contract farming systems, and have gained a reputation for exploiting local farmers through their exorbitant lending terms and poor pricing systems. Tenure reform alone cannot correct such systemic problems in rural development.

The Downside of Private Tenure

Our study demonstrates that the main beneficiaries of the conversion of customary tenure are, in fact, the urban elites and corporate actors. Moreover, lessons from Zambia's urban areas, such as Lusaka, where land is largely held in private hands, show that private tenure has merely served to profit a small and elite population, while the poor have been priced out of land and excluded (Chitonge and Mfune 2015). Similarly, as private tenure gains ascendancy in rural areas, cases of land grabbing and dispossession also appear to be on the rise. In all the study sites, cases of land changing hands from rural dwellers to urban elites were observed. The study also found cases of people's land (or part of it) being sold without their consent. Figure 3.1 presents the views of some respondents with respect to this trend.

Cases of land grabbing are, of course, not unique to Mungule. Recently there have been reports of large-scale land acquisitions from small-scale farmers for the purposes of commercial sugar production (Kalinda 2014) and game ranches. Similarly, at the regional level, Clements and Fernandes (2013) report cases of land grabbing in Mozambique. They note that with the rising cost of land, investing in sub-Saharan Africa has become attractive because fertile land here is extremely undervalued, and large tracts of it can be acquired under long-term leases. Land grabbing is a growing phenomenon (see Cotula et al. 2004), and the promotion of leasehold in the name of attracting investment (both foreign and local) is actually working to facilitate such grabbing. The result is often displacement of the poor from fertile lands; or in cases where unoccupied lands are being taken, the land may be unavailable for future rural generations.

Respondent 1: "Huh, we had plenty of land. Now this same issue that people want land … our land was sold" (widow in Malaka).

Respondent 2: "I have two hectares, it was larger than two hectares until my auntie sold part of it" (orphan in Malakata).

Respondent 3: "There was a man that bought part of my land through the headman without our consent" (Chibombela resident).

Figure 3.1: Cases of land sold without consent
Source: LURLAP Interviews 2014.

This is all reminiscent of the colonial era, when people were pushed off their fertile lands. While some actors tout "private" tenure as a means of fostering rural development, we must be cautious of promoting development that occurs in a climate of exclusion. There is a risk of creating glaring inequalities in the process. As Benjamin (2012) points out, where there is great property, there is great inequality. Lessons from Brazil demonstrate how such inequalities can be created (Clements and Fernandes 2013). As Moyo et al. (2013) also argue, grabbing land is not a solution for the large majority of humanity; and in the long run it cannot result in anything other than human catastrophe.

What Really Needs Reforming?

Although this chapter has demonstrated the importance of customary land to both the rural and urban poor, as noted in the introductory section this does not mean that the issue is untainted and not in need of reform. Customary-land tenure needs reform in many ways. Accordingly, this section turns to the question of what needs reform when it comes to customary tenure. Although numerous answers to this question may exist, this chapter focuses primarily on the views of the landholders who live and work the customary lands. From our study, three issues appear to be particularly important among rural actors. First, in the field, respondents were concerned that customary tenure occupies an inferior status, compared to leasehold, in the country's legal system. In particular, customary landholders cannot use their land as collateral to obtain loans. To do so, they must convert their land to leasehold. This concern was raised in all the FGDs conducted in Chongwe and Chibombo (LURLAP Focus Group Discussions 2014).

A second concern is the placing of land under the direct control of chiefs, who can legally grant permission to anybody to convert it to leasehold. This has created a situation in which chiefs have become a gateway to land acquisition in rural areas. It is important to note that customs and traditions vary considerably among the more than seventy Zambian ethnic groups. Likewise, local traditions concerning who holds power over land vary among these groups. The 1995 Lands Act places this power singularly in the hands of the chiefs. In many ways, this amounts to a standardisation of customary tenure. Of course, the idea of standardising customary tenure originates in the colonial perceptions of it. For example, Mvunga (1980) notes that the colonialists who bequeathed a dual-tenure system to the country lacked knowledge of how land was held under customary tenure. Instead, there was a generalised belief that indigenous people did not "own" land; rather, tribal land was viewed as "owned" by the chief. Although later studies revealed this to be a misconception, Zambia's contemporary land laws are still crafted in such a way that chiefs are viewed as "owning" land.

Our study shows that not all chiefs use this power to foster equitable distribution of land among their subjects or to benefit members of the chiefdom or wider society interests. Instead, many cases of corrupt practices, in which customary land has been fraudulently allocated to individuals or to corporate investors, have been reported. Sometimes village headmen (who are said to be the eyes of the chiefs) collude with individuals to sell land. For example, one respondent pointed out that headmen benefit from individuals who sell their lands. He pointed out, "At whatever price you sell, there must be a share for the headman to permit the person buying the land to establish themselves in the village" (LURLAP Interviews 2014).

Similarly, another respondent noted how headmen have placed customary lands on sale. He remarked, "Long ago, land was just given for free but later they [the chiefs and village heads] started charging. At first it was at K80 [(US$14)] then it increased to K800 [(US$140)] because of the population increase" (LURLAP Interview 2014). Another respondent pointed out that for "the two hectares I am negotiating now, they [the village headman] are asking for K10,000 [US$1670]" (LURLAP Interview 2014). These interviews demonstrate that fraudulent land allocations are rampant in customary areas. This has occurred primarily because too much power has been concentrated in the hands of the chiefs and their headmen. It appears also that these incidents are not restricted to our study sites. Other writers such as Metcalfe (2005) and Brown (2003) have noted similar scenarios elsewhere in the country.

The final issue that needs to be questioned regarding customary tenure is the patriarchal system of control and use of land. It was noted in all the study areas that inheritance rules favoured male family members. Women had access to land only through their fathers or husbands, rendering them vulnerable in the event of their fathers' or husbands' death.

These three concerns are just some of the elements of customary landholding that require reexamination, but it is important to point out that reform in no way equals a call for the wholesale dissolution of the practice. Furthermore, these three problematic issues concern customary *landholding*, not "customary tenure" itself. The problems outlined above associated with customary land appear to have emerged from the series of land reforms that have occurred since the colonial era. Successive governments have chosen not to carry out reform to strengthen the rights of customary landholders. Rather, many reforms have either weakened customary landholders' rights or subverted them to suit elite interests.

Conclusion

Our concern in this chapter has been the question of whether customary tenure remains relevant to Zambia's development. The chapter responds to current intense debates among scholars, the media, political elites, and other actors. At the time of writing, Zambia was in the midst of discussing a new draft constitution. One of the clauses dominating the debates dealt with the fate of customary land. Some argued that the clause demonstrated intent to bring customary land under state control by introducing "title deeds" for occupants of customary lands, i.e., the effective dissolution of customary tenure. Although the final adopted constitution retained customary tenure as before, the debate nonetheless brought to the fore the question of customary tenure's relevance today.

In contributing to this debate, this chapter has reexamined views that question the relevance of customary tenure to Zambia's development. The chapter has argued that such views are not new; they simply persist and are situated within the general fabric of dominant narratives concerning rural dwellers and the institutional arrangements that guide their access to and use of land (and other resources). Today, the state, corporate entities, and other elite actors draw on these narratives to advance their ideas of the "irrelevance of customary tenure" and the "good" of private tenure. As shown in this study, however, no evidence supports the view that customary tenure is irrelevant or validates the idea of private tenure as a "cure" for rural backwardness in Zambia. In fact, studies have noted that even in countries such as Kenya, which has long embraced the titling and registration of customary lands, evidence on the ground shows no correlation between land titling and an increase in investment (Cotula et al. 2004).

The crucial point in our findings is that despite twenty years of land reforms aimed at tilting landholding towards private tenure, customary tenure remains the principal route to land for many of the country's poor. Furthermore, the availability of land is crucial for both urban and rural dwellers. In a country with few economic opportunities outside the agricultural sector and that lacks a formal social-security system, easily accessible land on which farming and pastoral households can depend is vital. Moreover, over the past few years it has been the smallholders, relying on customary land, who have been responsible for the bumper harvests of the staple crop maize. As others have argued, smallholder agriculture remains the most important source of food production for most of the world's population (Martin 2013). Customary land, because of the locally suitable and flexible institutional arrangements that surround it, enables the poor to cope with livelihood uncertainty.

This chapter contends that if customary tenure does require reform, such reform should not be in the context of tilting customary land towards a tenure system that facilitates land grabs, fosters exclusion of the poor from fertile and productive lands, and reduces their capacity to cope with livelihood uncertainty. Instead, this chapter advocates reforms that seek to strengthen customary tenure itself (rather than dissolving it), giving it a status that increases the rights (including the right to use the land to access credit) of customary landholders regardless of their gender. Moreover, reforms to improve the well-being of the rural poor and to foster development should go beyond the issue of land tenure and address those historical structural forces that have been at the heart of rural underdevelopment in Zambia. As Murisa (2013) has shown in the case of Malawi, pro-poor rural-development and agricultural policies, such as the development of market infrastructure, agricultural loans, small-scale irrigation, road construction, primary water supplies, and rural electrification programmes, can increase rural productivity in customary areas and yield better dividends, compared to tenure reform alone.

References

Adams M., B. Cousins, and S. Manona. 1999. *Land Tenure and Economic Development in Rural South Africa: Constraints and Opportunities.* London: ODI.

Amanor-Wilks, D. 2009. "Land, labour and gendered livelihoods in a 'peasant' and a 'settler economy.'" *Feminist Africa* 12: 31–50.

Beitl, C. M. 2012. "Shifting policies, access, and the tragedy of enclosure in Ecuadorian mangrove fisheries: Towards a political ecology of the commons." *Journal of Political Ecology* 19: 94–113.

Benjamin, D. 2012. *Land Policy: Planning and the Social Consequences of Property.* Surrey: Ashgate.

Benjamin, E. C. 2004. Livelihoods and Institutional Development in the Malian Sahel: A Political Economy of Decentralised Natural Resources Management. PhD diss., University of Michigan.

Benjaminsen, T. A. 2011. "A critical political ecology of population growth, markets and land in Africa." In *The Political Economy of Environment and Development in a Globalised World: Exploring Frontiers,* edited by D. J. Kjosavik and P. Vedeld. Trondheim: Tapir Academic Press.

Birgegard, L. E. 1993. *Natural Resources Tenure: A Review of Issues and Experiences With Emphasis on Sub-Saharan Africa.* Uppsala: Swedish University of Agricultural Sciences, Institute of Agricultural Sciences and Rural Development.

Blaikie, P. 1985. *The Political Economy of Soil Erosion in Developing Countries.* Longman: Harlow.

Blaikie, P., and H. Brookfield. 1987. *Land Degradation and Society.* Methuen: London.

Bollier, D. 2013. "The commons as a new/old paradigm for governance, economics and policy." *Kosmos* Spring/Summer edition: 18–25.

Braun, V. J. 2007. "Rural-urban linkages for growth, employment and poverty reduction." Ethiopian Economic Association Fifth Conference on the Ethiopian Economy, June 7–9.

Brown, T. 2003. *Contestations, Confusion and Corruption: Market Based Land Reform in Zambia.* London: The IDL Group.
Bryant, R. L., and S. Bailey. 1997. *Third World Political Ecology.* New York: Routledge.
Burke, W. J., T. S. Jayne, and A. Chapota. 2010. *Factors Contributing to Zambia's 2010 Bumper Harvest.* Lusaka: Food Policy Research Project.
Central Statistical Office. 2012. 2010 Census Report. Lusaka: CSO.
Chileshe, J. 1998. "Land reforms and community based natural resources management." In *Enhancing Land Reform Strategies and Community Based Natural Resources Management,* edited by F. Mutefpa, E. Dengu, and M. Chenje. Harare: ZERO-Regional Environmental Organisation.
Chitonge, H., and O. Mfune. 2015. "The urban land question: The case of urban land conflicts in the city of Lusaka, 100 years after its founding." *Habitat International* 48: 209–218.
Chongwe District Council. 2005. Chongwe District Situation Analysis. Chongwe: CDC.
Clements, E. C., and B. M. Fernandes. 2013. "Land grabbing, agribusiness and the peasantry in Brazil and Mozambique." *Agrarian South: Journal of Political Economy* 2 (1): 41–70.
Cotula, L., C. Toulmin, and C. Hesse. 2004. *Land Tenure and Administration in Africa: Lessons of Experiences and Emerging Issues.* London: IIED.
Deininger, K., and H. Binswanger. 1999. "The evolution of the World Bank's land policy: Principles, experiences and future challenges." *The World Bank Research Observer* 14 (2): 247–76.
De Soto, H. 2000. The Mystery of Capital. Why Capitalism Triumphs in the West and Fails Everywhere Else. New York: Basic Books.
Devas, N., and D. Korboe. 2000. "City governance and poverty: The case of Kumasi." Environment and Urbanization 12 (1): 123–35.
Economic Association of Zambia. 2007. Equity and Development in Zambia. Lusaka: EAZ.
Ervine, K. 2011. "Conservation and conflicts: The intensification of property rights disputes under market-based conservation in Chiapas, Mexico." Journal of Political Ecology 18: 66–80.
Focus Group Discussions. 2010. Focus Group Discussions conducted in 2010.
Forsyth, T. 2003. Critical Political Ecology: The Politics of Environmental Science. New York: Routledge.

Golden Valley Research Trust. 2008. GART 2008 Year Book. Lusaka: GART.

Government of the Republic of Zambia. 2005. The Lands Act, 1995. Lusaka: GRZ.

Gyasi, E. A. 1994. "The adaptability of African communal land tenure to economic opportunity: The example of land acquisition for oil palm farming in Ghana, Africa." *Journal of the International African Institute* 64 (3): 391–405.

Hardin, G. 1968. "Tragedy of the commons." Science 168 (3859): 1243–48.

In-depth Interviews. 2010. In-depth Interviews conducted in 2010.

Kalikiti, W. S. 2013. "Colonial legacy: Post-colonial land policies, the rural masses and the peri-urban poor in Zambia, 1964-2012." *Journal of Humanities,* Special Issue of OSSREA Papers: 125–54.

Kalinda, T. 2014. "Acquisition of land for sugar production: Effects on the livelihoods of the Magobo small holder farmers in Zambia's Mazabuka district." In *International Land Deals in Eastern and Southern Africa,* edited by P. B. Mihyo. Addis Ababa: OSSREA.

Kean, S. A., and A. P. Wood. 1992. "Agriculture reform in Zambia. The dynamics of policy in the first republic." *Food Policy* 17 (1): 65–74.

Kruger, F. 1998. "Taking advantage of rural assets as a coping strategy for the urban poor: The case of rural-urban interactions in Botswana." *Environment and Urbanisation* 10 (1): 119–32.

Lesetedi, G. 2003. "Urban-rural linkages as an urban survival strategy among urban dwellers in Botswana: The case of Broadhurst residents." *Journal of Political Ecology* 10: 37–46.

Lusaka Times. 2014. "Zambia in bumper harvest as 2013/2014 production estimates show a 23 percent jump in maize output." Accessed July 6, 2014. https://www.lusakatimes.com/2014/05/05/zambia-bumper-harvest-20132014-production-estimates-show-23-jump-maize-output/.

Malekano, E. M. 2009. The Profession of Farming from a Small-Scale Farmer's Point of View. Paper presented at the Inaugural National Symposium on Agriculture held at the University of Zambia, Lusaka, April 7–8.

Martin, B. 2013. "Living in a theoretical interregnum: Capital lessons from southern African rural history." In *The Promise of Land: Undoing a Century of Dispossession in South Africa,* edited by F. Hendricks, L. Ntsebeza, and K. Helliker. Johannesburg: Jacana Media.

Mbilinyi, M., and G. Shechambon. 2009. "Struggles over land reform in Tanzania: Experiences of Tanzania gender networking programme and feminist activist coalition." *Feminist Africa* 12: 95–104.

Meinzen-Dick, R., and E. Mwangi. 2009. "Cutting the web of interest: Pitfalls of formalising property rights." *Land Use Policy* 26 (1): 36–43

Metcalfe, S. 2005. Landscape Conservation and Land Tenure in Zambia: Community Trusts in the Kazungula Heartland. Lusaka: Africa Wildlife Foundation Working Paper Series.

Metcalfe, S., and T. Kepe. 2008. "Dealing land in the midst of poverty: Commercial access to communal land in Zambia." *African and Asian Studies* 7: 235–57.

Mfune, O. 2014. "Managing common pool resources without state support: Insights from Shisholeka community in central Zambia." *Environment, Development and Sustainability* 16: 1263–2080.

Movement for Multiparty Democracy. 1991. Party Manifesto – 1991–1996. Lusaka: MMD.

Moyo, S., P. Jha, and P. Yeros. 2013. "The classical agrarian question: Myth, reality and relevance today." *Agrarian South* 2 (1): 93–119.

Murisa, T. 2013. "Prospects for smallholder agriculture in southern Africa." In *The Promise of Land: Undoing a Century of Dispossession in South Africa,* edited by F. Hendricks, L. Ntsebeza, and K. Helliker. Johannesburg: Jacana Media.

Mvunga, M. P. 1980. *The Colonial Foundations of Zambia's Land Tenure System.* Lusaka: NECZAM.

Ostrom, E. 1990. *Governing the Commons: The Evolution of Institutions for Collective Action.* Cambridge: Cambridge University Press.

Phiri, S. H. 1980. Some Aspects of Spatial Interaction and Reaction to Governmental Policies in a Border Area (Zambia/Malawi). PhD diss., Liverpool University, Liverpool.

Potts, D. 2005. "Counter-urbanisation on the Zambian copperbelt? Interpretations and implications." *Urban Studies* 42 (4): 583–609.

—. 2009. "The slowing of sub-Saharan Africa's urbanisation: Evidence and implications for urban livelihoods." *Environment and Urbanisation* 20 (1): 253–59.

Riddel, J. C. 2000. "Emerging trends in land tenure reform: Progress towards a unified theory." Food and Agriculture Organisation of the United Nations. Accessed March 20, 2015. www.fao.org.

Ruddle, K., E. Hviding, and R. E. Johannes. 1992. "Marine resources management in the context of customary tenure." *Marine Resources Economics* 7: 249–73.

Simon, R. B. 2004. Political Ecology of Living Aquatic Resources in LAO PDR. PhD diss., University of Sydney.

Vaccaro, I., and O. Beltran. 2010. "Conservationist governmental technologies in western European mountains: The unfinished transformations of the Pyrenees." *Journal of Political Ecology* 17: 28–41.

Zambia Agriculture Consultative Forum. 2010. Study on the Status of Customary_Land and How it Affects the Rights of the Indigenous Local Communities. Lusaka: Food Research Projects.

Zambia Agriculture Research Institute. 2008. Research Report on Agriculture and Climate Change in Zambia. Lusaka: ZARI.

Zambia Central Statistics Office. 2010. 2010 Census Report. Lusaka: Central Statistics Office.

Zambia Draft Constitution. 2014.

Zambia National Archives. 2010. District Notebooks. Lusaka: Zambia National Archives.

Zambia National Commercial Bank. 2014. Agriculture Finance Information Bulletin. Lusaka: ZANACO.

PART II:

CUSTOMARY LAND AND EMERGING LAND MARKETS IN ZAMBIA

CHAPTER FOUR

LAND-TENURE DYNAMICS IN AN EMERGING MARKET: OPPORTUNITIES AND CHALLENGES IN CHIBOMBO AND CHONGWE DISTRICTS, ZAMBIA

GEAR M. KAJOBA

Introduction

Most customary land in sub-Saharan Africa (SSA) has no registration of who owns it or who has rights to use it. Thus, in the past several decades many of the region's governments have set up programmes to formalise land rights on the premise that this would enhance tenure security and increase land-based investments and conservation of land (Toulmin 2009). In this regard, Zambia is not an exception. Although the process of formalising customary land in Zambia is not a state-driven programme, the conversion of customary land, which is administered by traditional leaders (i.e., chiefs and village heads), to leasehold tenure (formalisation) with title deeds for individuals or corporate entities, has gained momentum since the passing of the controversial Lands Act No. 20 of 1995 (1995 Lands Act).

At independence in 1964, Zambia inherited a dual land-tenure system that comprised Crown land and native reserves (see also chapter 3). The first category was Crown land. This consisted of land that had been reserved for European settlers and mining along a narrow strip of about twenty to thirty miles on either side of the railway line, which runs from Livingstone in the southern part of the country all the way to the Copperbelt into former Zaire (Toulmin 2009). This strip is commonly referred to as "the line of rail." The second category was native reserve and trust lands, set aside exclusively for indigenous people. Crown land was declared state land and comprised 6 percent of the nation's total land area.

Reserves and trust land were formally amalgamated in 1995 to form one category known as customary land, administered through traditional authorities. This comprised the remaining 94 percent.

However, since independence, the country's population has grown significantly and the monetary economy has expanded. Most of the state land along the line of rail, and especially in urban areas, has been taken up for various development initiatives. As a result, land for development and urban settlement is available only in customary areas. To make this land available for development to individuals and corporate entities, the state promotes conversions of customary land. The 1995 Lands Act provides for such conversions. Other than provisions for issuance of title deeds on formerly customarily held land, the act allows the alienation of land, including to non-Zambians, and provides for the establishment of a land market (GRZ 1995).

This chapter examines land-tenure dynamics in Mungule, Nkomesha, and Bunda-Bunda chiefdoms, focusing on both opportunities and challenges regarding rural livelihoods in the context of an emerging market economy in Zambia. Although the LURLAP study, from which this chapter draws, focused on Mungule and Nkomesha chiefdoms, residents of Bunda-Bunda chiefdom (formerly in Chongwe District but now in the new Rufunsa District) were also interviewed. This was because background information suggested that in Bunda-Bunda chiefdom, perceptions of the conversion of customary-land tenure to leasehold were somewhat more flexible than in Nkomesha chiefdom.

The discussions in this chapter are part of the broader review of trends occurring in Zambia concerning land conversion. The work is also part of a comparative research study on South Africa and Zambia, involving scholars from the Centre for African Studies at the University of Cape Town and those from the Department of Geography and Environmental Studies and the School of Agriculture at the University of Zambia (see chapter 1 for details). The research focused on land use and rural livelihoods.

The conversion of customary tenure in Zambia (details of the conversion process are presented in chapter 2 of this volume) has gained momentum since the passing of the 1995 Lands Act. At independence in 1964, a dual land-tenure system was embraced, in which former Crown land became state land (6 percent of total national land), and customary land was under the jurisdiction of traditional leaders in the reserves and trust land areas (accounting for 94 percent of the land). However, since independence the country's population has increased and the economy has expanded, with state land completely taken up. If more land is to be made available for development, conversion of most of the customary land is necessary; hence, the need for this study to explore the dynamics and trends accompanying the practice of converting customary land to leasehold tenure.

The chapter discusses land-tenure dynamics in terms that locate Zambia in the broader context of emerging markets in Africa (section 3). Section 4 reviews the drivers of land-tenure dynamics in customary areas. A discussion of the opportunities arising from the conversion of customary land follows. Section 6 addresses the challenges resulting from the practice of converting customary land into leasehold tenure, and section 7 concludes the conclusion.

Background to the Study

The data used in this chapter were collected during fieldwork in Nkomesha, Mungule, and Bunda-Bunda chiefdoms between January 2013 and June 2014. Information was collected through focus-group discussions (FGDs) and in-depth interviews with key informants, including headmen/women and other community leaders. For details of how the data were collected and the number of people who were interviewed and participated in the FGDs, see Table 5.1.

	Interviews And Focus Group Discussions (FGDs)				**Short Survey**
Chiefdom	*Male*	*Female*	*Headmen/ women*	*Total*	*Households*
Mungule	30	39	9	78	42
Nkomesha	11	9	2	21	23
Bunda Bunda	17	11	2	30	20
Total	**57**	**59**	**13**	**129**	**85**

Table 4.1. Number of respondents by chiefdom
Source: Compiled by authors based on LURLAP data and fieldwork notes

The main issues that were discussed in the FGDs included the following: land use, settlement, land size, cropping systems, tenure conversion, traditional governance in relation to land, tenure-security concerns, land use and food security, investment in land, non-farm income generation, gender relations around land, and food-security interventions. Participation in the discussions was based on availability, and all who turned up at the FGDs in the stated villages were welcomed and encouraged by the facilitator to express their views freely. The discussions were recorded and later transcribed, although individual researchers also took notes of the proceedings. In the FGDs, both men and women were represented, as were headmen and headwomen, village officials (including village secretaries), village-development committee members, church leaders, and youths.

To understand the opportunities and challenges created by the practice of converting customary land to leasehold tenure, we started by asking the residents about the village structure through which land is administered. In all the villages where we conducted fieldwork, residents confirmed that the village heads (women or men) are central, not just to the allocation and administration of customary land but in the day-to-day life of people in the village. They stated that close family members of the most recent previous village head appoint or choose the village heads (headpersons) according to the customs and traditions of each ethnic group or local traditional governance structure. For instance, headman Malakata of Kamalata village in Mungule chiefdom indicated that a village council made up of close relatives of the previous village head appoints a headperson. A village committee, which is elected by the people in the village, assists the village head in making decisions concerning village affairs. The village council also has the power to dethrone the village headperson when necessary. Thus, the village headperson becomes the local representative of the chief in the village and reports directly to the chief on any traditional governance matters affecting village members or subjects. The headperson also coordinates development matters with the village committee.

The Conceptual Framcwork: Zambia as an Emerging Market Economy

This chapter discusses land-tenure dynamics within the general framework of Zambia as an emerging market economy. According to Kvint (2004), the concept of emerging markets appeared after 1985 with the collapsc of dictatorships in Asia, Latin America, and the former Soviet Union. Thus, with the end of the Cold War between the East and the West, an emerging market is widely seen as one that makes the transition from a commandist state-controlled economy to a free-market economy. Kvint (2004, 38) goes on to state that to understand emerging markets, "it is necessary to consider the social, political, and business perspectives as well as the purely financial ones." But to define what an emerging market economy actually is, "it is…critically important to evaluate the level of development of capitalist institutions and business activity" (Kvint 2004, 40). These institutions and business activities might include banks, insurance companies, law firms, capital markets, accounting firms, and sound infrastructure that includes transport and communications to facilitate business transactions.

In political terms, Kvint (2004) believes that an emerging market economy enjoys democracy and democratic institutions such as a constitution, periodic elections, political stability, and a functioning democratic form of government. In addition, such a country allows foreign investment and investors to operate and has an environment conducive to an entrepreneurial spirit. Thus, Kvint (2004) seems to be of the view that an emerging market economy is characterised by a society in transition from a commandist economy (in which the state controls major sectors of the economy, including means of production) to a free-market-oriented economy that features increased levels of economic freedom, an expanding middle class, improving standards of living, social stability, tolerance, and an increase in cooperation with bilateral and multilateral institutions (such as the World Bank, the International Monetary Fund, and the United Nations).

Generally, "emerging market" is the term applied to rapidly developing economies such as the United Arab Emirates, Chile, and Malaysia, all of which are undergoing rapid growth. With respect to emerging markets such as Mexico and Turkey, Marois (2012) argues that financial considerations have become more significant; thus he has developed the idea of "emerging finance capitalism." To Marois it seems that in the countries he studied, the collective interests of finance capital shape the policies and choices of governments; these governments he refers to as state elites, which sit over and above the labour and popular classes.

Vercueil (2012) distinguishes the concept of "emerging economies" from "emerging markets." For him, an emerging economy displays, among other things, the following characteristics: an intermediate income that is between 10 and 75 percent of the average European Union per capita income; brisk economic growth in the last ten years and narrowing of the income gap with advanced economies; profound institutional transformations that have contributed to deeper integration into the world economy, as a result of globalisation. According to Vercueil (2012), more than fifty countries (representing 60 percent of the world's population and 45 percent of its GDP) matched these criteria by 2010, including those grouped as the BRICS, i.e., Brazil, Russia, India, and China, and South Africa.

For the purposes of this chapter, however, Kvint's (2004) broader concept of an emerging market applies more prominently to the situation prevailing in Zambia and the rest of Africa as a whole. The transitions from state-controlled economies to free-market economies (but with state interventions in the case of Zambia, including partial subsidies to smallholder farmers who produce most of the staple food, maize, and social cash-transfer schemes piloted in some parts of the country to cushion vulnerable groups) and the welcoming of foreign direct investments (FDI) in mining, agriculture, manufacturing, construction, tourism, and the communications sectors seem to be contributing to economic growth, the growth of a middle class, and the emergence of micro, small, and medium enterprises (SMEs) within the broader framework of regional and continental trade, integration, and globalisation. In her foreword to Kgomoeswana's (2014, vii) book *Africa Is Open for Business*, Maite Nkoana-Mashabane, Minister of International Relations and Cooperation in the Republic of South Africa, writes that countries or regions across the African continent have "turned the corner towards economic prosperity." In Zambia, since President Frederick Chiluba and the Movement for Multiparty Democracy (MMD) won democratic elections and removed the socialist-humanist economic policies of Dr. Kenneth Kaunda and his United National Independence Party (UNIP) in 1991, a shift towards economic liberalisation has helped usher in an economy that meets Kvint's above-noted characterisation of an emerging society and economy.

With respect to the dynamics of land tenure (discussed later in this chapter), one can also argue that an entrepreneurial spirit is now entrenched especially among the urban business elite in the country. Kajoba (1998) argues that since 1991, there has been a transition from protectionist policies that perceived land as a valueless resource that should not be bought or sold towards empowerment policies that view land as an economic asset with a market value.

The Drivers of Land-Tenure Dynamics

The drivers of the current customary-land tenure dynamics, among other factors, include population pressure caused by urban expansion of the capital city, Lusaka; rural-to-rural movements (as well as return migration) of people to the surrounding hinterland; land-use change from agriculture to industrial, business, and residential uses; and gradual changes in the attitudes of people towards customary land, which is increasingly perceived as having economic value.

Population Pressure

According to the 2010 Census of Population and Housing, the population of Zambia at that time was 13,046,508. Of this total population 7,978,274 people, or 61 percent, resided in rural areas, while 5,068,234 people, or 39 percent, resided in urban areas. The most densely populated province in Zambia in 2010 was Lusaka, whose density increased from 31.6 persons/km^2 in 1980, to 45.1 in 1990, to 63.5 in 2000, and to 100.4 in 2010, in contrast to the national average figure of 17.3 persons/km^2 in 2010 (see also chapter 10).

Given the expanding population density of the city of Lusaka and of the provincial hinterland, the resulting pressure acts as a driver of land-tenure dynamics in the surrounding chiefdoms, including Mungule (Chibombo), Nkomesha (Chongwe), and Bunda-Bunda (Rufunsa) chiefdoms.

When individuals such as retirees from Lusaka and other urban centres look for land on which to build houses and settle and when rural-rural migration occurs, the surrounding villages must accommodate settlers seeking land from the village heads. These movements may include return migrants, retirees, and those who choose to relocate in search of greener pastures. When participants in the FGDs were asked whether people from Lusaka had approached them asking for land, the responses were affirmative.

Some of those who retire from employment in the capital city (as in a case in Mungule, cited below) may look for a place to establish a smallholding and a modern house in the hinterland of Lusaka, instead of returning to their village of origin. They choose this option for numerous reasons. First, as Zambian citizens, they are free to settle in any part of the country as long as they are welcomed by the traditional authorities and they observe the formalities of approaching the chief via the village head to ask for land where they can settle.

Second, locations such as those in the study areas, which are in close proximity to the city, are preferable compared to remote places that are far from urban areas. This is because the retirees and their families are accustomed to urban amenities such as shopping facilities, banks, hospitals, and other modern necessities, all of which they can continue to access from nearby peri-urban locations.

Third, the retirees are likely in some instances to prefer to settle in an area away from their tribal kin because many years of urban living have weakened traditional kinship ties. Retirees often want to enjoy the benefits of retirement with their own immediate family, without undue claims on their wealth by tribal kin who are likely to anticipate a share of such benefits, per traditional norms under the system of communal village living.

Fourth, it is advantageous and considered equally important to settle close to the city so that the retiree can easily access urban markets and supermarkets. Being close to urban markets allows retirees and their families to supply produce and equipment that can support small-scale agricultural and livestock production at the retirement smallholding, with the retirement package being used as investment capital.

Land-Use Change

Land use may be defined simply as the use to which a portion of land is put under prevailing socioeconomic, technological, environmental, and other conditions. In the study areas, the majority of the people are the Lenje (in Mungule chiefdom) and the Soli (in the Nkomesha and Bunda-Bunda chiefdoms), who have traditionally grown *maila* (sorghum) as a staple cereal. However, since the advent of colonialism and the influence of modernisation, agricultural crops now include maize, cotton, cabbages, rape, tomatoes, and small livestock such as chickens, goats, and pigs, which are supplied to markets in Lusaka (see chapter 6). The increase in the rural population, the desire to generate farm incomes, and the demand for agricultural produce in the nearby urban markets may have contributed to land-use change.

It is worth emphasising that land-use change in the study areas has historically meant a change or transition from traditional subsistence-level agricultural production of *maila* (the staple cereal) to the adoption of maize. Muntemba (1977) states that in Bulenje society, the introduction of a peasant farmer scheme during the colonial period between 1946 and 1948 led to agricultural change in crops, land tenure, and agricultural technologies (see chapter 6 in this volume). Maize, rather than the traditional *maila*, was widely adopted as the major cash crop, and modern agricultural implements such as ox-drawn ploughs began to diffuse to the rural population. The dynamics of colonial land and agricultural policy, involving land alienation to make way for European settlement in the 1920s, caused congestion and land shortages in the Lenje native reserves. Thus, in Chief Mungule's area, the "peasant farmer scheme" could not be introduced due to insufficient land available (Muntemba 1977).

Because of land scarcity, land in areas adjacent to large urban settlements, including the Mungule area, had increased in value by the 1970s (Muntemba 1977, 359). In more recent years, land-use change has continued to reflect the desire of individuals (locals and foreign investors) to use the land for semicommercial or commercial productive activities. Retirees and other investors from Lusaka are establishing smallholdings that promote commercial agricultural, livestock, and poultry production. For instance, in Mungule a retiree has been farming since 1999 after the village head allocated land to him, which he then converted to leasehold tenure. He owns about eight hectares of land, on which he keeps 3,675 laying hens and collects sixty-one to ninety-one trays of eggs per day (one tray holds thirty eggs, which is 2,930 eggs each day). He also keeps 1,400 broilers, which he sells for ZMW17 at farm-gate price and at ZMW27 to supermarkets in Lusaka. This local farmer also has a piggery, grows tomatoes, and employs six workers.

Apart from increased commercial agricultural production, other types of land use include construction activities such as blockmaking, real estate, lodges, trading premises, maize milling, and sand quarrying. These income-generating activities are creating greater demand for land in the areas where the LURLAP study was conducted. Thus, land-use change there clearly relates to the increasing population of Lusaka and its hinterland and contributes to the land-tenure dynamics that are the subject of this chapter.

Change in Perceptions of Land

In the Mungule area, a key informant explained that the chiefdom faced a great challenge due to its proximity to Lusaka. He said that until 1980, the chief gave land free of charge to refugees from South Africa and Zimbabwe as part of a national policy to accommodate those fleeing oppressive white-minority regimes in the region. The informant further explained that when refugees had to return, especially following Zimbabwe's independence in 1980,

> the chief ruled that refugees could be given a token of money for the fields that they had been cultivating. But the people who got those fields started claiming that they bought land from the ex-refugees, and the headmen had no power to control those people who claimed to have bought the land. Such claimants even ended up asking for permission to get title deeds near the road (LURLAP Interviews 2013).

Given this historical background and the other dynamics reviewed above, especially those relating to population pressure, the desire in the Mungule area to convert and sell customary land and obtain title deeds seems to have gained momentum. Participants in the focus-group discussions during field research confirmed this desire.

In a study conducted by Kajoba (1994) in Chinena village, in Chief Liteta's area (in Chibombo District), increasing agricultural commercialisation has attracted more people to settle in the area, leading to land scarcity, land disputes, and a tendency towards individualisation of tenure. Similarly, a study by Malambo (2013) in Chibombo District (including the Mungule area) showed that individuals from the area and others from outside had benefited from changed attitudes towards customary land and from the legal provisions that enabled the sale and conversion of customary land to leasehold tenure. These shifts are taking place due to investments flowing to converted customary land. Newly established investments in the study area include a cooking-oil processing plant, filling stations and lodges, and other investments. Apart from creating employment, some local people are also selling portions of their land to raise money with which to improve their houses, to purchase solar panels, bicycles, motorbikes, radios, and cell phones, and to send their children to school and gain access to medical care.

As a result of the increased population of Lusaka city and its hinterland as well as local and foreign investors' growing demand for land, local people in the study areas are beginning to perceive customary land as an economic asset with marketable value. Changes in land use reveal that land is increasingly perceived as a valuable economic asset. In response, individual attitudes towards the resource are gradually changing in some areas. This is indeed the case in Mungule, although not so much in Nkomesha's chiefdom.

Opportunities Created

Livelihood and Investment Activities

Because the three chiefdoms included in the LURLAP study (Mungule, Nkomesha, and Bunda-Bunda) are in close proximity to Lusaka, the local people are able to engage in livelihood activities that benefit from the expanding market in the city and its hinterland. This growing demand should also be situated within the broader context of a market economy that has been emerging since 1991, when privatisation and economic liberalisation were introduced. Thus, different stakeholders are responding to opportunities created by these changes, such as participation in market gardening, in which men but more commonly women cultivate vegetables such as cabbage, rape, tomatoes, eggplant, and watermelon for the urban market. Others are involved in the cultivation of maize, cotton, sweet potatoes, groundnuts, and the raising of livestock to provide eggs, chicken, and pork to urban consumers via the supermarkets and ordinary open markets, such as those at Soweto Market in Lusaka. In addition, local people are raising non-farm incomes by participating in trade, charcoal production, sand quarrying, and stone crushing.

A key informant explained that there were about twenty to thirty investors who were allowed to operate in the chiefdom, including a Chinese firm that was involved in stone crushing and the production of toilet tissue. Apart from providing employment to local people, each investor was expected to contribute ZMW1500 per year to the Chiefdom Trust Fund, from which monies were allocated to the traditional annual Kulamba Kubwalo ceremony of the Lenje-speaking people.

Sale of Land

Individuals' changing perceptions of customary land have, in some cases, created opportunities to rent out land, while in other situations land is being sold and converted to private leasehold with title deeds. The proceeds from such transactions are used to build better houses and pay for domestic electrification, school fees, and medical expenses. The process of selling land in Nkomesha's chiefdom appears to be occurring in a clandestine manner between willing sellers and buyers, although without conversion to private titled land, as a result of participants' fear that traditional authorities will evict and banish them.

With respect to the sale of customary land, the village secretary in Kakubo, in Chieftainess Nkomesha's chiefdom, stated at the FGD, "those rich people from Lusaka come to buy land," adding that "pressure near Lusaka forces us to encourage the building of modern houses, so one may sell a portion of land to build a modern house."

When the FGD moderator asked about the implications of selling land with respect to customary regulations, the village secretary stated, "Now, it is difficult to find free land to settle on—yes, we are all breaking the regulations, but a chick learns to deposit droppings in the *kraal* from the mother!" This response implies that locals were following what the leadership was doing in the first place. Although land sales were taking place, the village secretary said, "people are fearful of losing their land, so they are being tempted to sell; but selling is underground, as the chieftainess can repossess land from those known to be selling." But one man told us, "there is a way of selling without attracting penalties or reprisals from the traditional authorities." At this same village meeting, a female participant added her voice to the discussion, stating, "Now, the houses we had traditionally were not strong—to build better houses we are tempted to sell a portion of land to raise money to build more modern houses and to send our children to school."

This process is thus perceived as a positive development. A discussant illuminated this as follows: "When you buy/sell land, the developer builds a better house, brings electricity, and those in the neighbourhood can imitate the development process and do the same." He further added that, in fact, "the chieftainess (Nkomesha) has told the headmen in the zone to process titles to individuals," but the process had not yet taken off.

In a study conducted in Southern Province, Sitko (2010) found that scarcity of arable land has led to the emergence of a clandestine market, which allows some individuals to consolidate land under their control and profit from it. The study also found that prominent local people, including village leaders, have benefited from land sales. The author argued that these people participated in this clandestine land market because, in their view, the chief was also participating in the de facto selling of land by accepting monetary tributes from individuals in exchange for land.

Similar land-tenure dynamics are occurring in other African countries such as Tanzania and Burkina Faso, where increasing agricultural commercial production has placed a higher premium on land, and both traditional authorities and individuals are borrowing, renting, and even selling or exchanging land for money—practices that were once unthinkable but are now becoming common (Mthaien et al. 2002; Odgaard 2002).

In Mungule and Bunda-Bunda, unlike in the Nkomesha chiefdom, people's attitudes (including traditional leaders) towards the titling of land are more favourable since they view the process as the only way to secure their interests given the expanding urban pressure for land in the hinterland of Lusaka. However, local people lamented that the costs of hiring surveyors, and other steps required to convert land, were prohibitive to most of those wishing to convert customary land and obtain titles.

Individuals and groups who are taking advantage of opportunities relating to the sale and conversion of customary land include the following:

- Those with some education who are aware of the economic opportunities in the country since the Movement for Multiparty Democracy (MMD) introduced economic liberalisation and a free-market economy in 1991. These people know that in Zambia, free-market imperatives are prompting enterprising individuals to consider land as a valuable economic commodity that requires security and investment.
- Those with leadership roles, such as teachers, religious leaders, traditional leaders, and micro- and small-business leaders.
- Those who are exposed to social changes occurring in urban environments, including workers in various urban-based institutions

> who have the knowledge and desire to improve themselves through hard work and their own initiative.

These groups could be perceived as part of the rural elite. Such people should not be demonised as aliens who disadvantage the people among whom they reside; rather, they should be considered innovative individuals able to take advantage of the opportunities around them (Rogers 2003). That is to say, these early adopters of innovation in a rural milieu are trendsetters. Such people set examples for others to follow as they attempt to improve themselves on a daily basis under prevailing circumstances.

Individuals in these groups include men, women, and even some enterprising youths. For instance, during an in-depth interview at Chombela School in Chieftainess Mungule's area in Chibombo, one man was asked the question, "Can you sell the land, are you faithful to your children or what is the story there?" The response was, "I don't intend to sell because already it's not enough for me and looking at the size of my family, I can't sell even if I were given an opportunity" (LURLAP Interview 2014). But the interviewee further disclosed that he was negotiating to *purchase* two hectares of land to increase his current holding of 6.5 hectares and that the landowners were asking for a sum of K10,000. He further remarked, "People with large sums of money come looking for land so you can be tempted to sell it" (LURLAP Interview 2014).

As for those individuals and groups who seem not to be taking advantage of the opportunities arising from land-tenure dynamics, Rogers (2003) presents a model of the diffusion of innovation that outlines a continuum of early adopters, early majority, late majority, and laggards. With the passage of time, with sensitisation, and with attitudinal change based on persuasion, even those individuals who are lagging behind may perceive things in a new light and seek to benefit from the new opportunities presented by the emerging market economy in rural communities. They, too, may then perceive the value of converting, selling, and buying customary land.

Challenges Arising from Land-Tenure Dynamics

Land Scarcity and Land Disputes

The research in the study areas showed that a major challenge arising from the current land-tenure dynamics, especially in Nkomesha's area (Chongwe), is land shortages. This arises from increasing population in the villages, which is occurring naturally and caused by in-migration.

Land shortages in these areas also stem from the fact that during the colonial period and after independence, the Nkomesha area ceded a large amount of land to Lusaka city authorities. Participants in FGDs explained that the population increase had resulted in village heads reducing the landholding size allocated to new settlers. Participants pointed out that in Chombela village (Mungule) in the 1980s, larger parcels of land (up to ten hectares) were allocated to individuals. But as the population increased, subdivisions occurred, and new settlers are thus allocated much smaller parcels of land. Further subdivisions occur as children inherit and share their parents' land.

An in-depth interview with headman Malakata (for Chieftainess Mungule) revealed that many people were seeking land in the area. The headman confirmed this, saying that many people go to the areas to ask for land, and he added, "A long time ago people were running away from the villages for fear of the witches and wizards but now witches and wizards are in town so they are coming back to the village" (LURLAP Interviews 2014). When he was asked, "What kind of people are buying land, are they only Zambians?" the headman responded, "Not just Zambians but also foreigners" (LURLAP Interviews 2014). In Chongwe, one male resident in Chieftainess Nkomesha's area, who had a three-hectare holding, admitted that the plots allocated to residents or newcomers are getting smaller. He further observed that in the future, "It will be a problem [to access land] because the headmen don't have any more land" (LURLAP Interviews 2014).

The research also showed that as a result of reductions in land size, land use was affected since villagers were no longer able to practise crop rotation. Productivity was therefore also affected. The focus-group discussions in all the study areas also revealed that villagers were experiencing land disputes relating mainly to encroachment and lack of secure boundaries, since customary rules forbid fences around homesteads. Participants in one FGD stated that disputes often arise as follows: "When someone's animals—for example cows—trespass on someone else's land and destroy their crops, or eat their bananas, a dispute may arise because that may be the only source of income for that person" (LURLAP FGD 2014).

Lack of proper records showing who owns which land under customary tenure contributes to land-tenure insecurity and land disputes arising from encroachments. Common practices such as planting trees and hedges do not adequately mediate such disputes because over time, trees marking the boundaries may be cut. Thus, stray livestock can destroy neighbours' crops, leading to disputes. A study by Kajoba (1994) in Chinena village (Chibombo), where agricultural commercialisation has led many new settlers to cultivate vegetables such as rape, tomatoes, and watermelon, showed that land scarcity was also leading to encroachments, resulting in further land disputes.

Tenure Insecurity and Access to Natural Resources

Data analysis from the study areas also suggests that as a result of the increased number of people from Lusaka seeking land, villagers are experiencing insecurity of tenure. Expansionary urban pressure for land is likely to lead to a situation where, contrary to customary rules, individuals are tempted to convert their land to private titled land or engage in clandestine land sales even without title, for fear that Lusaka will eventually swallow their customary holdings and force them to pay council rates and other fees.

In response to this tenure insecurity and the threat of Lusaka's urban expansion, headman Manenekela explained that in the Chombela area (Mungule), the traditional authorities are encouraging local people to apply for conversion in order to obtain title deeds to their land. The headman emphasised that there was no other way of securing people's land. He further added that given the pressures of urbanisation, in fifteen to twenty years' time no customary land would remain. When asked how he, personally, was preparing to respond to this urban pressure, he stated that he had not yet converted his parcel of village land but did have plans to do so.

Community members in the villages also commented on the challenge of accessing natural resources such as water and wood fuel (firewood), especially in areas where farm owners prevent them from cutting down trees for firewood and thatch grass. Because of this, women told researchers that they usually venture farther into the hills to access fuel sources. Furthermore, women in some areas complained that water was scarce. This is probably because numerous streams have dried up as a result of climate change. In a personal communication on June 15, 2015, with Dr. Henry H. Sichingabula of the Department of Geography and Environmental Studies at the University of Zambia, it was pointed out that the Chongwe dam dried up in the 2013–14 agricultural season as a result of low rainfall. This negatively affected the amount of water in Chongwe River, which lies within the Nkomesha study area in Chongwe District. A similar fate befell other streams, both within and beyond the study areas. This state of affairs negatively affects rain-fed agriculture and those who depend on simple irrigation methods that rely on river water. It was also pointed out that as a result of the women's challenges in accessing wood fuel, the price of charcoal (for cooking) was increasing. Yet, at the same time, there were limited sources of income for women, especially in areas where water is scarce for vegetable gardening.

Conclusion

This chapter has shown that in the study areas, land-tenure dynamics have created both opportunities and challenges within the broader framework of an emerging market economy in Zambia. These dynamics affect many stakeholders, including community members, retirees, local and foreign investors, and traditional leaders, who are responding to them in various ways.

Studies from other parts of Zambia and elsewhere in Africa record similar findings: a gradual change in perceptions of customary land pertaining to land conversion and the clandestine selling of land. This is especially the case in Chibombo and Rufunsa, rather than in the Nkomesha area. The proceeds earned contribute to livelihood improvements such as building (and even electrifying) homes, paying school fees for children, purchasing livestock, and even purchasing household luxuries such as mobile phones, bicycles, motorbikes, radios, and motor vehicles.

References

Central Statistical Office. 2011. Zambia 2010 Census of Population and Housing: Preliminary Population Figures. Lusaka: Central Statistical Office.

Kajoba, G. M. 1994. "Changing perceptions on agricultural land tenure under commercialization among small scale farmers: the case of Chinena village in Chibombo district (Kabwe rural), central Zambia." *Science Reports of Tohoku University* 44: 1, 43–64.

—. 1998. "The landmarks of Zambia's land tenure system: From protectionism to empowerment." In Proceedings of the International Conference on Land Tenure in the Developing World with a Focus on Southern Africa, edited by Michael Barry, 300–10. Cape Town: University of Cape Town.

Kgomoeswana, V. 2014. *Africa is Open for Business: Ten Years of Game-Changing Headlines.* Johannesburg: Macmillan.

Kvint, V. L. 2004. *The Global Emerging Market in Transition: Articles, Forecasts and Studies.* 2nd edition. New York: Fordham University Press.

Malambo, A. H. 2013. "Land administration in Zambia since 1991: History, opportunities and challenges." Global Advanced Research Journal of History, Political Science and International Relations 2 (4): 53–66.

Marois, T. 2012. States, Banks and Crisis: Emerging Finance Capitalism in Mexico and Turkey. Cheltenham: Edward Elgar.

Mthaien, P., M. Zongo, and L. Pare. 2002. "Monetary land transactions in western Burkina Faso: Commoditisation papers and ambiguities." *European Journal of Development Research* 14 (2): 109–28.

Muntemba, M. S. 1977. "Thwarted development: A case study of economic change in Kabwe rural district of Zambia, 1902–1970." In *The Roots of Rural Poverty in Central and Southern Africa,* edited by R. Palmer and N. Parsons, 345–64. London: Heinemann.

Odgaard, R. 2002. "Scrambling for land in Tanzania: Processes of formalization and legitimization of land rights." *European Journal of Development Research* 14 (2): 71–88.

Rogers, E. M. 2003. *Diffusion of Innovations. 3rd edition.* New York: Macmillan.

Sichingabula, H. M. 1998. "Rainfall variability, drought and implications of its impacts on Zambia, 1886." In *Water Resources Variability in Africa during the XXth Century,* edited by E. Servant, D. Huggers, J. M. Fritsch, and M. Hulme, 125–34. Proceedings of the International Conference on Water Resources Variability in Africa during the XXth Century held at Abidjan, November 16–19. Wallingford: International Association of Hydrological Sciences.

Sichingabula, H. M., and H. Sikazwe. 1999. "Occurrence, severity and magnitude of hydrological drought in Zambia: Impacts and implications." In *Hydrological Extremes: Understanding, Predicting, Mitigating,* edited by Lars Gottschalk, 297–305. Proceedings of the 20th General Assembly of the International Union of Geodesy and Geophysics, Birmingham, UK, July 18–30. Wallingford: International Association of Hydrological Sciences.

Sitko, N. J. 2010. "Fractured governance and local frictions: The exclusionary nature of a clandestine land market in southern Zambia." *Africa* 80: 1, 36–55.

Vercueil, J. 2012. *Emerging Countries Brazil, Russia, India, China – Economic Change and New Challenge. 3rd edition.* Paris: Breal.

Wikipedia. n.d. "Emerging market terminology." en.wikipedia.org/wiki/Emerging-Markets Terminology.

CHAPTER FIVE

EMERGING LAND MARKETS AND THE "CUSTODIANS" OF A FLEETING LAND RESOURCE: PERSPECTIVES FROM CHIBOMBO AND CHONGWE DISTRICTS OF ZAMBIA

DAVID KAFWAMBA

Introduction

Land, as the single most important resource for rural livelihoods in Africa (Potts and Mutambirwa 1990; Thebe and Rakotje 2013), is the foundation of customary governance. Since the colonial period, several forces have had a profound impact on African customary-land governance systems, especially with respect to property rights. Property rights are conceptualised in this chapter as enforceable claims underpinning individual action relating to land (Ostrom and Charlotte 2007). These rights place demands on others not to interfere with aspects of an individual's rights (Abdulai 2006; Cole and Grossman 2002; Obeng-Odoom 2012), such as the right to alienate land. Although this may be the case in principle, current increasing commoditised access to customary land in most parts of Africa is shifting the dynamics of customary-land governance.

In the Zambian context, the interplay between property rights and commoditised access to customary land creates dynamics that challenge conventional views of customary-land tenure. For instance, notions of individuals being unable to alienate and/or sell customary land are becoming highly contested. Therefore, this chapter explores the interplay of individual property rights and emerging land markets and its effect on Zambia's customary land. Furthermore, it examines customary authorities' responses to this shift in two contrasting contexts. This paper argues that, apart from creating a threat to customary-land governance, this interplay has generally created two interesting scenarios. First, formal land markets are gradually influencing the alienation of customary land to leasehold tenure, while informal land markets are increasingly individualising customary-land ownership. Second, some customary authorities' resistance to formal land markets is creating a clandestine land market in which locals secretly exercise their individual rights to property on customary land.

The chapter draws on data from two contrasting Zambian chiefdoms with respect to customary-land governance. The Mungule chiefdom in Chibombo District provides a context in which customary authorities allow formal and informal land markets to operate freely, while Nkomesha chiefdom in Chongwe District is a context of pronounced resistance by customary authorities, in principle, against commoditisation of customary land.

The chapter is organised into five sections. The first section briefly highlights the historical development of the current customary-tenure model with respect to property rights. The second shows the nature and intricacies of emerging land markets while exploring the increase of commoditised access to customary land. Here, our interest lies in questions relating to the nature of land markets in the two areas, participants in these markets, and the resultant effects. The third section shows the interaction of property rights with both informal and formal land markets, while the fourth examines the impact of this interplay on power relations within the current customary-tenure framework. The final section outlines the responses of customary authorities to the effects of this interplay.

The Colonial Foundations of the Current African Customary-Land Tenure Model

It would be very difficult to discuss the interplay of land markets and property rights with regard to contemporary customary land without considering the historical foundation of African customary-land tenure. To date, many narratives of customary-land tenure have been formed. For instance, customary-land tenure has often been deemed to be static, conservative, and incapable of adapting to change (see Birgegård 1993; Gyasi 1994; Peters 2009; see also chapter 2 of this book for an extended discussion). In contrast, several studies have shown these land-tenure systems to be dynamic and responsive to forces of change under varied contexts (see Floyd 1972 for Zimbabwe; see Morgan 1972 for Kenya). Hence, generic narratives tend only to mask the context-specific variations inherent in these systems.

A vital point is that systems of African customary-land tenure have historically been susceptible to certain influences, although writers seem to have various opinions on this. For instance, while some scholars assert large-scale modification to these systems by external forces such as European colonisation (Chimhowu and Woodhouse 2006; Joireman 2008; Mamdani 1997), others point to a combination of several local factors and colonial influences (Benjaminsen and Lund 2002; Bruce 1993; Cheater 1990; Cowen and Shenton 1991; Palmer 2003). However, both camps seem to agree that colonial influences had a profound impact on African customary-land tenure systems. In this regard, scholars have argued that certain tenets in most of these systems derive from perceptions and reports of early European settlers and writers (Chimhowu and Woodhouse 2006; Whitehead and Tsikata 2003, cited in Joireman 2008). These tenets can be noted in contemporary customary-land tenure, and they exemplify how the impact of these influences has transcended the colonial period.

Upon gaining political independence, most African countries inherited a modified customary-land tenure system. This had implications for the future of land governance in these new countries. For instance, some African governments replaced the existing customary-land tenure systems with private tenure, as occurred in Kenya (Morgan 1972); while others, as occurred in Zambia, opted to inherit and maintain the colonial land-administration structures (Mvunga 1980). This legacy involved a dual land-administration system consisting of both customary and private-tenure systems. Sitko (2010) notes that this dualism in Zambia's land administration was directly set up by "colonialists" who codified customary law over land for the indigenous African populations, while administering statutory law over Crown land for European settlers. This not only produced the current dual land-tenure administration system in the country, but it also introduced fundamental changes to vital elements of customary-land tenure. However, it should be noted that although it is not possible to perfectly describe the nature of precolonial African customary-land tenure, colonial influences are quite evident. For example, the creation of new customary-land tenure systems even where none existed before has had longer-term effects.

In several instances, narratives derived from both European settlers and African customary elders created versions of African customary-tenure systems. In this regard, Joireman (2008) more generally argues that customary authority over land was created where it did not exist, and modified where it already existed, mainly to suit the colonialists' interests. For instance, Sitko (2010) asserts that customary governance (traditional authorities) among the Tonga-speaking people of southern Zambia was a direct creation of the colonial powers as part of their system of indirect rule. Such creation and/or modification of customary-tenure systems had major impacts whose influences are still felt today. One of these influences involves a denial of the existence of individual property rights within the African customary-tenure framework. For instance, there was suppression of individual property rights to customary land and disproportionate empowerment of local customary authorities over that land (Joireman 2008). This trend has persisted and has widely shaped public views of customary-land tenure in Zambia. In Zambia, this debate has largely focused on the individual's ability to alienate customary land, and the debate is rooted in colonial practice and social engineering.

The major consequence of colonial influences on Zambia's customary-land tenure system seems to be the perpetuation of what Mamdani (1997) refers to as a "bifurcated state." This is a state where customary-land tenure is understood only in terms of local land users' membership in the broader kinship structure that confers their usufruct rights. The problem with this rendering is that it robs people of power to freely exercise their individual rights to property. In a way, this is meant to maintain the disproportionate power of customary authorities over customary land and, consequently, over their "subjects." However, in reality, there are overlapping bundles of rights within the customary-land framework, including individual property rights.

In Zambia, colonial influences diminished aspects of these individual property rights, such as the right to alienate customary land, while at the same time vesting customary-land rights under the control of customary authorities. In certain cases, for example in Nkomesha chiefdom, this has hindered the emergence of formal land markets and yet has led to the perpetuation of a highly clandestine land market, similar to that reported by Sitko (2010) in his case study of Nkandanzovu in southern Zambia. In contrast, Mungule chiefdom shows a widespread acceptance of both formal and informal land markets. However, this acceptance has largely been driven by local influences mainly involving the chiefdom's previous loss of huge swaths of land to the rapidly urbanising city of Lusaka.

A common point between the two contexts is that the existence of individual property rights is influencing individuals' participation in formal and informal land markets. Although much has been written on the existence of individual property rights within customary-land tenure (see Gluckman 1945 and Simpsons 1954, cited in Chimhowu and Woodhouse 2006), it is important to consider how they interplay with emerging land markets. However, to set the stage for that, we must first look at the nature and intricacies of these emerging land markets.

The Nature and Intricacies of Emerging Land Markets on Customary Land in Zambia

Land markets exist under both customary and statutory jurisdictions. On customary land, these markets are still emerging and developing since the adoption of neoliberal economic policies in 1991, which led to the enactment of the Lands Act No. 29 of 1995 (henceforth, 1995 Lands Act). However, this does not necessarily mean that land markets have a recent history in the country or in the African continent. When I refer to these markets as emerging, in the case of Zambia it simply means they have been developing for a long time.

Several factors have caused these markets to become more widespread in various contexts of customary tenure. Across the African continent, numerous factors have contributed to the development of these markets. In the case of Maseru, the capital city of Lesotho, land-use conversion spurred the development of a clandestine land market (see Thebe and Rakotje 2013). The main driving force behind this was the desire to enhance livelihoods, but the process was found wanting because of the failure of the formal land-delivery system to cope with social dynamics such as population pressure (Thebe and Rakotje 2013). Although land markets are generally not a new phenomenon in Africa, they are currently becoming more widespread, as evidenced by the increasing trend towards commoditised access to land. However, scholars reflect no universal agreement on the factors behind this trend (Chimhowu and Woodhouse 2006). Despite this lack of consensus on which factors have led to this increasing commoditisation of customary land across the African continent, numerous factors are quite obvious in the case of Chibombo and Chongwe Districts.

In Zambia, since 1991, the formal land market, which is rooted in neoliberal ideology, has been driven by the 1995 Lands Act, while the informal land market is partly a product of individuals' inability to access and/or engage in the formal markets (see Chimhowu and Woodhouse 2006 for the historical development of vernacular, or informal, land markets). It should also be noted that other policies have previously influenced Zambia's land-tenure system. For instance, in the 1975 land reforms, Zambia adopted a "no-value" land policy whose impact has lingered in the view that customary land cannot be bought. This policy removed the sale value of land, with the implication that land could not be sold as a commodity on the market. Of course, this policy was rooted in socialist ideology. For instance, when a piece of property was sold, only improvements on that land, such as buildings, had monetary value attached to them, while the land on which they rested was merely transferred to new owners at no cost. This policy still influences the development of current land markets. A major impact of this policy, which is vital for this chapter, is that the idea of attaching no value to customary land has persisted in the mindset of most Zambians. That is why it seems inconceivable that an individual could possess rights even to alienate, let alone sell, customary land. However, a contrasting scenario has developed. Local dynamics such as population pressure are rapidly increasing the commoditisation of customary land in Chibombo and Chongwe. People are realising that if state land can be sold, then the same must be true of customary land. For instance, a village headman from the Mungule area argued that "Since the Chiluba time [when neoliberal policies were introduced in Zambia], headmen have [had the] power to sell [customary] land just as council houses were sold cheaply to sitting tenants [by the government]" (LURLAP Interview 2014). This statement indicates that the adoption of neoliberal policies introduced markets for both state and customary land, contrary to the no-value policy adopted in the 1975 land reforms.

The change from socialist to neoliberal policies in 1991 steered the country's land-tenure policies from the no-monetary value policy to those that recognised this value and established land as a commodity to be traded on the market. Since then, not only does the law permit the sale of state land, it provides for the conversion of customary-land tenure to leasehold (see chapter 2). This is a major driver of the emergence and development of informal land markets in Zambia. Hence, all land now has monetary value, although the country's formal land policy limits this value to land held under leasehold. These dynamics bring with them dualities in the country's land markets. Just as two land-tenure systems run parallel, land markets have adopted a similar dual nature comprising formal and informal land markets. However, in reality these have complex linkages as they interact and influence each other in several ways.

Land markets for customary land are not a new phenomenon. They have operated in Africa within the customary-tenure framework for several decades (Chimhowu and Woodhouse 2006), although they are still emerging in Zambia. Despite this, during the colonial period, the colonial powers suppressed African participation in land markets, thereby confining individual access to land via the tribal authorities. However, currently in Zambia, the implementation of neoliberal policies is a major driver, while population pressure and land shortages spurred by the expansion of Lusaka city have a compounding effect on the development of these markets in the case-study areas. Furthermore, the local contextual direction of development and operation of these markets depends heavily on customary politics, as noted above in the cases of the Nkomesha and Mungule chiefdoms. A common element in both chiefdoms is that most customary land is bought on the informal land market in order to convert it to leasehold tenure later (see chapter 2). The only difference is that in the Mungule area, conversions are successfully completed by those with enough money to pay for the conversion. On the other hand, those with inadequate financial resources can only hope to be able to do so in the future.

In both chiefdoms, however, "subjects" and customary authorities (village heads and chiefs) have been involved in formal and informal land transactions, often involving money. This has occurred despite the framework of the "idealised" customary-tenure model strictly forbidding such practices. Participation in informal land markets occurs largely through the sale and rental of customary land (LURLAP Interview 2014). Not only does such participation point to people's rights to alienate customary land (Peters 2009), it challenges de Soto's (2000) contention that customary land is "dead capital."

In the case of Mungule chiefdom, not only are the local people individually involved in land sales, rentals, and the overall process of land conversion from customary to leasehold tenure, but village heads encourage such involvement. A focus-group discussant in the Mungule area remarked, "We have different problems. Sometimes you may encounter problems, and the selling of land becomes one thing to do" (LURLAP FGD 2014). Another added, "we sell land to town dwellers" (LURLAP FGD 2014). These statements exemplify how people openly admit, in the presence of village heads, to selling customary land, without receiving any objection from them. However, other comments implied that although the sale of customary land is prohibited, local people had the choice to exercise their individual property rights. In this regard, a focus-group discussant commented, while being supported by more than 50 percent of the other discussants, "tradition does not allow the selling of land, unless the owner of that land really wants to, then they can sell that land...though it is not allowed" (LURLAP FGD 2014). Furthermore, signifying individuals' power over land, a female interviewee contended, "if I want to sell part of it, I will just inform him [the village head] but he has to receive a share also" (LURLAP Interview 2014). A village head affirmed these land sales by commenting, "It's just up to you [to sell or not]" (LURLAP Interview 2014). Those who chose not to sell their customary land either claimed it was for their children's inheritance or that the land simply was not of sufficient size to warrant the sale of any part of it.

However, in Nkomesha chiefdom there was a ban on the conversion of customary land to leasehold. A male focus-group discussant stated, "the chiefs [referring to Chieftainess Nkomesha] do not even support the idea of title deeds because this is customary land" (LURLAP FGD 2014). Nevertheless, although conversion was not permitted in this area, people secretly engaged in customary-land sales. Many of these land sales in the area were either directly for money or in exchange for valuables such as houses or vehicles. A male interviewee reported, "Others sell [land] in order to change [their] status or build better structures" (LURLAP Interview 2014).

The evidence above shows that individuals in both areas exercised their agency and rights to property by participating in land markets. In Mungule chiefdom, customary authorities could be informed about such transactions only after the sales agreements between buyer and seller were finalised. In Nkomesha area, ordinary individuals largely concealed their informal transactions from the authorities unless the traditional leaders were involved. However, a common element in all areas was the involvement of traditional leaders, especially the village heads, in the sale of land. Therefore, although both the formal and informal land markets exist in these areas, the choice to engage in any market was largely left to individual landowners, while the level of transparency for such transactions depended on the context. Having considered the nature and intricacies of emerging land markets, I now examine how they contribute to property-rights dynamics in Chibombo and Chongwe Districts.

Individual Property Rights: Their Interplay with Emerging Land Markets

As noted, individuals in both areas engage in land markets even when they do not have the consent of the customary authorities (LURLAP Interviews 2014). However, in Nkomesha chiefdom, other factors and the "supposed" lack of individual property rights under the area's customary-governance regime have made land markets undesirable to customary authorities. Thus, punitive measures have been devised against individuals engaging in the sale of customary land, as the practice is deemed "unacceptable and against local custom" (LURLAP Interviews 2014). Given the stifled formal land market in this area, only a clandestine market exists, not because individuals lack individual rights to freely participate but because they fear the punitive action of the customary authorities, which often involves complete dispossession of land "owned" by the individual. This exclusion from participation in the formal land market spurs the existence of informal land markets, in which people informally and secretly exercise individual rights to property (LURLAP Interviews 2014).

Free participation in the land markets would require the freedom to exercise individual property rights, which, unfortunately, are stifled in much of current customary-land governance in Zambia. In this regard, individuals engage in land-rental agreements and land sales mostly without the consent of village heads. As a result, many people from outside these peri-urban districts have been accessing land directly via locals without following the "normal" customary-land acquisition channels (LURLAP Interviews 2014). Place (2009) shows that such changes to land acquisition in many African countries are part of the dynamism of land-tenure systems. In the Mungule area, where the sale and rental of customary land and its conversion to leasehold tenure are not necessarily restricted, the land markets operate freely. In this area, informal land markets occur outside the process of land sales prescribed by the state, which distinguishes them from formal land markets (LURLAP Interviews 2014).

It is evident that property rights have a strong relationship with emerging land markets. This interplay has led to the development of other societal dynamics such as land grabs and conflicts. Ironically, although the village heads explicitly stated that the sale of customary land was prohibited, they nonetheless engaged in the activity themselves. A woman interviewee from the Nkomesha area commented, "[I had] about 53 hectares [of land] before the death of my husband, but after his death, and now that I am a widow, my land is being depleted by the headmen who keep selling the land.... They even chase people and sell off their land" (LURLAP Interview 2014). Village heads confirmed these land sales; however, the land they sold was deemed "idle," "unoccupied," or, at times, it was simply grabbed from the locals. Hence, apart from enabling customary authorities to engage in land markets at a time of land shortages in these peri-urban areas, land grabs indicate the existence of individual property rights in customary tenure. Embedded in the phenomenon of land grabs is the notion of prior ownership of a piece of land and the dispossessed individual having possessed individual property rights and, therefore, the ability to engage in land markets.

The existence of such individual property rights has enabled knowledgeable and empowered individuals to contest the land grabs. For instance, locals have often contested dubious land transactions, at the country level, via the Zambian Lands Tribunal (Brown 2005), although very few local residents are reported to have knowledge of this process. Since Brown's (2005) paper was published, an official from the Zambia Lands Tribunal, the statutory body mandated by the state to resolve land conflicts, indicated that conflicts over customary land have intensified (LURLAP Interview 2015).

Furthermore, this official indicated clearly that where land sales involved conversion of customary land to leasehold, such contestations have often led to the revocation of title deeds on the grounds of "illegal conversion." These illegal conversions were characterised by exploitation of the poor or vulnerable and demonstrate disregard for the proper formal rules and channels that demand the existence of a willing seller and buyer. For instance, an interviewed headman from the Mungule area contended that "sometimes a title [deed to land] is good… [but] if that person always brings trouble [and] is not cooperative, the headman through the chief can revoke the title" (LURLAP Interview 2014). This suggests the existence of conditions under which a title deed can be cancelled within a certain period after issue. It does not, however, mean that title deeds can be cancelled at the whim of the village head or any other customary authority. Such notions of the village head's ability to cancel title deeds or reverse land sales only served to instil fear among local subjects by making them believe that all land, whether on leasehold or customary tenure, belonged to customary authorities (LURLAP Data 2014). Such notions profoundly influenced the interplay of property rights and land markets.

The intention behind instilling such ideas and fears was to force acquiescence to the customary authorities' demands among locals who never really understood the implications of possessing individual land rights in the first place. Where it occurred, the individual dispossessed of land usually remained aggrieved, while the authority responsible for the grab found a pretext for doing so. In Chibombo and Chongwe Districts, incidents occurred in which land was grabbed on the pretext of punishing an individual for breaking societal rules (LURLAP Interview 2014). These dynamics point to the existence of individual property rights and personal agency in land markets.

The existence of land grabs in both areas challenges the view that customary land belongs to customary authorities. The very fact that land is grabbed implies that an individual has rights of claim and ownership to it. Conversely, this may loosely indicate that the individual never had a claim to ownership but, rather, held usage rights only by virtue of group membership in society. However, the fact that land was grabbed and sold to another individual challenges the preceding idea in that markets significantly influenced the issue. The fact that customary authorities mediated land conflicts is evidence that individual rights to land needed protection, and, in some way, this may signify the protection of the individual's participation in land markets.

The interplay of property rights and land markets has led to conflicts resulting from overlapping claims to adjacent customary land within and between villages. Land disputes reported in the study area often involve encroachment onto a piece of land that another individual actively defends as their own. If people did not have individual property rights, such disputes would never exist, and there would be no need for customary authorities to intervene to resolve the conflict. Customary authorities' intervention in land conflicts, which is quite common, serves as an indirect acknowledgement of the existence of and need to protect these individual property rights. The prevalence of conflicts and resolution mechanisms reveals people's demands for enforcement to make their property rights clear and secure (Joireman 2008).

If people's demands for clear and secure property rights in customary tenure are important and evident, why have they been difficult to implement on customary land? The answer is plain and simple and has to do with the developed "idealised" type of customary tenure discussed above. Therefore, property rights entail the ability to prohibit others from interfering with an individual's rights.

Evidence from the two districts reveals that such conflicts involved boundaries between adjacent properties and occurred because of a lack of permanent boundaries such as permanent geographic features. If usufruct rights alone were available to customary landholders, these conflicts would not exist, as this category would accommodate others wanting to use the land whenever and however they wished. That is not to say that people do not enjoy usufruct rights to land beyond that which they personally own; rather, it means that limiting their rights in that category would be misguided.

Land grabs and disputes seem to be the overriding factors that create a sense of insecurity regarding customary land. The following remark by a woman interviewed from the Nkomesha area evidences this: "Because of boundary disputes... I look forward to having a title to my land.... The Lenje who claim to be the owners of…land and have lost most of their places… forcefully occupy other people's land" (LURLAP Interview 2014). In addition to conflicts driven by tribal claims to land, arbitrary and non-permanent boundaries on customary land give people the sense that private titles have benefits in that they lead to a situation where "land conflicts reduce" (LURLAP Interview 2014) due to the existence of clear and indisputable boundaries. However, this insecurity regarding customary land is a construct rooted in the "idealised" nature of customary tenure that has developed since colonial times.

The existence of property rights also brings about the exclusivity and excludability of rights. Conflicts are a consequence of competition for land, and they reveal the existence of overlapping individual property rights over land (Peters 2009). Therefore, not only are there dynamics to customary-land relations (Thebe and Rakotje 2013), but there are individual property rights to customary land and exclusivity to such rights (Thebe and Rakotje 2013 also show this in the case of Lesotho). This exclusivity empowers locals to transfer land rights to their next of kin or through monetary transactions. In both districts in the LURLAP study, the children of the landowners were more likely to inherit the land (LURLAP Interview 2014). In the Nkomesha area, a female focus-group discussant commented, "Some of us inherited the land from our parents" (LURLAP FGD 2014); another added, "in the event of death…the widow and children can inherit the estate" (LURLAP FGD 2014). Despite preferences regarding who was eligible to inherit land, which depends on local customs, the fact of inheritance further consolidates claims of the individuality and exclusivity of property rights in the study areas. However, this is not the case in all sub-Saharan contexts, such as in Lesotho, where norms and customs differ from those in the studied areas (see Thebe and Rakotje 2013).

Although this evidence is not exhaustive, it debunks the argument that individuals cannot alienate and sell customary land. Therefore, land does not necessarily belong to the chief or other customary authority. The evidence as presented above is not restricted to contemporary settings. Historically, during the early days of mining development in several parts of the African continent, chiefs often became involved in land deals and had to negotiate with their subjects on matters of land allocation to mine developers (Simutanyi 2008). Such negotiations indicate the historical existence of property rights that gave individuals power to participate in the alienation and sale of customary land.

Removing individual property rights from customary tenure cuts the link between people and their land. However, Peters (2013) seems to believe that these ties to land by both customary authorities and their subjects are a colonial creation that never really existed in precolonial times. I partly disagree with this assertion, although I agree that colonial influences over customary tenure should be noted. For example, in the case of Zambia, the colonial administration confined whole tribes to areas where they then appointed rulers over them, as part of a system of indirect rule (Mvunga 1980). In such areas, precolonial systems of customary tenure were modified by vesting all land rights in a customary authority deemed to be a custodian within the context of an "idealised" model of customary tenure. However, I disagree with this assertion insofar as it suggests that people's rights to land have not always existed; people's livelihoods are and have always depended on land resources. In most customary African societies, livelihoods are normally land-based (Potts and Mutambirwa

1990; Thebe and Rakotje 2013). In the case of Chibombo and Chongwe Districts in Zambia, residents were of the opinion that land was life and that without it there would be no livelihood (LURLAP Interview 2014). Most people in the two districts derive their livelihoods from direct and indirect use of land, primarily by engaging in agricultural activities. Perhaps this was the impetus for trying to secure and enforce their property rights.

These individual property rights form the basis of people's engagement in both formal and informal land markets. In practice, commoditised access to land is actually more widely practiced than is often thought. This is all the more so because, in some instances, customary authorities have been captured by market dynamics in which the former "token of appreciation" they received for granting access to land has become a lucrative commercial activity from which they benefit. For instance, people now have to pay huge sums of money to the headmen to access land (LURLAP Interviews 2014). Thus, commoditised access to land now predominates over the norm that was perpetuated under the "idealised" customary-tenure systems. In this regard, Chimhowo and Woodhouse (2006) also rightly perceive the current customary-tenure model as an "idealised" communal tenure. In both Chibombo and Chongwe Districts, property rights are, in principle, vested in customary leadership, with the chief at the top of the social structure. In both areas, the sale of customary land is unwelcome in "principle" and is punishable under customary law despite the fact that some ordinary residents as well as chiefs conduct land sales (LURLAP Interviews 2014). Land markets continue to thrive in these areas, so to label customary societies and their structures as static and lacking in individual property rights is a serious stereotype that impedes a comprehensive understanding of such systems. Perhaps now it is vital to understand the implications of how the interplay of property rights and land markets affects customary authority and power.

Effects of the Emerging Land Market on Customary Authorities

Emerging markets for customary land have the potential to threaten the power of those customary authorities deemed to be "custodians" of customary land under the "idealised" customary tenure. These markets promote increasingly commoditised access to land, often overlooking the control and power of customary authorities. This has resulted in customary-land scarcity in both Chibombo and Chongwe Districts. "There is no land," commented one headman from the Mungule area (LURLAP Interview 2014). This sentiment was shared in both areas, signifying that a land shortage is emerging gradually, partly due to the operation of these monetised land transfers. A burgeoning population in peri-urban areas resulting from inward migration has been a major product of the land markets (LURLAP Data 2014). The increase in land sales and rentals in both Chibombo areas contributes to the scarcity of customary land, leading some residents to migrate to peri-urban areas.

Furthermore, emerging land markets promote increased individual control over land and conversion of customary land to leasehold, while increasing the potential to negatively affect local social relations. According to Hailey (1946, xix, cited in Chimhowu and Woodhouse 2006, 350), "acceleration of progressive individualization may hasten the disintegration of the present social structure and thus weaken the basis on which the institutions of local self-government are now being built." In these peri-urban districts, this situation may eventually result in the complete transfer of customary land out of the control of customary authorities, thereby inhibiting their powers to allocate and regulate its use.

Control over land is the lifeblood of several forms of customary authority in Africa. Thus, within the existing framework of customary-land governance, land markets and conversions to leasehold tenure effectively transfer power from customary authorities to individuals. The loss of customary authority and power caused by emerging land markets has attracted varied responses and reactions. Although the 1995 Lands Act engages customary authorities to be part of land sales and the land-conversion process to leasehold tenure, these authorities are very aware of the consequences of such involvement. One respondent in the Mungule area said, "if you get a title the headman has no control over that [land]. He cannot come to you and say where is [money] for the Kulamba Kubwalo [ceremony] – meaning their powers are shrinking" (LURLAP Interview 2014). A headman in the same area affirmed this by stating,

> Once you acquire a title [deed] you are assured of having a much stronger power over that land.... We are threatened because [in] converting the customary land into private [ownership] we are giving away our powers.... It will be bad on my part and the chief because ...losing customary lands means having no control, no power (LURLAP Interview 2014).

Cognisant of this loss of power emanating from individualising customary land, customary authorities in the Nkomesha area do not permit residents to sell customary land and convert it to leasehold tenure. As one interviewee put it, "Getting a title [deed] is forbidden because the land is in the chiefdom area. So they refuse [conversion] because that land will be out of the chiefdom" (LURLAP Interview 2014). This perceived loss of power creates a situation in which land markets are engaged in an environment not conducive to their development. In many sections of these peri-urban areas, land markets are seen as a vehicle for wresting power away from the "custodians" of customary land. Since there can be no customary power without control of customary land, resistance to land markets has stalled their further development in areas such as Nkomesha in Chongwe. However, on the contrary, in Mungule chiefdom, the land market has partly served to the advantage of its "custodians," as will be noted in the following section.

In principle, much of the land allocation in some peri-urban areas of Zambia has remained under the power of customary authorities, and yet in practice evidence reveals that land is allocated by those who are not members of these customary bodies. Individuals in Chibombo and Chongwe, for example, privately sell land, and this entails a reallocation to other users (LURLAP Interview 2014). Consequently, most peri-urban areas in Zambia, as demonstrated in this paper, are now home not only to original groups of people but have incorporated people from "outside." With such a high degree of social integration among people from a greater variety of social backgrounds, demographic change is part of the dynamic that drives and influences customary-tenure-based relations. These changing demographics also add to the perceived loss of customary authority.

Traditionally, land is power, and the lack of it fosters powerlessness. Interestingly, these power dynamics largely concern questions of "power to whom?" and "power over whom?" It is worth noting that customary authorities are gradually facing this sense of powerlessness, as they wield progressively less power over the people they rule. One can safely say that the larger the physical domain controlled, the greater the power that customary authorities have. Any reduction in the size of this domain, therefore, points to eventual collapse of the social structure of which customary authorities are custodians. If current trends towards more individual control over land continue, an inevitable devolution of power from customary authorities to individuals will occur. As one interviewee put it succinctly, "there could be no chiefs without land" (LURLAP Interview 2014). Under the current dominant view of customary tenure, customary authorities' loss of control over land inevitably leads to loss of power over people. However, will this loss of control over land result in the annihilation of customary authority? Probably, but this thinking is in line with the static customary-tenure model. If we agree that customary tenure is dynamic, then it is possible that customary authority itself can adapt to prevailing conditions. In the case of Mungule chiefdom, customary authorities have fully embraced the land market as well as the gradual conversion to individual control over land. This is probably working to their advantage. As one man from Mungule argued, "Let us all have title deeds to ensure security of our property [and our] land as the city is expanding" (LURLAP FGD 2014). A village head in the same area added, "Once you acquire a title you are assured of having a much stronger power over that land. Actually we encourage [them], looking at the way the town is expanding, because their lands are not secure" (LURLAP Interview 2014).

The real threat to customary authority stemming from its loss of control over customary land, however, is not simply the result of the conversion process or the land markets; the threat comes from the perception that customary tenure does not confer individual property rights and that power and control over land are vested in customary authorities. Misunderstandings over the type of property rights available to individuals are both a primary factor behind and a root cause of these perceived power insecurities, which are themselves auxiliary outcomes of the stereotypes currently attached to customary-land tenure. This situation has compelled customary authorities to devise ways of coping with the effects of emerging land markets, even though in reality, they do not own the land.

Responses of Customary Authorities to the Emerging Land Markets

In this section, I discuss the coping strategies that customary authorities have adopted in response to emerging land markets. The responses include overwhelming acceptance of land markets, extended customary claims to titled land, social integration, and forbidding of land markets.

Acceptance and Encouragement of Land Markets

Customary authorities in the Mungule area were very assertive in encouraging people to acquire title deeds to land as a way of protecting themselves from outside groups coming to take over their land (LURLAP Interview 2014). Customary authority thus encourages formal land markets under the premise of securing people's land rights, as noted. Customary authorities acknowledged that such a move would take away their powers, and yet they encouraged the practice. However, this adaptive move is actually intended to protect their own power over the land. By securing their subjects' land rights through acquisition of title, they were ensuring that their people would not be displaced in the future as a result of the expansion of Lusaka city (LURLAP Interview 2014). In so doing, they have developed new forms of social relations with their people, relations that act to guarantee a customary authority structure independent of customary-land relations. Historically, the Lenje-speaking people of the Mungule area have been displaced by Lusaka's continuing expansion (LURLAP Interview 2014), so conversion of their land to leasehold has been adopted as a countermeasure against further displacement, although very few have successfully done so. The major outcome of this failure to attain large-scale conversions to leasehold is the widespread practice of informal land markets, which has served as a platform for land transfers to outsiders. Customary authorities' encouragement of the land markets, however, may be seen as having a hidden personal benefit for the involved customary authority and the locals.

Extended Customary Claims to Titled Land

Customary authorities have created perceptions among locals that the land held under leasehold tenure still belongs to customary authorities. For instance, a focus-group discussant in the Mungule area argued, "we still say the owner of the territory is the headman" (LURLAP FGD 2014). This is one of many claims that were widespread among both customary authorities and their subjects. Thus, notions of customary authorities' ability to revoke land on leasehold title from individuals breaking village rules were widespread. However, this view was held only in the Mungule area, given the historical background of the Lenje-speaking people, who had previously lost land to the expansion of Lusaka city.

Social Integration

With regard to informal land sales, village heads have also accepted buyers' registration in the village register as a form of acceptance in the community. Village heads try to unite all people under their authority and enforce customary norms for both people on customary and titled land, although this was deemed a threat to the efficacy of land markets. One woman responded to a question on norms governing land usage by stating, "there are some laws that are traditional, for instance, contributions towards our ceremonies such as Kulamba Kubwalo. Everyone is to pay for such activities through the headmen" (LURLAP FGD 2014). However, as previously discussed, this integration with other non-indigenous groups has the potential to dilute and erode the powers of customary authorities.

Forbidding Land Markets

In the Nkomesha area, the response is very different: land markets are strictly forbidden in an attempt to prevent the loss of customary power. However, as noted, this response has led to the development of a clandestine land market. In response to this informal land market, punitive measures have been devised against individuals engaging in the practice, if discovered. Nonetheless, individuals and village heads involved in clandestine markets often got away with the practice due to their ability to conceal land sales.

A common element of these various responses by customary authorities is the perpetuation of land markets, whether formal or informal. However, whereas the authorities are trying to secure their power over land, individuals are losing land to outsiders. Hence, land ownership is gradually shifting from the indigenous groups to outsiders through the conversion process to leasehold, which often starts with the informal land markets. This process has significant implications for rural livelihoods.

Conclusion

In this chapter, I have shown how emerging land markets interplay with individual property rights and how customary authorities are responding to the effects of this interplay. Emerging land markets are part of the dynamics of customary-land tenure, and market-based systems of land allocation have developed in areas where private tenure is encouraged and in those where it is frowned upon. The difference between the two environments where these markets have developed is the perceived benefit or loss to customary authority. Customary-land tenure and customary-authority structures are not static, as implied by studies trying to show how rigid customary norms are; these structures are dynamic and respond to various pressures and forces acting on them over time.

Although the current customary institutions seemingly do not, in principle, recognise individual property rights on customary land, there is overwhelming evidence for their existence and practice. Not only do such rights exist, they form the basis for the existence of land markets in peri-urban areas. The existence of such individual property rights on customary land has enabled individual customary landholders to have power to engage in land markets. Emerging land markets interplay with individual property rights to customary land. The interplay of property rights and emerging land markets has created two contradictory scenarios: 1) formal and informal land markets complement each other on customary land in the Mungule area, and 2) resistance to formal land markets and individuals' rights to alienate customary land in the Nkomesha area has paved the way for the emergence of a clandestine land market.

The involvement of individuals in land markets, whether in secret or openly, has been seen as diminishing the power of customary authorities, especially when that land is converted to leasehold tenure. However, the threat to customary authority does not simply result from the conversion process from customary to leasehold tenure. The perpetuation of notions of insecurity attached to customary tenure poses the greater threat. Customary authorities' denial of the existence of individual property rights in customary tenure largely creates these notions. This has inhibited people's freedom to openly exercise individual agency in informal and formal land markets, as was the case in the Nkomesha area.

Furthermore, I argue that the interplay of property rights with emerging land markets can negatively affect customary authorities. Thus, intolerance of these property rights translates into intolerance of people's agency and participation in land markets. In the Nkomesha area, the ban on land markets and on the conversion of land to leasehold tenure has led to the development of informal land markets. Conversely, customary authorities' tolerance of the land markets in the Mungule area has been a way of securing their own future control over land in the face of the very real threat of assimilation by the expanding city of Lusaka. I argue that lawmakers need to acknowledge and legally enforce individual property rights to customary land in order to protect the poor, given the failure of formal titling.

Finally, I argue that given these dynamics, the notions of "no chiefs without land" and "no traditional authority without customary control to land" are constructs rooted in the idealised form of customary-land tenure. Hence, they may gradually become outdated as societal changes proceed; no society has ever remained static. Therefore, as these areas respond to various socioeconomic pressures, modifications to their systems of governance will likely occur. Land governance and social relations dependent on it will eventually adapt to the continued individualising of land ownership in peri-urban areas. The only worry in the meantime is the increase of landlessness for the majority of the poor if current trends remain unregulated.

References

Abdulai, T. 2006. "Is land title registration the answer to insecure and uncertain property rights in sub-Saharan Africa?" *RICS Research Paper Series* 6: 6, 1–27.

Benjaminsen, T., and C. Lund. 2002. "Formalisation of land and water rights in Africa: An introduction." *European Journal of Development Research* 14: 2, 1–10.

Birgegård, L. E. 1993. *Natural Resource Tenure: A Review of Issues and Experiences with Emphasis on Sub-Saharan Africa*. Uppsala: International Rural Development Centre.

Brown, T. 2005. "Contestation, confusion and corruption: Market-based land reform in Zambia." In *Competing Jurisdictions: Settling Land Claims in Africa*, vol. 6, edited by S. Evers, M. Spierenburg, and H. Wels, 79–107. Leiden: Brill Academic Publishers.

Bruce, J. 1993. "Do indigenous tenure systems constrain agricultural development?" In *Land in African Agrarian Systems*, edited by T. J. Basset and D. E. Crummey, 35–56. Madison: University of Wisconsin Press.

Cheater, A. 1990. "The ideology of 'communal' land tenure in Zimbabwe. Mythogenesis enacted?" *Africa* 60: 2, 188–206.

Chimhowu, A., and P. Woodhouse. 2006. "Customary vs. private property rights? Dynamics and trajectories of vernacular land markets in sub-Saharan Africa." *Journal of Agrarian Change* 6: 3, 346–71.

Cole, D., and P. Grossman. 2002. "The meaning of property rights: law versus economics?" *Land Economics* 78: 3, 317–30.

De Soto, H. 2000. *The Mystery of Capital*. New York: Basic Books.

Floyd, B. N. 1972. "Land apportionment in southern Rhodesia." In *People and Land in Africa South of the Sahara: Readings in Social Geography*, edited by R. M. Prothero, 225–39. London: Oxford University Press.

Gyasi, E. A. 1994. "The adaptability of African communal land tenure to economic opportunity: The example of land acquisition for oil palm farming in Ghana, Africa." *Journal of the International African Institute* 64: 3, 391–405.

Joireman, S. F. 2008. "The mystery of capital formation in sub-Saharan Africa: Women, property rights and customary law." *World Development* 36: 7, 1233–46.

LURLAP Survey Data. 2014. Land Use and Rural Livelihoods Africa Project Primary Data. Chibombo and Chongwe Districts, Zambia.

LURLAP Focus Group Discussions. 2014. Land Use and Rural Livelihoods Africa Project Primary Data. Chibombo and Chongwe Districts, Zambia.

LURLAP Interviews. 2014. Land Use and Rural Livelihoods Africa Project Primary Data. Chibombo and Chongwe Districts, Zambia.

LURLAP Interviews. 2015. Land Use and Rural Livelihoods Africa Project Primary Data. Chibombo and Chongwe Districts, Zambia.

Mamdani, M. 1997. *Citizen and Subject. Contemporary Africa and the Legacy of Late Colonialism.* Oxford: James Currey.

M'membe, F. 2005. "The Zambian land tenure system and the process of land alienation: The need for land reform in Zambia." BA thesis, University of Zambia, School of Law, Lusaka.

Morgan, W. T. W. 1972. "The 'white highlands' of Kenya." In *People and Land in Africa South of the Sahara: Readings in Social Geography*, edited by R. M. Prothero, 208–24. London: Oxford University Press.

Muniesa, F. 2011. "A flank movement in the understanding of valuation." *The Sociological Review* 59.S2: 24–38.

Mvunga M. P. 1980. *The Colonial Foundations of Zambia's Land Tenure System*. Lusaka: NECZAM.

Obeng-Odoom, F. 2012. "Land reforms in Africa: Theory, practice, and outcome." *Habitat International* 36: 1, 161–70.

Ostrom, E., and H. Charlotte. 2007. *Private and Common Property Rights.* School of Public and Environmental Affairs Research Paper No. 2008-11-01, Indiana University. Bloomington: Indiana University.

Palmer, R. 2003. "Struggling to secure and defend the land rights of the poor in Africa." *Austrian Journal of Development Studies* XIX (1): 6–21.

Peters, P. E. 2009. "Challenges in land tenure and land reform in Africa: Anthropological contributions." *World Development* 37: 8, 1317–25.

—. 2013. "Conflicts over land and threats to customary tenure in Africa." *African Affairs* 112: 449, 543–62.

Place, F. 2009. "Land tenure and agricultural productivity in Africa: A comparative analysis of the economics literature and recent policy strategies and reforms." *World Development* 37: 8, 1326–36.

Potts, D., and C. Mutambirwa. 1990. "Rural-urban linkages in contemporary Harare: Why migrants need their land." *Journal of Southern African Studies* 16: 4, 677–98.

Simutanyi, N. 2008. *Copper Mining in Zambia: The Developmental Legacy of Privatisation*. Institute for Security Studies, Paper No. 165. Pretoria: Institute for Security Studies.

Sitko, N. J. 2010. "Fractured governance and local frictions: The exclusionary nature of a clandestine land market in southern Zambia." *Africa* 80: 1, 36–55.

Thebe, V., and M. F. Rakotje. 2013. "Land strategies and livelihood dynamics in peri-urban communities: Challenges to land and agricultural policy in Lesotho." *African Studies* 72: 3, 399–415.

Toulmin, C. 2009. "Securing land and property rights in sub-Saharan Africa: The role of local institutions." *Land Use Policy* 26: 1, 10–19.

PART III:

LAND, MINING, AND RURAL LIVELIHOODS

CHAPTER SIX

POLICY, LAND USE, AND LIVELIHOOD INTERPLAY IN CUSTOMARY AREAS IN ZAMBIA: THE CASE OF SMALLHOLDERS IN CHONGWE

ORLEANS MFUNE AND DAVID KAFWAMBA

Introduction

A central focus of the chapters in this book is the conversion of customary land to leasehold tenure, which is taking place in Zambia and other countries in Africa. The starting point for this discussion is the dual land-tenure system that originates in colonial land and economic policies. Other chapters in this book demonstrate that postcolonial policies have sustained this dualism despite emerging attempts to create unitary tenure systems. What has not been discussed, however, is that beyond tenure reform, colonial policies also sought to shape land-use decision-making at the household level in rural areas. In agriculture, for example, colonial policies sought to change local agronomic and livelihood practices in order to suit colonial interests (Blaikie and Brookfield 1987). Some of the features and impacts of these policies persist in rural Africa today. Using the colonial era as a starting point, we discuss in this chapter the link between macro-level policies and local land-use changes in rural areas. We examine how land use and livelihoods in rural Zambia have, over the years, changed in tandem with major policy shifts. We argue that since colonial times, policy shifts have often failed to meet rural people's expectations because of the policymakers' failure to engage with the ecological and livelihood dynamics that characterise rural areas.

Our contention in this chapter is that macroeconomic policies or sectoral policies that are intended to improve or change other aspects of the economy often have secondary effects on rural land use and, hence, people's livelihoods and welfare (World Bank 2008). For instance, policies aimed at tilting the entire economy towards socialist or neoliberal ideologies may bring significant change in rural land-use patterns. As Ayele

(2001) argues, macro policies made at the national or international level may influence land-use decision-making at the micro level (such as the farming household). Although the literature acknowledges the links between macro (and sectoral) policies and local land-use practices, in Zambia these remain poorly understood. Because of the centrality of land to agriculture, which is the main livelihood source for more than 60 percent of Zambians, we focus on land use in the context of semisubsistence, or smallholder, farming. In this chapter, we focus primarily on land use in customary areas where most rural people live.

Analysing Links Among Policy, Land Use, and Livelihoods

To examine these questions, the chapter uses an analytical framework that considers the linkages between macro policy shifts and land-use changes (Figure 6.1). We start with the basic premise that rural people, as other papers in this book have already shown, depend heavily on land resources for their livelihoods (see chapters 1, 7, and 10). The notion of "livelihood" as used in this chapter needs explanation. Chambers and Conway (1992) have been credited with the popularisation of the concept of livelihoods. In particular, their idea of the five categories of assets (natural, financial, human, physical, and social capital) that form the basis for rural actors' construction of livelihood has been highly influential in rural-development scholarship (see also Ellis 2000; Scoones 2009). In this framework, while local actors often draw on a combination of these sets of assets to achieve sustainable livelihood outcomes, any changes in the asset portfolio will have either negative or positive effects on such livelihoods. Land fits into this framework as one of the most important livelihood assets that rural actors draw on to construct their livelihoods.

A livelihood approach often requires that we examine livelihoods in their broadest sense (i.e., in the context of all five groups of assets). In this chapter, we focus mainly on land as a critical livelihood asset, although we remain fully aware of the importance of the other assets for viable rural livelihoods. We also focus on livelihood diversification but in the context of land-based livelihoods.

Given that more than 60 percent of the population of Zambia relies on agriculture (GRZ 2013), land is truly one of the most important livelihood assets in the country. In this regard, changes in land use and the availability or quality of land will always affect the livelihoods of rural people. Among the factors that can influence these changes are policy shifts, both at the macro and micro levels. Figure 6.1 presents our framework for analysing these issues, focusing on macro policy shifts, changes in land resources (and its use), and livelihood outcomes. We start our analysis by examining some of the most important policy shifts in the history of Zambia (and our study area) in terms of their bearing on land use and livelihoods. Second, we analyse the links among such policies, changes in land use, and other factors associated with land. As Figure 6.1 shows, policy shifts may trigger changes in the land-resource base that include not only land use but also the mode of access, availability, and quality of land. Changes in land use (and its size, availability, and quality) will, therefore, significantly alter the livelihoods of rural people and affect their welfare. In particular, the changes may influence the returns from the land and, consequently, livelihood outcomes. These changes may result from the dynamic interplay of factors that include macroeconomic and sectoral policy shifts.

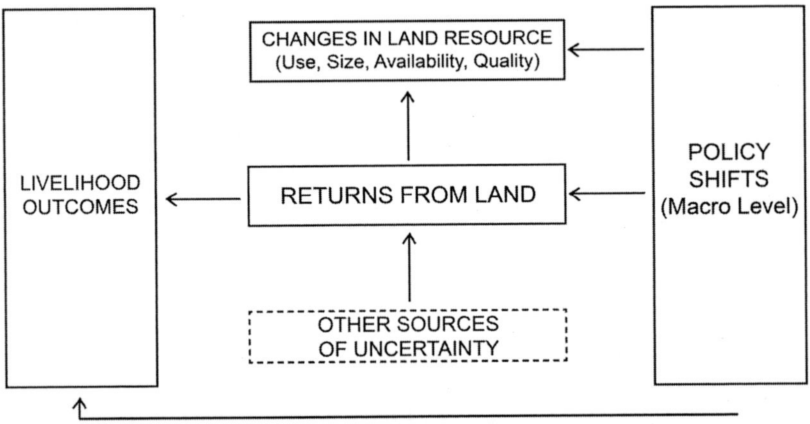

Figure 6.1: Macro policy shifts and land use in rural areas
Source: Mfune and Kafwamba (2015) LURLAP Research Project

The major policy shifts that affect land use were identified through an examination of archival data (mostly declassified government documents that date back to the colonial era), and these are complemented by other policy documents and interviews with key actors associated with land and rural livelihoods (macro-level data). This data set is compared to local actors' experiences of such policy shifts (micro-level data). To examine the nature of changes that have occurred in the study area, we use micro-level data gathered from interviews with residents who have lived in Bunda-Bunda and Nkomesha chiefdoms of Chongwe District since colonial times and from other key informants. This data set was collected in two phases.

The first study was conducted in 2010 in four areas of Chongwe District. This represented the first engagement with land use and livelihoods in Chongwe. Data collected in 2013 and 2014 through the LURLAP project complement the first study.

The Evolution of Land Use and Livelihoods in Chongwe District

Chongwe District is mainly inhabited by the Soli people, who have lived in the area for more than five centuries. Local narratives indicate that over the past century, the livelihood characteristics of the Soli have changed significantly. While very little information exists concerning the nature of their livelihoods before the advent of colonialism, the traditional names by which the different groups of the Soli were identified shed some light on this. The Soli existed in three groups: (1) the *Soli-wamanyika*, oriented to the Lenje tradition, (2) the *Soli-futwa* (food growers), and (3) the *Soli-shamifwi* (hunters with bow-and-arrow). Such names indicate that the Soli pursued crop cultivation and hunting as their dominant livelihood activities. For example, according to local elders, Shisholeka village, in the Chieftainess Nkomesha's area, started as a hunting camp for Soli hunters before they decided to settle permanently. Similarly, in another area in Bunda-Bunda, local elders noted that although the area was tsetse-fly infested, settlers were attracted because of the abundant game and forests, which played a crucial role in their local livelihood system. These local narratives show a long history of local actors' dependence on natural resources.

According to the local elders who participated in the LURLAP study, before the advent of the colonial period the Soli cultivated mainly sorghum and millet, which formed part of their staple diet. Maize, which is currently the staple food of the Soli, occupied a rather peripheral position in this agronomic system and became an important food crop only in the 1940s, when colonial administrators began to encourage its cultivation. Trapnell and Clothier (1999) confirm this, observing that the traditional agriculture system of the Soli centred on bush and village gardens. Bush gardens were created by cutting tree branches, piling them around trunks and stumps, and then burning them. This was similar to the *Chitemene* system practised in Northern Province and described in detail by Allan (1965). On these patches of land, intercropping and mixed cropping were practised; sorghum or millet (as the main crops) with small amounts of maize were intercropped with pumpkin and other cucurbits. According to Chidumayo (2001), these bush gardens were abandoned after two to four years to be reclaimed by natural vegetation. The village gardens, on the other hand, were cultivated on a continuous basis by women, who grew maize, pumpkins, sweet potato, and sorghum (Chidumayo 2001; Trapnell and Clothier 1999). From Trapnell and Clothier's (1999) description of Soli agronomic practices, it is clear that a diversified cropping pattern, rather than a mono-cropping one, characterised their system. In addition, there was a distinction drawn between village gardens (where cultivation was continuous) and bush gardens (where long fallow periods were observed).

Today, the livelihoods of the people in the area are more diversified. However, as Chitonge's chapter on land use and livelihoods shows (see chapter 10), to a large extent people's livelihoods remain highly dependent on land resources. Crop cultivation and livestock rearing continue to be the most important livelihood sources in Chongwe. In this regard, land for agriculture and pasture is critical to the livelihoods of people living in the district.

Policy, Land Use, and Livelihood Interplay in Chongwe

Colonial Engagement with Land Use and Livelihoods

The present rural land-use and livelihood patterns in Chongwe bear the mark of state policy interventions. During colonial times, perhaps the most significant policy shift that affected rural land use and livelihoods in Chongwe was the land-alienation policy. The Soli, along with several other tribal groups, experienced the alienation of some of their best land during colonial rule. Before the advent of colonialism, Soli tribal land included much of the land on which the city of Lusaka is located today. In fact, the city of Lusaka derives its name from one of the Soli headmen who occupied the area (Headman Lusaaka). This land was alienated in the 1930s to establish the city. Furthermore, to the east of Lusaka, vast areas of fertile land were alienated for the benefit of white settler farmers. After independence, land policies did not alter the colonial patterns of landholding, so these lands never reverted to the Soli people; they are now the site of large private commercial farms that can be seen between the city of Lusaka and our study sites in Nkomesha chiefdom.

To appreciate the implications of such policies not only for Chongwe District but in a broader national context, it is important to consider two critical issues regarding the colonial government's land policy in Zambia. First, access to the land (and its associated natural resources) of the occupied territories was a major attraction for the settler, which in turn led to colonialism itself. The territory's land resources were seen as a vital source of raw materials to feed the then-expanding industries of Western Europe (Rodney 1972). In this regard, land, forests, and minerals were all subjected to patterns of exploitation and management that deviated from those practiced by the indigenous people. The colonial administration's interest in land was reflected in a massive alienation of communal tribal land for the benefit of European settlement, through export-oriented agricultural production. Between 1928 and 1964, large tracts of highly productive land were set aside and designated as Crown lands for the exclusive use of the European population. The rest of the territory's land was classified as native reserves for the benefit of the indigenous population (Adams 2003; Chileshe 2005). The land policy adopted by the colonial government was strongly driven by what has been termed "the white settlers' dream" (Adams 2003; Banda et al. 1997; Chileshe 2005). As part of this "dream," the colonial administration anticipated an influx of European settlers into Northern Rhodesia (now Zambia) and set aside more land for European settlement than was required. Banda et al. (1997) note that the "white settlers' dream" was well expressed in the following words of Cecil Rhodes, the head of the BSA Company:

> My cherished idea is a solution to the social problem, that is, in order to save 40 million inhabitants of the United Kingdom, we colonial statesmen must provide new lands to settle the surplus population to provide new markets for the goods produced in the factories and the mines (cited in Banda et al. 1997, 36).

This view was reinforced by the Duke of Fife, who was reported to have predicted in 1893 that

> before many years are over, thousands of our countrymen who are overcrowded here (Britain) will take advantage of the enormous space, healthy climate, and immense resources which the territory (Northern Rhodesia) offers to those who will go in and possess the land (cited in Banda et al. 1997, 36).

These statements make clear that the settlers' dream was part of a solution to myriad social problems facing *Britain* at that time. By drawing on the militant biblical words "go in and possess the land," the colonialists signalled that British interests would come first in their engagement with the land (and other resources) of the colonised territories. Much like Moses in the Bible, the "colonial statesmen" viewed themselves as would-be saviours of 40 million Britons.

In the Zambian case, the predicted influx of Europeans never occurred, although huge tracts of land had already been alienated. European settlers who were already in the territory acquired disproportionately large portions of land. Nonetheless, vast swathes of Crown land remained vacant and came to be known as the "silent lands" (Chileshe 2005).

In contrast, in areas where tribal lands were appropriated as Crown lands, indigenous people were deliberately overcrowded in native reserves (Chileshe 2005; Phiri 1980). Evidence from archival documents reveals that colonial policy was the genesis of inequitable land distribution in Zambia. Although Crown land comprised only 6 percent of the total land in Zambia, it was also the best land for agriculture and the best serviced. Much of what was termed customary land was characterised by hostile physical conditions (scarps, swamps, mountains, and poor soils) (Zambia Agriculture Consultative Forum 2010). Sadly, even today, much of what is alienated for the benefit of farming blocks and private investment constitutes the best land (ZACF 2010). Given this situation, it is important to note that although some commentators view customary landholding as inhibiting agricultural development, these same commentators often ignore the fact that customary lands tend to have very low economic potential.

In some parts of the country, conditions in the native reserves could not adequately support and sustain people's livelihoods. Arable lands were in short supply. The available literature (Adams 2003; Banda et al. 2002; Chileshe 2005; Mulolwa 2002; Phiri 1980) and official correspondence between colonial administrators well document this fact (Zambia National Archives 2010). These sources reveal that land clearance for farming and harvesting of wood resources in these areas increased to serve a large population, leading to environmental degradation. However, rather than implicate their own land and resettlement policies as the source of this environmental degradation in the reserves, colonial administrators argued that this had resulted from overproduction by the "natives" (i.e., production had outstripped the carrying capacity of the available agricultural land). In this regard, the government sought to deal with environmental degradation in the reserves by restricting people's livelihoods through a reduction in their cultivated acreage. Thus, the idea of keeping farming systems within the "ecological carrying capacity" of the land was used to support decisions aimed at disrupting livelihoods in the reserves.

In Chongwe, this policy altered people's land-use and livelihood patterns significantly. The land-alienation process and the forced concentration of indigenous populations into native reserves meant that hunting and shifting cultivation could not be practised in the same way as before. Thus, according to Chidumayo (2001), the bush gardens began to be replaced by more permanent fields, and the distinction between village gardens and bush gardens tended to disappear because both were cultivated on a more-or-less continuous basis. Today, shifting cultivation is no longer the norm in Chongwe.

Besides land alienation and forced resettlement, the next important issue is that colonial and postcolonial policies significantly influenced changes in cropping patterns on land used by indigenous populations. While sorghum and millet constituted the main crops in Chongwe, government policies favoured maize. In part, the growing of maize was promoted to meet the demands of urban labourers, especially those working in the mines, despite the fact that sorghum and millet were better suited to local ecological conditions. The *District Notebooks* (ZNA 2010) reveal that changing or replacing indigenous crops with crops that suited colonial interests was a widespread trend in Zambia. In Feira, for example, there were major attempts to introduce perennial crops such as banana and pawpaw. The writings of the district commissioner of Feira District, a neighbouring district of Chongwe, reveal major attempts to introduce targeted crops through a policy of forced planting between 1905 and 1935. The colonial government punished headmen who delayed planting or refused to plant such crops. But these projects, according to the district commissioner, were a disaster. The "forced" crops were ill-suited to the physical conditions of the areas in which they were planted, where high temperatures and low rainfall prevailed. But the failure of such crops was then attributed to the natives' laziness. However, in a 1934 letter to the chief secretary of Livingstone (then the capital of Northern Rhodesia), district commissioner Cooke ruled out that the failure resulted from the native farmers' laziness—the project was overseen by a European! Instead, he argued that in experimenting with new crops, colonial agricultural officers had never considered local ecological conditions. He noted that "after sixteen years in Northern Rhodesia, I have yet to meet the native who prefers hunger to crop cultivation," adding that before new crops were introduced, it was important to first ask what the local farmers grew, why they grew that particular crop, why they did not grow particular alternative crops, and whether any new crops introduced would withstand the local severe climatic conditions. Lastly, concluded Cooke, "not all natives are fools as regards their agriculture" (Cooke 1934).

Cooke's (1934) arguments and objections are important, since they demonstrate how colonial governments in Africa attempted to change people's agronomic practices without critically engaging local environmental dynamics that characterised these areas. Understanding why local people use their land the way they do and why they grow particular crops is always important before embarking on radical change.

During the first phase of the fieldwork for the LURLAP study, on which this chapter is based, we observed that people in the study areas constructed their land-based livelihoods by taking advantage of the ecological diversity and seasonal changes that characterise their surroundings. Land use, in this regard, is patterned to best exploit opportunities offered by prevailing ecological conditions, while also accounting for that same environment's limitations. Different types of land attract different types of land use, depending on the season and allowing for livelihood diversification. Table 6.1 presents an example of how people use the opportunities offered by their local ecology:

Land type	**Season**	**Use**	**By whom**
Forest/ bushland	*Dry season*	Firewood; construction poles; fibres; fruit; grazing of animals; small animal trapping; (Charcoal production in Munyeta)	Men and women (firewood mainly women)
	Wet season	Firewood; construction poles; fibres; fruit, mushrooms; wild vegetables	Men and women (mushrooms, vegetables and firewood by women)
Seasonal ponds	*Wet season*	Livestock watering	Men and boys
Streams	*All seasons*	All year stream-side gardening (vegetables and maize); livestock watering; domestic water source	Men and women
Crop land	*Wet season*	Crop production; wild vegetables (weeds)	Men and women, wild vegetables by women
	Dry season	Livestock foraging; Mice trapping	Men
Homestead	*Wet season*	Home gardens for pumpkin and okra; fruit trees; small livestock grazing; poultry rearing; trees with medicinal value	Women and men
Wetland (Chinyika)	*Grazing*	Grazing and used for keeping sweet potato seedlings	Men and boys

Table 6.1. Land use types in the Chongwe study
Source: Field data (2010).

Table 6.1 shows, in addition to ecological diversity, the importance of seasonality in the pursuit of local livelihoods. Chongwe, like all other districts in Zambia, is characterised by a single rainy season from November to April. Also associated with seasonality is the area's susceptibility to climate-related stresses such as the unpredictable length of the season, frequent dry spells, and occasional drought. The LURLAP study revealed that these environmental dynamics are a key determinant of local land-use arrangements and livelihoods. Sorghum and millet, for example, were grown because of their tolerance of low rainfall and high temperatures. To foster sustainable livelihoods, governments need to engage these environmental dynamics. Unfortunately, government policy and intervention have failed to do this.

The Postcolonial Government's Engagement with Land Use and Livelihoods

Archival data and interviews with various actors show that while post-independence governments attempted to reduce the inequalities between Crown lands (which were renamed state lands after independence) and customary areas, they also sustained elements of colonial policy that were ill-suited to rural livelihoods. We examine post-independence policies in the context of former president Kenneth Kaunda's socialist policies and the subsequent neoliberal policies adopted after the fall of his government in the 1990s.

Socialist Policies, Land Use, and Livelihoods

At independence, the government's policy focused on modernising the rural economy through the establishment of productive infrastructure and mechanised agricultural-production systems. Clearly, the development paradigm adopted at this time was that of modernisation and industrialisation. The focus was on creating an economic base to stimulate industrialisation and economic growth (EAZ 2007). During this period, agriculture was believed to have great potential to boost economic growth and improve the quality of rural life. Investment in agricultural technology became the dominant rural-development strategy. The economic system adopted was also guided by the philosophy and political ideology of "humanism" developed by President Kaunda, which included strong socialist perspectives of social and economic equity and the need to control capitalist tendencies (Kean and Wood 1992). In this regard, modernisation and industrialisation had to be achieved within the equality-oriented approach of the humanistic philosophy. To achieve these pro-socialist goals, the government adopted an interventionist strategy and became the main investor in all sectors of the economy (EAZ 2007). The government sought to increase market-oriented agriculture and mechanise the agricultural system through the expansion of agriculture-extension services, the creation of a network of agriculture-marketing depots, the introduction of subsidised tractor-ploughing services, and increased subsidies on fertilisers (EAZ 2007; Kean and Wood 1992).

While these policies seemed radical at the time and were hailed as important for boosting the rural economy, they still retained colonial elements as far as land use was concerned. Such policies sustained the colonial ethos of emphasising maize production (particularly to benefit the urban population) on customary lands. Moreover, the state encouraged the development and production of high-yielding hybrid maize varieties at the expense of local varieties and other crops. Hybrid maize varieties fetched higher prices and were well supported by subsidies. Again, local environmental and livelihood dynamics were ignored. Moreover, crops viewed as having little market value, such as sorghum and millet, were ignored. In total, maize production accounted for an estimated 70 percent of all crop land (World Bank 2012).

In Chongwe, this led to a further decline in the cultivation of sorghum and millet, and the area quickly became a maize belt. Furthermore, with the promotion of mechanised farming, the Soli adopted the plough for cultivation, as maize became the dominant crop. Today, the area has lost some of its most important agrogenetic resources and the indigenous knowledge associated with them. This has been replaced by the monocropping of maize, which has become the custom. The indigenous genetic resources not only included sorghum and millet but also vegetatively propagated crops that were ignored as a result of agricultural technological development (Interview with SADC Gene Bank 2010). Furthermore, the loss includes indigenous maize varieties that were often planted because of their capacity to withstand extended dry spells and a short rainy season. Government policies favoured "certified hybrid maize varieties," a situation that continues today.

The shortsightedness of these policies was exposed in the 1970s, when the copper price tumbled drastically and the economy took a downturn. The government was forced to borrow to support public expenditures and to subsidise maize production (MTNR 1998). By the mid-1980s, as hopes of a recovery began to fade, the provision of subsidies was no longer sustainable. Real GDP fell drastically (by more than 50 percent), inflation escalated, and by 1992 Zambia had become one of the most heavily indebted poor countries in the world (MTNR 1998). The country was characterised by rising poverty levels, as urban employment shrank and agricultural production declined. In the long run, the modernisation project had yielded very little return.

Neoliberal Policies, Land Use, and Livelihoods

Zambia was forced to reexamine its policies when a new government came to power in 1991. In a departure from Kaunda's socialist policies, the new government embraced a free-market economy framework that was characterised by reduced state intervention in various sectors of the economy, including agriculture. Agricultural subsidies were drastically reduced. Again, these policies had serious effects on land use and livelihoods in areas such as Chongwe. Indeed, according to the farmers who participated in the LURLAP study, lack of access to farming inputs (fertiliser, seed, herbicides, etc.) and agricultural credit is among the most important effects experienced by smallholders during these economic reforms (LURLAP FGD 2014). Farmers still view these as the most important limitations to their livelihoods (see chapter 10). As one respondent noted, "the reason we cultivate smaller portions [of land] is because the farm inputs are hard [expensive] to acquire" (LURLAP Interviews 2014).

The importance of subsidies for land use and livelihoods should not be underestimated. In some places, such as the Nkomesha area, soils are poor and unsuitable for growing maize without fertiliser. One respondent confirmed this, saying, "[Soil] fertility is low, thus we use fertilisers to improve the yield" (LURLAP Interviews 2014). Indeed, in all the study sites in Chongwe, respondents reported a reduction in the quality of land, as measured by a perceived loss of fertility by those farming it. Moreover, a reduction in agricultural subsidies has forced farmers to reduce the amount of maize planted; this, in turn, has led to a decline in maize yields. While this appeared to be an opportunity for farmers to diversify, the importance that maize now occupies in the lives of Zambians means that the declining yields can lead to political tension (i.e., the blame for poor maize production has been placed on the government). Consequently, the state is compelled to continue the supply of inputs supporting maize production.

This appears to be an example of policy dualism; on the one hand, the government seeks to increase private-sector involvement in agriculture, while on the other, it continues to intervene. In this regard, in 2009 and 2010, when fertiliser subsidies were increased, Burke et al. (2010) reported that maize yields increased substantially, by 48 percent, as the areas where maize was planted also increased. Thus, the narrow focus on using land for maize production emerged once more. We must note, however, that despite this resurgence in maize cropping, its production remains, as ever, vulnerable to climatic shocks and stresses. We contend that the reliance on maize prevents the diversification of rural livelihoods not only through crops resilient to both climatic and economic shocks but also in terms of livestock farming, which government policy largely ignores.

Reduced state intervention in agriculture has affected not only crop production; it has also affected the provision of veterinary infrastructure and associated services. In Chongwe, for example, the veterinary infrastructure (e.g., livestock dipping tanks) that the state had previously developed and maintained is now ruined because the private sector has failed to fill the vacuum. Furthermore, livestock farmers lack access to subsidised vaccines and other veterinary treatments. Consequently, livestock farmers have been unable to contain diseases such as foot-and-mouth (FMD), which has drastically reduced their head of cattle and had the secondary effect of reducing the amount of draught power (Interviews with district veterinary office 2010). The livestock sector in the area appears to have collapsed. Two decades ago, many households owned cattle, but LURLAP data indicated that only fifteen of those households interviewed now own cattle, less than 50 percent of the total area households participating in the study.

Because we are discussing agricultural policies, it is important to note that market-based policies have focused not only on agriculture but also on land-tenure reform, which has already been discussed in preceding chapters. In contemporary times, these land conversions (as a key feature of market-based policies) are also producing new dynamics of land use in Chongwe. The LURLAP study reveals that the new dynamics are gradually altering rural land-use patterns and affecting the livelihoods of the local people. In particular, respondents in the study area identified increased land scarcity, land fragmentation, and the enclosure of communal spaces as land-reform outcomes that have affected rural land use and livelihoods. These are inducing changes in land use and the availability and quality of land in customary areas.

Land Scarcity and Reduced Land Size Held by Smallholders

Our study results demonstrate that the conversion of customary land to leasehold is affecting the availability of farmland in Chongwe. In Chief Bunda-Bunda's area, for example, where traditional authorities have allowed conversion, some respondents noted that land was becoming scarce (i.e., it was becoming difficult for people moving into the area to access land for agriculture), while others have noted that the parcels of land allocated to households are becoming smaller. Although a general increase in population exacerbates this problem in part, the LURLAP FGDs clarify that outsiders (mainly elite urban dwellers) are buying land both from the headmen and from individual households (leading to reduced amounts of land held by some farmers). This appears to have a ripple effect on agricultural land use: unallocated land at the village level is diminishing, while simultaneously some households are experiencing reductions in the amount of land they hold. Land-use patterns are changing as households adjust to land scarcity and reductions in their land holdings. For some farmers, this reduction has meant a move towards agricultural intensification. Indeed, when one farmer was asked what the current trend means for him, he noted "that we are cultivating on one plot. As a result, the harvest is becoming lower for the soil fertility is low, and fertiliser is not enough for the crop" (LURLAP Interviews 2014). Here the farmer implies that households are increasingly finding it difficult to own more than one farm plot or to expand their fields because opportunities to do so have been drastically reduced.

While agriculture intensification has its merits, some scholars have observed that without sufficient access to external inputs, intensification has also led to yield deterioration resulting from loss of micronutrients (Carswell 1997). This occurs as fallow periods are shortened. Thus, it is not surprising that our respondents linked low crop yields to intensification. In addition, reduced farm-plot sizes and intensification have implications for crop diversification; when land is in short supply, farmers choose to focus only on the staple crop: maize. This, in turn, affects farmers' ability to achieve sustainable livelihoods.

Land Fragmentation and the Enclosure of Communal Spaces

An important aspect of land use in Chongwe is that some plots are under communal use (see chapter 3). Such pieces of land include grazing areas, village woodlands, riverbank areas, and grazing sites. Furthermore, village members tend to have secondary rights to some land resources controlled by individual families (e.g., the right to use a footpath, cut thatch grass, or use a water point in someone's field) (see Meinzen-Dick and Mwangi 2009 for an extended discussion of such issues). Communal spaces are critical to the construction of rural livelihoods, but the trend towards land conversion affects such spaces and causes disruption. The problem manifests when people who have converted customary land to leasehold erect fences. The resulting enclosure blocks others from using communal spaces such as riverbanks or from gaining access to communal resources such as thatch grass (which, by custom, have been accessible to other community members through the secondary-rights system). The following sentiments from one survey respondent exemplify this scenario: "Titles have robbed us of the freedom we had … we used to fetch firewood, thatch grass and had freedom of movement; but now we can't because the owners have fenced off the land" (LURLAP Interviews 2014). Moreover, there is evidence that in some cases, village headpersons are fraudulently selling land in areas that village members previously reserved as communal space. For example, representatives from the lands tribunal noted that the most common disputes brought before them include land sales in communal spaces and along riverbanks. The allocation of land in communal spaces is also triggering the problem of land fragmentation, which in turn affects livelihoods requiring large amounts of land. For example, communal grazing areas for cattle have reduced in size. In fact, in one village, communal grazing land has totally disappeared, which has negatively affected livestock-based livelihoods. Some farmers have responded by rearing goats (and other small livestock) instead of cattle. But while goats require relatively smaller pieces of land, they do not offer access to draught power. These results suggest that land fragmentation and the loss of communal space are affecting both livestock- and crop-based livelihoods and impeding farmers' capacity to achieve sustainable livelihoods.

Conclusions

In this chapter, we have examined the major policy shifts that have influenced land use and agriculture-based livelihoods in some customary areas of Zambia. Our study has shown that sometimes policies are developed and implemented without any attempt to understand the local dynamics that characterise rural areas. Over the decades, this trend has predominated in Africa, and rural farmers now must live with the long-term consequences of these policies. Of specific interest here is how successive postcolonial governments have *sustained* postcolonial policies (that served elite colonial interests). When the colonialists engaged the rural land-use and livelihood question, they disregarded local ecological and livelihood dynamics and, instead, sought to impose their preferred agronomic systems to suit their own interests. The introduction of maize in areas where sorghum and millet had been the dominant crops exemplifies this practice. The colonial policies discriminated against the production of crops that allowed farmers to cope with uncertainties in their environment. Likewise, postcolonial governments have continued to mirror those colonial policies that tied land use and livelihoods to colonial metropolitan interests. In colonial times, this was achieved through a policy of forced planting and direct intervention in land use. Postcolonial governments have perpetuated this situation through subsidies and marketing policies that continue to favour maize production. Such policies have constrained the possibility for livelihood diversification among the rural population. It is our view that policymakers failed to realise that the high-input dependence of maize production would create huge problems in the future when the state could not afford to sustain this dependence. The 1990s are a case in point.

The study also shows that not only policies on cropping systems affect rural land use; so, too, do land reforms associated with the government's neoliberal policies. Land policies favouring the conversion of customary land, for example, have implications for the availability, quality, and size of agricultural land available to farmers. Furthermore, these factors have the potential to disrupt the use of communal lands (e.g., riverbanks and grazing areas). Some farmers have been unable to expand their farms or acquire new ones due to land scarcity triggered by policies that allow conversion of customary land to leasehold tenure. While this may not be the case in all parts of the country where conversion is taking place, it certainly is in Bunda-Bunda chiefdom and in Chibombo District where the LUR-LAP study was conducted. It is important to note that these areas are close to Lusaka and have, therefore, become a target for seekers of land.

The study shows that policies aimed at engaging rural land livelihoods in Zambia need to be rethought. It is our view that governments would have better success in improving livelihoods and meeting the expectations of the rural poor if they engaged more with local dynamics. A major challenge for governments today is to address the distortions and disruptions to rural livelihoods that were created by colonial engagement with rural land use and livelihoods.

References

Adams, M. 2003. *Land Tenure Policy and Practice in Zambia: Issues Relating to the Development of the Agriculture Sector.* Oxford: Mokoro Ltd.

Allan, W. 1965. *The African Husbandman.* Edinburgh and London: Oliver & Boyd.

Allison, G., and A. Agunya. 2001. *Conservation Agriculture and Agro-Forestry.* Lusaka: PELUM Association.

Assan, J. K., C. Caminade, and F. Obeng. 2009. "Environmental variability and vulnerable livelihoods: Minimising risks and optimising opportunities for poverty alleviation." *Journal of International Development* 21: 403–18.

Ayele, S. 2001. "The consequences of structural adjustment and debt for desertification and food security in Africa: A literature review and discussion." *International Journal of Economic Development* 3: 4, 1–28.

Banda, J. A., P. Banda, and B. Tengnas. 1997. Agro-Forestry Manual for Extension Workers in Central and Lusaka Provinces. Nairobi: Regional Soil Conservation Unit.

Benjamin, D. 2012. *Land Policy: Planning and the Spatial Consequences of Property.* Surrey: Ashgate.

Benjamin, E. C. 2004. Livelihoods and Institutional Development in the Malian Sahel: A Political Economy of Decentralised Natural Resources Management. PhD diss., University of Michigan.

Blaikie, P., and H. Brookfield. 1987. *Land Degradation and Society.* London: Methuen.

Burke, W. J., T. S. Jayne, and A. Chapota. 2010. Factors Contributing to Zambia's 2010 Bumper Harvest. Lusaka: Food Policy Research Project.

Carswell, G. 1997. Agriculture Intensification and Sustainable Rural Livelihoods: "A Think Piece." IDS Working Paper No. 64. Brighton: Institute for Development Studies.

Chambers, R., and G. Conway. 1992. *Sustainable Rural Livelihoods: Practical Concepts for the 21st Century.* Brighton: Institute of Development Studies.

Chidumayo, E. 2001. Land-Cover Transformation in Central Zambia: Role of Agriculture, Biomass Energy and Rural Livelihoods. Paper presented at the International Symposium titled "Area studies: Past experiences and future visions." January 19–22, Kyoto International Community House, Kyoto University, Kyoto, Japan.

Chidumayo, E., I. Masialeti, H. Ntalasha, and O. Kalumiana. 2001. Charcoal Production in Southern Africa. Lusaka: CHAPOSA Final Report.

Chileshe, R. A. 2005. Land Tenure and Rural Livelihoods in Zambia: Case Studies of Kamena and St Joseph. PhD diss., University of Western Cape, Bellville.

Economic Association of Zambia. 2007. *Equity and Development in Zambia.* Lusaka: EAZ.

Ellis, F. 2000. *Rural Livelihoods and Diversity in Developing Countries.* Oxford: Oxford University Press.

Government of the Republic of Zambia. 2013. Zambia National Agriculture Investment Plan (NAIP) 2014–2018. Lusaka: GRZ.

Government of the Republic of Zambia—Ministry of Natural Resources and Tourism. 1998. Zambia Forest Action Plan. Challenges and Opportunities. Lusaka: GRZ.

Hanyoma, S. 2002. "Farmers find new ways of fighting cattle diseases." *Groundup* 1: 8–10.

Kean, S. A., and A. Wood. 1992. "Agriculture reform in Zambia. The dynamics of policy reform in the first republic." *Food Policy* 17: 1, 65–74.

Kirby, J., P. O'Keefe, and C. Howorth. 2001. "Introduction: Rethinking environment and development in Africa and Asia." *Land Degradation and Development* 12: 195–203.

LURLAP Data. 2014. Data collected through the LURLAP research project. Chibombo and Chongwe Districts, Zambia.

LURLAP Focus Group Discussions. 2014. Focus Group Discussions conducted by the LURLAP research project. Chibombo and Chongwe Districts, Zambia.

LURLAP Interviews. 2014. Interviews conducted by the LURLAP research project team. Chibombo and Chongwe Districts, Zambia.

Meinzen-Dick, R., and E. Mwangi. 2009. "Cutting the web of interest: Pitfalls of formalising property rights." *Land Use Policy* 26: 1, 36–43.

Mulolwa, A. 2002. Integrated Land Delivery: Towards Improving Land Administration in Zambia. Delft: Delft University Press.

Nief, A. 2004. "The significance of diversification for rural livelihood systems." *Food Policy* 29: 321–38.

Phiri, S. H. 1980. Some Aspects of Spatial Interaction and Reaction to Governmental Policies in a Border Area (Zambia/Malawi). PhD diss., Liverpool University, Liverpool.

Rodney, W. 1972. *How Europe Underdeveloped Africa.* Washington: Howard University Press.

Scoones, I. 2009. "Livelihood perspectives and rural development." *Journal of Peasant Studies* 36: 1): 171–96.

Southern African Development Community Gene Bank. 2010. Interview with representative. Lusaka.

Tembo, G., A. Chapota, T. Jayne, and W. M. Weber. 2009. Fostering Agriculture Marketing Development in Zambia. Paper presented at the Inaugural National Symposium on Agriculture under the theme "the potential of agriculture to meet the increasing demand from a growing population." April 7-8, University of Zambia, Lusaka.

Trapnell, C. G., and J. N. Clothier. 1996. The Soils, Vegetation and Traditional Agriculture of Zambia, Volume 1. Bristol: Redcliffe Press Ltd.

World Bank. 2008. Poverty and the Environment: Understanding Linkages at the Household Level. Washington DC: World Bank.

—. 2012. "Agriculture and rural development indicators." Accessed March 29, 2015. data.worldbank.org.

Zambia Agriculture Consultative Forum. 2010. Study on the Status of Customary Land and How it Affects the Rights of the Indigenous Local Communities. Lusaka: Food Research Projects.

Zambia National Archives 2010. District Notebooks. Lusaka: ZNA.

CHAPTER SEVEN

PLATINUM, GOLD, AND AGRARIAN CHANGE IN ZIMBABWE: NEW LIVELIHOODS AFTER THE FAST TRACK LAND REFORM PROGRAMME[1]

GRASIAN MKODZONGI

Introduction

A major outcome of Zimbabwe's Fast Track Land Reform Programme (FTLRP), implemented in 2000, is that it allows resettled farmers to use formerly inaccessible natural resources under a dualistic agrarian structure inherited at independence in 1980 (Hanlon et al. 2013; Mkodzongi 2013a; Moyo et al. 2009; Scoones et al. 2010). In the aftermath of the land reform, newly resettled farmers have thus been able to diversify livelihoods at a time when agriculture alone could not sustain them.

In general, mineral-resource extraction has increased across Zimbabwe since land reform began. These range from the diamond mines in the Marange area in Manicaland Province, platinum mines operated by various companies (Anglo Platinum, MIMOSA, and Zimplats) along Zimbabwe's great dyke, and the widespread gold-panning sites concentrated along the gold belt (near the towns of Kwekwe, Kadoma, and Chegutu) frequented by farmers and other unemployed people.

Empirical data gathered in Mhondoro Ngezi District, in Mashonaland West Province, show that off-farm activities such as mining have become a key economic activity undertaken by a differentiated peasantry (Mkodzongi 2013b). Some farmers have discovered minerals on their plots and are thus running integrated mining and agricultural enterprises. This has stimulated accumulation from below. Other farmers are employed as wage labourers at platinum mines operated by the South African-owned Zimbabwe Platinum Mines (Zimplats), while some are artisanal miners involved in gold panning across the wider Mhondoro Ngezi area.

Mining has become central to Zimbabwe's economy, especially in the aftermath of the land reform. However, despite the importance of mining to the economy, very little empirical research has been undertaken to examine its political economy in terms of who has benefited from what type of mining and its economic contribution overall. Media claims of elite corruption and environmental banditry have largely influenced debates about mining (BBC News 2012; *Standard* 2011; *Telegraph* 2013), but these lack empirical evidence. While allegations of corruption, especially in the Marange diamond fields (Nyamunda and Mukwambo 2012; Towriss 2013), cannot simply be dismissed, more empirical research is required to address the gap in the literature on mineral-resource extraction following the FTLRP. For example, the current literature has not addressed the kinds of mining activities occurring across Zimbabwe's countryside and how these have influenced new livelihoods and accumulation among newly resettled farmers. Other questions whose answers require empirical data include who is benefiting from which type of mining and the class and gender dynamics of such processes. Questions such as whether farmers' involvement in mineral resource-extraction activities such as gold panning signal a process of deagrarianisation and depeasantisation, as observed by some scholars, need to be debated using current empirical evidence. However, this chapter does not aim to engage these wider debates but, rather, to investigate how mining activities have influenced the livelihoods of peasant households in the aftermath of the FTLRP.

This chapter contributes to ongoing debates about livelihood diversification among peasant households in sub-Saharan African countries by examining how mineral-resource extraction has influenced agricultural investments among a differentiated peasantry in Mhondoro Ngezi District of Zimbabwe. The chapter argues that farmers' involvement in mining activities does not necessarily signal a process of deagrarianisation, as some scholars claim. Interviews with such farmers show that capital gained from mining is further invested in agricultural activities. While these findings might be difficult to generalise, they show that debates about the peasantry as an analytical category and about livelihood diversification across sub-Saharan Africa should take into account the diversity of experiences.

The chapter is structured in three parts. First, it explores how mining activities have unfolded in the wider Mhondoro Ngezi District. Second, it examines how mining has influenced new livelihood trajectories among A1 farmers as well as accumulation among A2 farmers.[2] Third and last, the conclusion highlights the broader economic benefits brought to the local area by mining activities and the long-term socioeconomic and environmental challenges associated with such activities.

Livelihood Diversification Among Peasant Households in Sub-Saharan Africa: Conceptual Debates

The engagement of peasant farmers in small-scale and artisanal mining (ASM) across sub-Saharan Africa has generated an ongoing scholarly debate. This debate is centred on how to conceptualise the peasantry given the dynamic changes taking place across the African countryside (Beinstern 2003; Branchrigah and Hilson 2009; Bryceson 2000; Moyo and Yeros 2005; Veltmeyer 2005). At the core of this debate is the paradox of permanency or temporariness; does the phenomenon of "branching out" (Branchrigah and Hilson 2009) into mining activities signal a permanent shift from peasant farming to mining? Or is this a temporary rupture, with miners reverting back to agriculture? Or are these livelihood activities intertwined and taking place simultaneously? For purposes of clarity, the word "peasantry" here is loosely used to denote small-scale producers who largely rely on family labour to produce crops for sale and for personal consumption (Bernstein 1979; Moyo and Yeros 2005).

In their study focusing on livelihood diversification in sub-Saharan Africa, Banchrigah and Hilson (2009, 160) argue that "in rural sub-Saharan Africa, a growing number of smallholder farmers are struggling to subsist on earnings generated from the sales of crops. Such farmers are branching out into non-farm activities to supplement their incomes." According to these scholars, the involvement of farmers in non-farm activities is due to changing market dynamics engendered by neoliberal structural adjustment programs (SAPS) that led to the "opening up of crop parastatals to private sector competition, reductions in export crop taxes, the devaluation of local currencies and the removals of crop subsidies" (Banchrigah and Hilson 2009, 160). They conclude that smallholder agriculture is no longer viable and that policymakers and donors must move away from attempts to "re-agrarianise" the African countryside and should, instead, support artisanal mining activities, which offer better returns than farming does.

Similarly, Bryceson and Johnsson's (2009, 384) study of small-scale miners in Tanzania shows how a process of "de-agrarianisation" characterised by "a surge in new mining opportunities and the evolution of mining career patterns" is taking root. Based on biographies of individual miners, their study indicates a career trajectory of miners who often move from one goldmining site to another. This mobility, they claim, weakens the miner's familial bonds, which are replaced by new social networks and ties to their coworkers and goldmining sites.

These studies have provided important empirical detail showing how rural livelihoods across sub-Saharan Africa are undergoing a transformation as mining gains prominence as a source of income for rural households. However, scholars contest claims that livelihood diversification is tantamount to deagrarianistion and depeasantisation (Courville and Patel 2006; Moyo and Yeros 2005; Petras and Veltmeyer 2001). Some scholars argue that the crisis triggered by neoliberalism in the 1990s has led to the resurgence of rural movements and the repoliticisation of the peasantry across the countries of the South, in particular Latin America and the former settler colonies of southern Africa (Moyo and Yeros 2005; Petras 1997; Petras and Veltmeyer 2001). These studies show that rural movements have adopted land-occupation tactics as a strategy to challenge World Bank-supported neoliberal orthodoxy in agrarian policymaking. Through such land occupations, rural movements have pressured governments to fast-track agrarian reforms and give landless peasants access to lands that were previously inaccessible as a result of colonial enclosure. For example, in some Latin American countries such as Brazil, during a fifteen-year peasant struggle, "half a million landless workers were mobilised to occupy land, negotiate its legal expropriation and put it into production" (Veltmeyer 2005, 305). More recently in Zimbabwe, war veteran-led land occupations of white-owned commercial farms largely benefited landless peasants who had been denied access to such land by a colonial agrarian structure inherited at independence. These studies show that a trajectory of repeasantisation is taking place across the countries of the South. However, although farmers are diversifying livelihoods by engaging in off-farm activities such as mining (especially among the rural poor in Africa), agriculture remains at the centre of their social-reproduction strategies (Moyo and Yeros 2005). Moreover, studies undertaken in southern Africa show that artisanal mining is intertwined with agriculture, with the former playing a key role as a source of capital for agrarian investment (Maponga and Ngorima 2003; Mkodzongi 2013b; Mondlane and Shoko 2003).

Mineral-Resource Extraction after the FTLRP in Mhondoro Ngezi

In Mhondoro Ngezi, mineral resource-extraction activities significantly increased after the implementation of the FTLRP in 2000. The increase in mining activities in this area is attributed to the area's location on the great dyke, a "layered mafic intrusion of igneous, and metal bearing rock … that extends more than 550km northeast to southwest, across the centre of Zimbabwe varying from 3–12km in width" (Earth Observatory 2010, 1). According to geological survey data (Earth Observatory 2010), layered mafic intrusions such as the great dyke (see Figure 7.1) are usually associated with platinum group metals (PGM) such as chromium, nickel, copper, platinum, titanium, iron, rhodium, vanadium, and tin. In Mhondoro Ngezi, the most common PGMs are platinum, palladium, rhodium, and gold (Zimplats 2013a).

On Zimbabwe's great dyke are located four igneous complexes (see Figure 7.1) known to contain PGM and base-metal deposits, and several mining companies are currently exploring them. These include the Wedza complex (Mimosa Platinum Mine), the Selukwe complex (Anglo Platinum), the Hartley Geological complex (Zimplats Mine in Mhondoro Ngezi), and the Musengezi complex to the north, which is currently not being mined.

Among the four complexes, the Hartley Geological complex located near Mhondoro Ngezi contains more than 80 percent of known PGM deposits held by Zimplats, a wholly owned subsidiary of the South African platinum-mining company Impala Platinum (Implats).

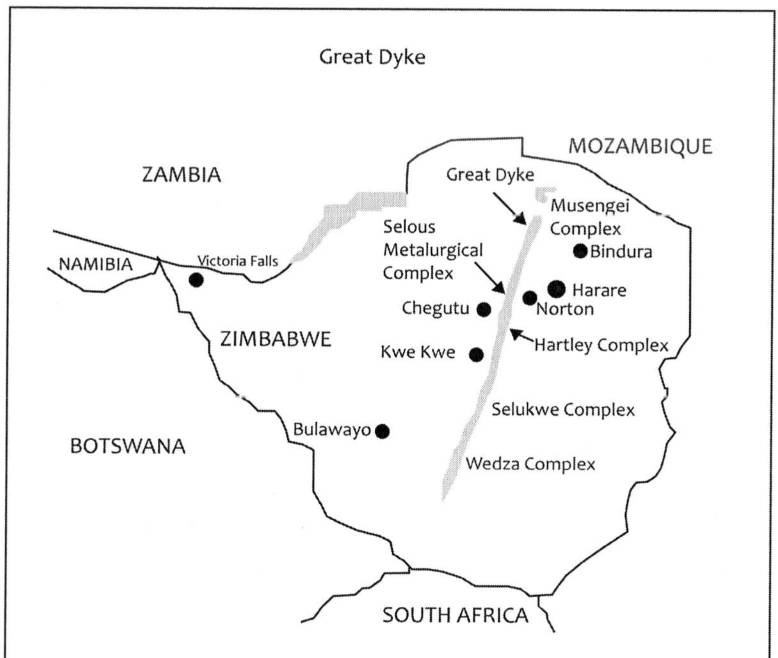

Figure 7.1. The location of Zimbabwe's great dyke and PGM-bearing complexes

Figure 7.1 shows the location of PGM reserves on Zimbabwe's great dyke. As shown on the map, the Hartley complex in Mhondoro Ngezi holds the largest reserves of PGM deposits found on the entire great dyke, which is why Zimbabwe's largest platinum mines operate in the area.

Although platinum was discovered in the Mhondoro Ngezi area in the 1980s, it was not until the 1990s that platinum mining started. In 1994, a joint venture between Australian companies Delta and BHP opened the Hartley Platinum Mine at Selous, to the north of Mhondoro Ngezi. However, the mine abruptly closed in 1999 after failure to meet production targets (Zimplats 2013a). After the closure of the mine, a local company known as Delta formed Zimbabwe Platinum Mines (Zimplats), which was later acquired by South Africa's Impala Platinum (Implats) when its shareholding increased to 87 percent. The acquisition of Zimplats led to rapid development of platinum-mining operations in Mhondoro Ngezi, from the open-pit strip mine opened in 2000 to four underground mines and a concentrator by 2013 (Zimplats 2013b).

Zimplats's mining operations in Mhondoro Ngezi coincided with the implementation of FTLRP, at a time when the country was facing economic and political crisis. The socioeconomic crisis was characterised by hyperinflation, economic decline, and political instability amid Western-imposed sanctions that left the country isolated and unable to borrow from the World Bank and International Monetary Fund (Hammar, Raftopoulos, and Jensen 2003; Moyo and Yeros 2005; Moyo and Yeros 2007; Scoones et al. 2010). However, this difficult socioeconomic situation did not necessarily deter the company from expanding its platinum-mining operations, which rapidly developed during the period. Between 2001 and 2010, four underground mines were opened (Ngwarati, Rukodzi, Bimha, and Mupfuti), and a concentrator (for milling the ore) was constructed at Ngezi, including staff accommodation and dams at Turf Village (Zimplats 2013a).

The rapid growth in Zimbabwe's PGM extraction industry during a period of socioeconomic and political instability can be attributed to two factors. First, PGM deposits on the Bushveld complex of South Africa are nearing depletion; minerals there are too deep to extract, making the maintenance of the mines expensive. Second, PGM production in South Africa has been affected by costly and at times violent industrial actions (*Financial Mail* 2013; *Mining Weekly* 2014), which in 2013 led to the now-infamous Marikana massacre of mine workers by South African police (*Mining Weekly* 2014). Labour unrest has led to significant losses in production. On the other hand, Zimbabwe, which has relatively large reserves of untapped PGM deposits, offered potential for growth with its stable labour market despite a hostile political environment underpinned by indigenisation policies (Platinum Review 2013, 15).

Besides platinum mining, a wide range of medium- and small-scale mining activities has increased during and after the land-reform process, although these have received limited publicity. For example, there is the Chinese-owned ZIMASCO Mid Reef chrome mine as well as small-scale gold, chrome, and silica mines operated by individual farmers.

Due to the availability of alluvial gold deposits in the wider Mhondoro Ngezi area, local farmers are also involved in gold-panning activities, locally known as *chikorokoza*. Despite being mostly illegal, this is a major livelihood activity undertaken by a differentiated peasantry, especially during the dry season when farming activities are low. Much of the gold panning takes places along riverbeds near the towns of Kwekwe and Kadoma (see Figure 7.1), where alluvial gold deposits are easily found.

As highlighted above, diverse mining activities are taking place in Mhondoro Ngezi and surrounding areas. These have influenced a new trajectory of rural livelihoods and accumulation among a differentiated peasantry. As discussed further below, many farmers in Mhondoro Ngezi are employed as wage labourers at the platinum mines operating in the area, while others are involved in *chikorokoza*. Other farmers, particularly the rich and politically connected, operate their own gold, chrome, and silica mines, and these have provided sources of capital to expand their farming operations into capitalist enterprises. Such farmers have used mining as a basis for their own accumulation strategies.

Below I analyse how mining activities have influenced the trajectory of agricultural investments and livelihoods of both A1 (peasant) and A2 (small-scale commercial) farmers who were resettled in Mhondoro Ngezi. A baseline survey targeting forty households in each group was undertaken. This survey sample constitutes 44 percent of A2 farmers resettled at the Solitude Farm and 22 percent of A1 farmers resettled at Damvuri.

Wage Labour, Artisanal Mining, and Livelihood Diversification Among A1 Farmers at Damvuri

This section explores the dynamics of mineral-resource extraction among A1 farmers resettled at the former Damvuri Conservancy. The conservancy was occupied by war veterans in 2000 during the implementation of FTLRP. It was subsequently demarcated and allocated to 175 peasant households (A1 model). Those who were allocated land came from diverse locations such as the old resettlements nearby, the Mhondoro Ngezi communal area, urban areas such as Kwekwe and Kadoma, and other communal areas as far as Sanyati and Gokwe to the west of Zimbabwe.

A key demographic feature of these farmers was their social differentiation. This differentiation has influenced how individual farmers invested in their newly acquired land. Among this group are richer peasants (5 percent of the surveyed households) who had the capital to quickly clear the land, build houses, set up new businesses, and hire labour. People in this group also tended to occupy positions of authority in local authority structures such as village-development committees, councils, local ZANU PF, and war-veteran structures. This group also included others who had jobs in cities and were able to invest from their own savings.

A large number (84 percent) of the new farmers consisted of worker peasants who generally struggled to invest in their land. Such people straddle livelihoods between farming and wage labour as well as other income-generating activities such as cross-border trade and petty commodity trade. These people rely mainly on family labour to work on the land, although some among them periodically hire labour on a temporary basis. At the time the fieldwork was carried out in 2010, these farmers had only managed to clear part of the land and make some initial investments, including the purchasing of assets such as livestock. However, given the difficult socioeconomic environment underpinned by sanctions and the lack of government support, such farmers faced difficulties in acquiring farming inputs and other means of production. Off-farm activities were thus important for people in this group to provide a source of finance for investment in their land.

There is also a group of poor peasants (11 percent of surveyed households) who constituted a rural proletariat[3] struggling to access land and waiting to be resettled or who had land but lacked the means to utilise it. Such people lacked draft and the financial resources to buy agricultural inputs. This rural proletariat managed to survive as wage labourers for their richer counterparts and generally were exploited by those with the means to farm (Mkodzongi 2013b).

Table 7.1 shows the trajectory of agricultural investments and livelihood dynamics among A1 farmers. As the data show, these farmers are socially differentiated. This affected their ability to utilise their newly acquired land. A major challenge that all the farmers have confronted, regardless of their class, is the severe economic crisis in Zimbabwe since the beginning of the land-reform exercise. Since the beneficiaries of FTLRP are on "contested" land (Mkodzongi 2013a), this meant that they were not eligible for donor support, unlike their counterparts in communal areas.

	Rich peasants	Peasant workers	Rural proletariat
Percent of surveyed households	5	84	11
Place of origin	Gokwe, Sanyati	Gokwe, Sanyati, old resettlements, urban areas	Old resettle-ments,urban areas, occupied farms
Average livestock owned	25 head of cattle	5 head of cattle, other small livestock	one head of cat-tle,other small livestock
Crop produc-tion and average yields	25 tonnes of maize, 15 bales of tobacco, 20 bales of cotton	5 tonnes of maize,100kg of small grains, 3 bales of cotton	500kg maize, 50 kg small grains
Moveable property owned	Tractors, ploughs, ox-drawn carts	Ploughs, ox-drawn carts, hoes	Ploughs, hoes
Investments and business ownership	Grocery shops, bottle stores, grinding mills, butcheries	Petty commodity trade	None
Involvement in off-farm activities	Hire in wage labour	Hire out wage labour, gold panning	Barter, hire out wage labour, goldpanning

Table 7.1. Socioeconomic differentiation among A1 farmers
Source: Compiled by author from baseline survey

Thus, they cannot access farm inputs and other support offered by NGOs funded by Western countries and entities such as the United States and the European Union (EU). International and local NGOs were barred from supporting farmers resettled under the FTLRP. Moreover, given the difficult socioeconomic situation, government support in terms of inputs and extension services was limited. This led many farmers to take the initiative to survive on their own. The limited government support has generally benefited those with the best political connections. As a result, many A1 farmers resettled at Damvuri are involved in off-farm activities, particularly related to mining.

But how have mining activities influenced new livelihood trajectories and agricultural investments and livelihoods? As noted above, a wide range of mining activities are taking place across Mhondoro Ngezi District. A survey undertaken at Damvuri (Mkodzongi 2013a) shows that approximately 20 percent of surveyed households are employed at the Zimplats mines. According to interviews with the farmers, they use income gained from wage labour to acquire livestock and other farm implements to improve their agricultural operations. The interviews also demonstrate that part of the wage-labour income is used to pay for social needs such as *lobola* (bride price), school fees, and food.

Apart from wage labour at the Zimplats Mine, some worker peasants are involved in illegal gold panning (*chikorokoza*). Gold panning is risky but pays huge dividends in the event of finding a sizeable amount of gold. Approximately 10 percent of the farmers were engaged in gold panning across Mhondoro Ngezi and Kadoma Districts. Some used shallow opencast mines on their own plots or along riverbeds near the towns of Kadoma and Kwekwe. According to some respondents, gold panning in the wider area predates land reform. People from the Mhondoro Ngezi communal area, and some from as far as Gokwe, frequented gold-panning sites near Kadoma during the dry season as a way of mobilising capital to acquire farming inputs ahead of the planting season. This practice has increased as a result of the opening up of many areas that were formerly enclosed before land reform. Despite the hazards involved, such as the murder of gold panners by criminal gangs, police arrests, extortion, and state violence (Mawowa 2013), gold panning has continued to flourish on account of the high monetary rewards. If one finds reasonable amounts of gold, the proceeds from the sale of gold are used to buy, among other things, livestock and other domestic goods. Below is a summary of selected interviews recorded during fieldwork that shows how artisanal mining has influenced livelihoods among this group (the names of interviewees have been changed to protect their identities).

Mr. Marxwell Bonza owns an A1 farm in Village 5 at Damvuri. He has been involved in gold panning ever since he moved from the Mhondoro Ngezi communal area in 2000:

> I have been involved in gold panning since 2000 when I got a farm here. It is a very tough job but I am used to it. I have been able to acquire livestock and a grinding mill. I also use money gained from mining to buy food for my family and to pay fees for my kids. Mining is important for us because we can use the money to buy farming inputs (Bonza interview 2014).

Mr. Magaya owns an A1 farm at Village 8. He was allocated an A1 farm at Damvuri in 2003 after leaving the Sanyati communal area in search of better-quality land:

> I am involved in both farming and gold panning. However, gold panning is a part-time activity. During the farming season I go back home to farm as it is always risky to mine when it is raining. I use money from mining to acquire farming inputs and to hire labour (Magaya interview 2014).

Mrs. Chitima and her husband moved from the town of Kadoma and were allocated an A1 farm at Village 3 in 2001. Although she is not a gold panner, she is an illegal gold buyer who frequents gold-panning sites to buy gold for resale at a profit:

> I have been buying gold across many gold panning sites in Kadoma and Mhondoro Ngezi since 2000, before we were allocated land at Damvuri. Although the returns are high, buying gold is a risky enterprise; if one is caught by the police you can be imprisoned for five years. Gold buying has been a major source of my family income. We use the money to acquire farming inputs, food and other domestic needs. We also hire labour since we are both working. We need people to look after our farm as we always travel across gold panning sites. My ambition is to own a gold mine one day (Chitima interview 2014).

The interviews, summarised above, show how *chikorokoza* is an important source of income used to acquire agricultural inputs and to pay for other domestic needs. The interviews also show that although *chikorokoza* is a major source of income, it is not necessarily replacing agriculture as the main livelihood among the peasantry, as supporters of the deagrarianisation thesis claim (Branchrigah and Hilson 2009; Bryceson 1996, 2000).

Another important dynamic of *chikorokoza* is the way it has indirectly transformed gender relations in favour of women. Interviews with women show how they have been able to take advantage of business opportunities at gold-panning sites to trade a wide range of commodities purchased locally or imported from neighbouring countries. Such commodities include mobile phones and chargers, solar panels and solar chargers, secondhand clothing, toiletries, meat, food, and wild fruit gathered across the newly opened areas. Some women have managed to accumulate enough capital to purchase livestock, household goods, and agricultural implements. This has transformed them from being passive housewives to contributors to household income, thus enhancing their ability to make decisions at the household level.

The benefits of mining are thus broad; some farmers have benefited from mining through wage labour, others as artisanal miners, and the wealthier ones through running local businesses. Some farmers, such as those in the rich peasant group (5 percent of the newly resettled farmers), are not directly engaged in mining but have benefited by opening retail businesses such as grocery stores, grinding mills, butcheries, and bottle stores. These businesses have benefited from the increased business activities driven by more incomes generated locally from mining wages and other related activities.

However, although most A1 farmers are involved in gold panning, agriculture remains at the core of their social-reproduction strategies. Gold panning tends to be conceived as a means to an end rather than an end in itself. A major reason for this is that gold panning is perceived as an illegal and risky source of income; *makorokoza* often rely on middlemen to sell their gold, making them vulnerable to extortion and arrest by corrupt police officers.

Below I explore the way mining has influenced accumulation among small-scale commercial farmers (A2 farmers) who were resettled in 1999 at the Solitude Farm, which neighbours the former Damvuri Conservancy.

Mineral-Resource Extraction and Accumulation among A2 Farmers at Solitude Farm

Unlike their A1 counterparts, small-scale commercial farmers (officially called A2 farmers) were resettled at the Solitude Farm in 1999, just before the onset of the FTLRP. Selected biographies of the farmers show that their "resettlement" was not an easy process. Despite being officially allocated land in 1996, they ended up "occupying" their plots in 1999. Although they were "officially" offered land by the government, these farmers generally tend to conceptualise the way in which they were resettled as a form of *jambanja* (force or violence) similar to the one that characterised land reform and resettlement under the FTLRP.

The way this group occupied their plots shows the dynamics of land reform and resettlement in Zimbabwe in the late 1990s. During this period, the Land Reform and Resettlement Programme (LRRP), implemented immediately after independence, had generally stalled. Funding constraints, a shift in government thinking about land reform, and donor pressure shifted the focus of land reform from decongesting crowded communal areas to providing land to the peasantry and other black people who had the capacity to farm productively. According to Moyo (2000, 75), "a key policy trend seemed to be a gradual revision of what was a radical strategy of compulsorily expropriating underutilised land … towards a more liberal market based land policy." Under this new context, the government of Zimbabwe adopted a "bifurcated approach of transferring land to better-off black farmers and to landless or poor but capable farmers in overcrowded communal areas" (Moyo 2000, 75).

Although these farmers were offered land on the basis of their ability to farm commercially, they immediately confronted many challenges after occupying their plots. Their plots lacked basic social and physical infrastructure to facilitate production and sale of the produce. This meant that they had to start from scratch to clear the land, construct roads, find water sources, and start farming operations with very minimal government support. Moreover, in the late 1990s when these farmers were resettled, Zimbabwe was experiencing the socioeconomic aftershocks of the World Bank-sponsored structural adjustment programs (SAPs), fiscal fatigue following the country's involvement in the DRC war, payment of war veterans followed by depreciation of the Zimbabwean dollar, and a decline in foreign domestic investment (FDI) that triggered hyperinflation and shortages of farming inputs and basic commodities. In addition, unlike farmers who were resettled under Zimbabwe's old resettlement schemes of the 1980s, these farmers received limited post-settlement support in terms of inputs and extension services. They had to rely on their own resources to invest in their newly acquired plots. Thus, despite their more privileged backgrounds, these farmers faced similar challenges to those faced by their A1 neighbours at Damvuri who were resettled under the FTLRP.

Interviews[4] show that in terms of their socioeconomic and geographic backgrounds, most of the farmers (75 percent) came from Sanyati, a rural area to the west of Kadoma. Others (14 percent) came from the nearby Mhondoro Ngezi communal areas, and a few (1 percent) came from urban areas such as Kadoma and Kwekwe. A total of ninety small-scale commercial farmers were resettled on fifty-hectare plots following the demarcation of the 4,500-hectare Solitude Farm. Among them were eighteen war veterans (20 percent) and war collaborators (locally known as *mujibhas* and *chimbwidos*), demonstrating the influence of war veterans in the land reform of the late 1990s.

These farmers are socially differentiated, just like their A1 counterparts. Most (97 percent) have become agricultural capitalists combining businesses, farming, and hiring of labour. A notable difference between these farmers and their A1 counterparts is the small percentage of worker peasants (6 percent), which is a predominant category among A1 farmers (84 percent). Another important socioeconomic feature of this group is that most of them hire labour; this includes worker peasants who periodically hire labour during the planting and harvesting seasons. However, the number of hired labourers varies from one household to another.

	Agrarian capitalists	**Rich peasants**	**Worker-peasants**
Percent of surveyed households	3	91	6
Place of origin	Gokwe, Sanyati and urban areas	Gokwe, Sanyati, old resettlements, Mhondoro Ngezi community area, urban areas	Gokwe, Sanyati, old resettlements, Mhondoro Ngezi community areaurban areas
Average livestock owned	200 head of cattle, 40 goats and sheep and other small livestock	50 head of cattle, 25 goats and sheep,10 pigs and other small livestock	10 head of cattle, other small livestock
Crop production and average yields	150 tonnes maize and 40 bales of cotton	50 tonnes of maize,15 bales of cotton and 20 bales of tobacco	10 tonnes of maize, 500kg ofsmall grains, 10bales of cotton
Movable property owned	Tractors, trucks, ploughs, earth-moving equipment, ox-drawn carts, grinding mills, water pumps, electricity generators	Tractors, ploughs, ox-drawn carts, grinding mills, water pumps, electricity generators	Ploughs, ox-drawn carts, hoes
Investments and business ownership	Grocery shops, mines, hardware shops, mine-relatedcontracting businesses, bottle stores, grinding mills, butcheries, poultry and horticulture	Grinding mills, butcheries and retail shops	Petty commodity trade

	Agrarian capitalists	**Rich peasants**	**Worker-peasants**
Involvement in off-farm activities	Hire in wage labourrun mine-related companies	Hire in labour, involvement in retailing businesses	Hire out wage labour and goldpanning
Hold politicalpositions	War veterans, ZANU-PF councillors and local ZANU-PF leaders	Village heads, Village Development Committee (VIDCO) and war collaborators	Ordinary members of local ZANU-PF structures

Table 7.2. Accumulation and socioeconomic differentiation among A2 farmers

Table 7.2 shows the trajectory of agricultural investments and the dynamics of accumulation among this group. In terms of agrarian investments, these farmers were also affected by the prevailing socioeconomic difficulties. As a result, some were more successful in their farming operations and have become agrarian capitalists (3 percent), while others generally struggled. This was caused by their differentiated access to agricultural inputs and mining benefits. Those with political positions in the ZANU PF Party, such as war veterans or local party representatives, had better access to capital and farming inputs; while those with property in the cities benefited from a steady monthly rental income, which they were able to invest in agriculture. Some farmers discovered mineral resources on their plots and are now running integrated and mechanised agriculture and mining operations.

But how has mineral-resource extraction influenced agricultural investments and accumulation among this group? Since these farmers are socially differentiated, some (especially those with minerals on their plots) have benefited from mining more than others have. Revenue generated from mining is deployed to acquire farming equipment such as tractors and trucks, mining equipment, and to hire labour.

Some of the politically connected farmers have started small companies supplying a wide range of commodities to Zimplats, such as plumbing materials, construction services, electrical goods, and bricks. Some of these companies are owned and run by women. For example, one group of women set up a brick-moulding cooperative that was awarded a lucrative contract by Zimplats to supply bricks for the expansion of its employee-housing scheme. These local companies, set up by the more politically connected farmers, have benefited from Zimplats's local supplier-development scheme, which is part of its wider corporate social responsibility (CSR) program.

The mine-related business enterprises have thus led to the emergence of a local agrarian bourgeoisie that runs integrated businesses. For example, Mr. Kazembe, a local ZANU PF councillor, used his political influence to secure a contract to supply silica, which he mines at his farm, to Zimplats (silica is used in the processing of platinum). As a result, Mr. Kazembe has become a successful businessman, employing fifteen full-time workers and more than thirty-five casual labourers. His Stalack Enterprises business has made him the "poster boy" of local economic empowerment. During an interview, he narrated his humble beginnings, from being a struggling A2 farmer to a thriving businessman, following the discovery of silica at his farm in 1999:

> I started small with nothing. Things changed when we discovered silica here in 1999. I received technical support and capacity development in silica mining from Zimplats. Earnings from silica mining have allowed me to invest in a horticultural enterprise. This has created employment for local people. Mining has allowed me to run a diversified enterprise which includes silica mining, poultry production and a horticultural enterprise. I also run a retailing business involving a butchery, grocery shop and a bottle store. I have also used revenue generated from mining to acquire tractors, earth-moving equipment and haulage trucks to transport minerals and agricultural produce (Kazembe interview 2014).

Mr. Kazembe's story is typical of farmers who have benefited from mining and are accumulating from below. However, not all farmers in this category attribute their success to mining alone. Other factors, such as the individual farmer's financial endowment, have influenced success among this group. For example, some farmers have relied on a combination of their own savings and wage labour to invest in their land and to accumulate assets.

Mr. Mumba, who has pioneered tobacco production in the local area, is a good example. He initially relied on his pension (savings) after retiring from his job as a meter reader for the Zimbabwe Electricity Supply Authority (ZESA). During his interview he reflected,

> I started from scratch, I did not have any prior knowledge of tobacco production. I went for tobacco production training at Kutsaga Research Station (KRS) in Harare. I used the tobacco production field guide which I bought at KRS. The tobacco field guide is my extension officer. I have used it to set seedbeds and transplant tobacco and to build a barn. I have an excellent tobacco crop, as you can see. I owe this to my extension officer (Mumba interview 2014).

In addition to producing tobacco, Mr. Mumba runs an integrated farming enterprise including horticulture and poultry production. He has also acquired equipment such as a grinding mill, which he uses to prepare poultry feed. His homestead is outstanding, with a tin-roofed bungalow, flushing toilets, and electricity. He has also sunk a borehole and has plenty of water for his horticultural enterprise. Although he has largely relied on his own income and savings from his pension, he has also benefited from mining since his two sons are employed at the Zimplats mines. Their wages are used to hire labour and to acquire agricultural inputs. Mining has also provided a market for his poultry and horticultural business.

Some farmers, such as Mr. Madhaka, have benefited from mining by working (as a manager) at the silica mine owned by fellow farmer and local councillor Mr. Kazembe. Mr. Madhaka's association with Mr. Kazembe, a ZANU politician and businessman, has earned him more than just wages. It has helped him to access inputs that are generally expensive to acquire. Interviews at various farms in the area revealed that many complained about the scarcity of fertiliser, yet Mr. Madhaka had recently acquired more than 500kg of fertiliser and herbicides. His maize crop was in relatively good health compared to those of other farmers, who were struggling to acquire fertiliser. During his interview he said,

> The main challenge facing people here is farming inputs. I have managed to acquire fertilisers and herbicides because I work at the silica mine. If I was not working, life could be much more difficult. My maize crop would be not this good (Madhaka interview 2014).

Mr. Madhaka instrumentalised his relationship with the local ZANU PF councillor to access farming inputs. This shows that a wide variety of factors have influenced agricultural investments and accumulation among this group of farmers. Although some among these farmers are already accumulating from below, their agricultural enterprises remain vulnerable to the ongoing economic challenges facing Zimbabwe more generally.

The presence of platinum mines and opportunities for gold panning in Mhondoro Ngezi has generally created competition in the wage-labour market. While this is good for farm workers (poor peasants) who are normally exploited by rich capitalist farmers, labour has become relatively expensive and in short supply. Many A2 farmers interviewed during fieldwork complained of labour shortages. They were now competing for labour with large mining companies that generally offered better wages. Moreover, some farm workers were opting to engage in gold panning, as it was perceived to offer better returns. For example, during an interview, Mr. Nhira, an A2 farmer, complained,

> These big mining companies are a threat to our farming operations. It is difficult to recruit labour as people now prefer to work in mines or engage in gold panning. Moreover, labour has become relatively expensive as a result. This is not good for us as new farmers (Nhira interview 2014).

These dynamics of mining, explored above, show how mining contributes to accumulation among A2 farmers. However, some farmers have benefited from mining more than others have. Such farmers have been able to utilise their own financial resources and their income from mining to mechanise their farming operations, acquire farming inputs, and hire labour. Mining has also contributed to the rising labour costs that have affected capitalist farmers whose accumulation is based on the exploitation of a rural proletariat.

Mineral-Resource Extraction and its Impact on Local Communities

In Mhondoro Ngezi, the benefit of mining goes beyond gaining income from working at mines, gold panning, or owning a small-scale mine. Mining has generally brought broader economic benefits to the local area at a time when many rural communities across Zimbabwe are struggling due to the difficult socioeconomic situation.

An important point is the way in which discourses of indigenisation popularised by ZANU PF have allowed local farmers to pressure mining companies to invest in local communities as a form of payment for natural-resource exploitation. For example, in Mhondoro Ngezi, Zimplats has responded to this "pressure from below" by implementing a wide range of CSR programmes benefiting local people. By 2013, CSR investments in Mhondoro Ngezi totalled US$152 million (Zimplats PR Brief 2013), a relatively large sum in Zimbabwean terms given the fiscal challenges facing the country. In 2013 alone, the company invested US$4.2 million in local projects, including the construction of schools, roads, clinics, and a laboratory (Zimplats Financial Report 2013).

Table 7.3 shows the trajectory of CSR investments by Zimplats in Mhondoro Ngezi between 2011 and 2013. It is significant that within this three-year period, Zimplats came under intense political pressure from ZANU PF and local people to indigenise its operations and to invest in local communities. Its CSR programmes can be interpreted as a response to political pressure, with the company seeking to manage its existence within a volatile political environment, especially in the run-up to the 2013 harmonised elections.

As highlighted above, many farmers (both A1 and A2) are employed at the Zimplats mines. Employment is competitive, but a local lobby led by chiefs and local councillors has forced Zimplats to reserve a certain number of jobs for local people as part of its wider CSR programme (Mkodzongi 2013a).

	FY 2013	FY 2012	FY 2011
Education	3,062,160	3,282,818	755,000
Sports	53,779	35,000	26,856
Income generating projects	80,025	46,732	303,000
Health	668,050	873,471	223,000
Other	339,641	1,071,079	40,794
Total CSR	4,203,655	5,309,100	1,348,650
Direct donation to CSOT	2,500,000	3,300,000	1,348,650
Total CSR	6,703,655	8,609,100	2,687,300

Table 7.3. Trajectory of CSR investment in a three-year period (US$)
Source: Zimplats Financial Report (2013b).

In general, mining has contributed to the local economy's growth by creating employment opportunities and infrastructural development at a time when most rural areas' infrastructures have deteriorated due to economic conditions. Thus, Mhondoro Ngezi has one of the best roads in Zimbabwe, which links the area to major towns and cities; a vibrant shopping centre with banks and clinics; and a connection to the electricity grid. The area now has mobile connectivity, which has allowed local farmers to use mobile phones and access local and global news and other information important for agricultural and other businesses activities. Zimplats also funded the installation of a fibre-optic cable, which has brought broadband internet to the local area. This has allowed some local farmers to access high-speed internet and some local businesses to boost their operations through internet connectivity. Moreover, infrastructure such as the tarred roads provided by Zimplats has made it easy for local farmers to transport their produce to markets that include the tobacco-auction floors, in Harare, about 150km away.

In 2013, Zimplats complied with Zimbabwe's indigenisation- and economic-empowerment regulations and donated US$10 million to the newly created Mhondoro Ngezi Chegutu Zvimba Community Share Ownership

Trust (CSOT). This money has added further financial resources for local development projects. However, access to the benefits of CSR investments is contested among a wide range of classes, ethnicities, and genders. For example, I have explored elsewhere how local chiefs have contested with political elites for control of the US$10 million donated by Zimplats to the local CSOT. This chapter does not explore this in detail, but before generalisations can be made, a nuanced analysis is necessary concerning how various classes, ethnicities, and genders contest with one another to benefit from mining and indigenisation.

Although mining has brought broader economic benefits to the Mhondoro Ngezi area, its long-term social and environmental impact cannot be ignored. Mine sites are generally associated with high incidences of HIV/AIDS infections. Survey data show that HIV/AIDS cases have risen across the Mhondoro Ngezi area as a result of high labour mobility and the miners' engagement in risky sexual relations with so-called "temporary wives." The long-term impacts of HIV/AIDS require further research.

The emission of toxic gases during the mining and processing of minerals pollutes the air, ground and surface water, and has potential short-term and long-term health implications. For example, the Zimplats Financial Report (2013b, 7) shows that sulphur-dioxide emission levels at its smelter remain "above recommended levels and that emission levels are increasing." The report does not, however, indicate the health implications of such emissions or when corrective measures will be put in place. Moreover, levels of naturally occurring radioactive materials (NORM) associated with the mining and processing of PGMs pose health hazards to local communities and to Zimplats's employees. Although Zimplats reports that it hired the South Africa Nuclear Energy Corporation (NECSA) to conduct a radiological survey at its mines and processing plants, NORM exposure levels and their health implications for employees and local communities remain unknown. This might have long-term health consequences for those exposed to radioactive material long after the company has left.

Although Zimplats's mining operations have not, to date, led to the displacement of large numbers of households, its continued expansion is likely to compromise rural livelihoods, for example, by taking away productive and common grazing land from local communities. For example, the building of the 30,500 megalitre Island Dam at Silver Star and the expansion of staff housing led to the relocation of twenty-eight households (approximately 280 people). Although those who were relocated were offered full compensation, including new houses with sanitary facilities, the long-term livelihood implications of such removals are unknown.

There are other social implications of mine expansion; for example, the Island Dam construction led to the closure of the nearby Silver Star cemetery because of the risk of flooding. The closure of the cemetery directly conflicts with local tradition, given that ancestral graves play an important role in the lives of the living. Flooding also affects the accessibility of graves, making it difficult for people to conduct annual rituals such as the *kurovaguva* ceremonies, which are undertaken to appease the spirits of the dead. While this ritual might be irrelevant to the mine, it has spiritual implications for local people because rituals are important for creating a sense of belonging and a connection to the land.

Another worrisome aspect of the Zimplats mines expansion is the increasing level of water use. Milling the platinum-bearing ores is a water-intensive process. Although the mine has established a water-recycling system, the demand for water is increasing on an annual basis as more mines are opened and ore production reaches full capacity. For example, in FY2013, water consumption increased by 31 percent (Zimplats 2013b, 64). Given the recurrent droughts associated with climate change, platinum-mining operations pose a direct threat to water security for local households. This also requires further research.

While artisanal mining has become an important source of rural income for many local farmers, most gold-panning activities around Mhondoro Ngezi take place along riverbeds and open pits. This leads to the discharge of mercury (which is used during the processing of gold) and other toxic waste into water consumed by local residents and domestic animals. Moreover, disused mine pits pose a health hazard to the farmers' livestock, miners, and the public: people and their animals often fall into the abandoned shafts. Land exposed to gold panning is generally degraded and requires rehabilitation to be of any use. Further research needs to be undertaken to explore the impact of artisanal mining on the environment.

Mining-based livelihoods are mostly short term given that minerals are a finite resource. At some point they will run out, leaving behind an army of unemployed people, a polluted environment, and a subsequent collapse of local infrastructures and markets. Moreover, global commodity markets tend to fluctuate in economic cycles; sometimes this can lead to mine closures and resultant unemployment. As in South Africa, the platinum sector in Zimbabwe faces a wide range of challenges. These include, among other things, labour unrest, overproduction, and a fall in platinum prices on the global commodity markets. All of these outcomes will likely cause viability challenges in the long term (*Mail and Guardian* 2011). Such viability challenges might affect local farmers whose livelihoods are now intertwined with mining as a source of income. This demonstrates the risky nature of mining as a source of rural income.

There is also the question of what happens to the town that has developed around the mine if the company suddenly ends its operations. For example, in 1999 the Delta-BHP GV platinum operation at Chegutu abruptly ended as a result of its failure to meet production targets, leaving behind a ghost town and many unemployed former workers. This shows the problem of reliance on mining as a rural livelihood. While its short- and medium-term benefits to local communities should be celebrated, its long-term socioeconomic and environmental implications must be considered. Such issues are beyond the scope of this article, but they illustrate the potential hazards of mining-based livelihoods. Total disinvestment from agriculture among local farmers can spell trouble in the long term, which is one reason why local farmers are cautious about completely abandoning farming in pursuit of mining careers.

Conclusions

In the aftermath of Zimbabwe's land-reform programme, mining has become a key economic activity pursued by a differentiated group of farmers (both A1 and A2 categories). However, it has not replaced farming as the main livelihood activity. The farmers generally view mining as a means to an end; among the A1 farmers, mining is a key source of income used to help acquire farming inputs, food, and other domestic needs, while among the A2 farmers mining has become a key driver of accumulation from below. However, among the latter group, mining has brought competition in the wage-labour market that has made labour relatively expensive. Mining has also brought broader economic benefits to the Mhondoro Ngezi area, although access to such benefits is contested among various classes and genders.

Nonetheless, mining activities have a negative environmental and social impact on local communities. These negative aspects cannot be overlooked and require further research. The Mhondoro Ngezi case study explored in this chapter demonstrates that generalisations about livelihood diversification across sub-Saharan Africa must account for a diversity of experiences.

Notes

[1] This article is based on ethnographic data gathered in Mhondoro Ngezi District as part of a doctoral thesis submitted to the University of Edinburgh in March 2013, and follows on fieldwork undertaken in 2014.

[2] Under Zimbabwe's FTLRP, the A1 farm category generally denotes a peasant farm, while A2 denotes a wider spectrum of commercial farms of varying sizes.

[3] The rural proletariat here comprises those who have not yet accessed land and those with land but insufficient means to utilise it. People in this group derive their livelihoods mainly from wage labour.

[4] Interviews were conducted from 2010 to 2014 using a baseline survey, formal and informal interviews, and personal observations.

References

Banchirigah, S. M., and G. Hilson. 2010. De-agrarianization, re-agrarianization and local economic development: Re-orientating livelihoods in African artisanal mining communities. *Policy Sciences* 43: 2, 157–180.

BBC News. 2012. "Zimbabwe's Marange diamond fields 'plundered.'" BBC News, November 13. Accessed May 13, 2014. www.bbc.com/news/world-africa-20305537.

Bernstein, H. 1979. "African peasantries: A theoretical framework." *The Journal of Peasant Studies* 6: 4, 421–43.

—. 2003. "Farewells to the peasantry." *Transformation: Critical Perspectives on Southern Africa* 52: 1, 1–19.

Bryceson, D. F. 1996. "De-agrarianisation and rural employment in sub Saharan Africa: A sectoral perspective." *World Development* 4: 1, 97–111.

—. 2000. "Peasant theories and smallholder policies, past and present." In *Disappearing Peasantries? Rural Labour in Africa, Asia and Latin America*, edited by D. F. Bryceson, C. Kay, and J. Mooij, 1–36. London: Intermediate Technology Publications.

Bryceson, D. F., and B. J. Jonsson. 2009. "Gold digging careers in rural east Africa: Small-scale miners' livelihood choices." *World Development* 38: 3, 379–392.

Courville, Michael, and Raj Patel. 2006. "The resurgence of agrarian reform in the twenty-first century." In *Promised Land: Competing Visions of Agrarian Reform*, edited by Peter Rosset, Raj Patel, and Michael Courville, 3–22. New York: Food First Books.

Earth Observatory. 2010. "The great dyke." Accessed May 3, 2014. http://earthobservatory.nasa.gov/IOTD/view.php?id=46341.

Financial Mail. "Bushveld complex a mining battle." *Financial Mail.* Accessed May 13, 2014. www.financialmail.co.za/business/money/2013/07/25/bushveld-complex-a-mining-battle-ground.

Hilson, G. 2009. "Small-scale mining, poverty and economic development in sub Saharan Africa: An overview." *Resources Policy* 34: 1–5.

Interviews with Residents of Damvuri. 2014. January 15–18. Damvuri, Mhondoro Ngezi.

Maponga, O., and C. F. Ngorima. 2003. "Overcoming environmental problems in the gold panning sector through legislation and education: The Zimbabwean experience." *Journal of Cleaner Production* 11: 2, 147–57.

Mawowa, S. 2013. "The political economy of artisanal and small-scale gold mining in central Zimbabwe." *Journal of Southern African Studies* 39: 4, 921–36.

Mining Weekly. 2014. "Platinum producers slam acts of violence as tensions mount in platinum belt." *Mining Weekly.* Accessed May 13, 2014. www.miningweekly.com/article/platinum-producers-slam-rising-acts-of-violence-as-tensions-mount-in-the-platinum-belt-2014-05-12.

Mkodzongi, G. 2013a. *Fast tracking land reform and rural livelihoods in Mashonaland West province of Zimbabwe: Opportunities and constraints 2000–2013*. PhD diss., University of Edinburgh.

—. 2013b. "New people, new land, new livelihoods: A micro-study of Zimbabwe's Fast Track Land Reform: Agrarian South." *Journal of Political Economy* 2: 3, 1–22.

Mondlane, S., and D. S. M. Shoko. 2003. "The socio-economic and environmental impacts of artisanal and small-scale mining in Mozambique." In *The socio-economic impacts of artisanal and small-scale mining in developing countries*, edited by Gavin M. Hilson, 265–280. Lisse: A. A. Balkema.

Moyo J. 2011. "Zimbabwe politicians scramble for trusts control." *Mail and Guardian,* May 16–22. Accessed October 10, 2011. http://mg.co.za/article/2011-10-24-zim-politicians-scramble-for-trust-control.

Moyo, S. 1994. *Economic Nationalism and Land Reform in Zimbabwe.* Harare: Sapes Books.

—. 2000. *Land Reform Under Structural Adjustment in Zimbabwe.* Upssala: Nordic Africa Institute.

—. 2011a. "Changing agrarian relations after redistributive land reform in Zimbabwe." *Journal of Peasant Studies* 38: 5, 907–34.

—. 2011b. "Land concentration and accumulation after redistributive reform in post settler Zimbabwe." *Review of African Political Economy* 38 (128): 257–76.

Moyo, S., W. Chambati, T. Murisa, D. Siziba, C. Dangwa, K. Mujeyi, and N. Nyoni. 2009. *Fast Track land Reform Baseline Survey in Zimbabwe: Trends and Tendencies 2005/06.* Harare: AIAS.

Moyo, S., and P. Yeros. 2005. "Land occupations and land reform in Zimbabwe: Towards the national democratic revolution." In *Reclaiming the Land: The Resurgence of Rural Movements in Africa, Asia and Latin America*, edited by S. Moyo and P. Yeros, 165–208. London: ZED Books.

Nyamunda, T., and P. Mukwambo. 2012. "The state and the bloody diamond rush in Chiadzwa: Unpacking the contesting interests in the development of illicit mining and trading, *c.* 2006–2009." *Journal of Southern African Studies* 38: 1, 145–66.

Petras, James 1997. "Latin America: The resurgence of the left." *New Left Review* 223: 1, 17–47.

Petras, James, and Henry Veltmeyer. 2001. "Are Latin American peasant movements still a force for change? Some new paradigms revisited." *Journal of Peasant Studies* 28: 2, 83–118.

Scoones, I., N. Marongwe, B. Mavedzenge, J. Mahenene, F. Murimbarimba, and C. Sukume. 2010. *Zimbabwe's Land Reform: Myths and Realities*. London: James Currey.

Standard. 2011. "ZANU PF chefs, chief fight over Zimplats shares." *The Standard,* September 24. Accessed January 20, 2014. www.thestandard.co.zw/2011/09/24/zanu-pf-chefs-chief-fight-over-zimplats-shares/.

Steyn, L. 2014. *Golden Goose or Dying Duck*. Johannesburg: M&G Media Ltd.

Telegraph. 2013. "Zimbabwe mining taxes disappear." *The Telegraph,* Platinum Review, June 19. Accessed May 13, 2014. www.telegraph.co.uk/news/worldnews/africaandindianocean/zimbabwe/10129989/Zimbabwe-mining-taxes-disappear.html.

Towriss, David. 2013. "Buying loyalty: Zimbabwe's marange Diamonds." *Journal of Southern African Studies* 39: 1, 99–117.

Veltmeyer, Henry. 2005. "The dynamics of land occupations in Latin America." In *Reclaiming the Land: The Resurgence of Rural Movements in Africa, Asia and Latin America*, edited by S. Moyo and P. Yeros, 165–208. London: ZED Books.

Zimplats. 2013a. *Zimplats Holdings Sustainability Report.* Accessed November 13, 2014. http://www.zimplats.com/Zimplats%20sustainability%202012%20.pdf

—. 2013b. *Financial Report 2013*. Harare: Zimplats Head Office.

Chapter Eight

The Implications of Large-Scale Mining on Customary Land in Zambia

Moonde Kabinga

Introduction

Since the late 1990s, Zambia has witnessed the expansion and development of new large-scale mines. Between 1996 and 2011, four large-scale mines were opened (Ministry of Mines, Energy and Water Development 2013).[1] The development of these mines came after the privatisation[2] of the mining sector in the early 1990s and, starting from the early 2000s, increasing copper prices on the global market have attracted more investments in mining. The increased mining activities are evident from growth in the production of copper, which tripled from about 250,000 tons in 2000 to about 750,000 tons in 2007 (IMF Zambia Report 2015).

The large-scale mining of copper in Zambia has always played a central role in the national economy and the political landscape. This is due to the centrality of the mining industry, which since colonial times has remained the main foreign-currency earner in the country, contributing close to 80 percent of total foreign-currency earnings (ACET 2014). In addition, because of the crucial role that mining plays in the Zambian economy, the government has always treated this sector as a special case, prioritising it over other sectors in various ways, including the process of acquiring land for mineral prospecting and development. As a result of the mining industry's elevated position in the country, mining investments are often negotiated without much thought given to the impact of mining activities on local communities.

While mining is essential for economic growth and development in Zambia, I argue in this chapter that balancing national interests and the interests and plights of people in local communities where mining activities occur seems to be a problem. I situate this discussion in the broader debate of land grabs and forced removals in the context of large-scale mining ventures. Cases of land grabs and forced removal are not unique to Zambia and are reported in many other African countries, such as Ghana and South Africa, where mining constitutes a significant segment of the economy. One question is how mining and the interests of local people can be reconciled so that all stakeholders (i.e., investors and the local communities in the mine areas) benefit fairly from the mining activities. As discussed further below, government officials, and in some cases traditional authorities, often overlook the rights of the local people when mining rights are granted to local and foreign investors.

By examining the implications of mining for local communities, this chapter aims to highlight certain challenges that should be considered to ensure that local communities' interests are protected and not sacrificed for profit and national growth. The chapter also argues that although mining can bring economic benefits to local communities, such as employment opportunities, such benefits come at a huge cost to the locals, including the loss of the land, which is the major source of their livelihoods.

The chapter is divided into five sections. Section 2 provides the background and gives an overview of the mining sector in Zambia, the history of mining, and some mining policies. Section 3 discusses the land situation in Zambia. Section 4 examines the social and economic implications of large-scale mining with regard to customary land and the livelihoods of surrounding communities. The chapter focuses on current debates over the implications of mining on customary land and possible approaches to reconciling the management of large-scale mining and the interest of locals in the mining areas. The final section offers concluding remarks.

Background

An Overview of the Mining Sector in Zambia

Zambia is a country rich in mineral-resources, with a wide range of mineral deposits, including copper, cobalt, zinc, lead, iron, manganese, gold, nickel, platinum, titanium, and gemstones (mainly emeralds and alluvial diamonds). These resources (especially copper, cobalt, lead, and zinc) contribute greatly to the country's economy in general and state revenue in particular, accounting for about 70 to 80 percent of the country's foreign-export earnings (Simutanyi 2008; Mususa 2012). "The mining industry has been the economic and social backbone of Zambia since the first major phase of exploration of the copper deposits commenced in the early 1930s" (ZEITI 2012, 7). Zambia also plays an important role in the global copper-mining industry, as the country is known to contain the largest reserves of copper in Africa and holds about 6 percent of the copper reserves in the world (UKaid and World Bank Report 2011).

Mining activities in Zambia can be grouped into three phases: Phase I, mining in the colonial era (1920s–1964); Phase II, mining in postcolonial Zambia under the mixed economy regime (1964–1991); and Phase III, mining under the liberalised economic regime (1991 to the present). This chapter focuses on mining during phase III, under the liberalised economy, as this marks the crucial era when the 1995 policy reforms came into effect, namely the 1995 Mining Policy and the 1995 Lands Act.

The Development of Mining in Zambia

From the inception of large-scale copper mines operating in the Copperbelt in Zambia in the 1920s, the country experienced a surge in mining activities that propelled it into a "modernising economy" (see Ferguson 1999). Lungu (2009) argues that after independence, the ruling United National Independence Party (UNIP), under former president Kenneth Kaunda, raised hopes of significant development in the country due to the favourable copper prices on the world market in the 1960s and 1970s. Cunningham (1981) notes that during the 1960s and 1970s, the copper-mining sector in Zambia accounted for over 95 percent of export earnings and over 60 percent of government revenue. At that time, Zambia was classified as a "middle-income country," and it had the highest gross domestic product (GDP) in Africa (Ferguson 1999, 6), which was higher even than that of countries such as Brazil, Malaysia, and South Korea (Lungu 2009, 544). According to Ferguson (1999, 1), "no place was emerging faster or more hopefully than Zambia during that period," and in Africa this was referred to as an "industrial revolution." Ferguson further suggests that the socioeconomic transformations led by the mining industry resulted in the emergence of new, modern mining towns in the Copperbelt.

However, the history of mining in Zambia is that of a boom followed by decline (Lungu 2009; Simutanyi 2008) and then revival. In the 1970s, Zambia produced approximately 700,000 tons of copper, but by 1998 production had been reduced to about 255,000 tons (UKaid and the World Bank 2011). As early as 1968, the economy had already begun showing signs of decline, and former president Kaunda had become concerned. The decline of the mining industry and, therefore, Zambia's economy can be attributed to the fall in copper prices on the international markets and to poor management. This led to a reduction in employment, declining imports, and huge foreign debts (Limpitlaw 2011). President Kaunda decided to nationalise the copper mines in 1969 in the hope that nationalisation would direct profits towards building social and economic infrastructure (Lungu 2009). This was achieved through the Mines and Minerals Act of 1969, which gave the Zambian government absolute control over the mining industry (Ndulo 1986). Unfortunately, nationalisation did not help much. The country eventually found itself in an economic crisis; consequently, the opposition party, the MMD, led by late former president Fredrick Chiluba, was able to use the worsening economic conditions to dislodge the UNIP from power in the 1991 elections.

Immediately after coming to power, the MMD implemented one of the most ambitious and aggressive privatisation programmes in the world, so that by the end of the 1990s the MMD government had privatised 273 state-owned companies, including the mines. The Zambian government adopted the privatisation process after the introduction of the structural adjustment programmes (SAP) and other reform programmes suggested by the World Bank (WB) and the International Monetary Fund (IMF). The 1995 Lands Act was one of the programmes enacted as a result of the SAP, to pave the way for land conversions from customary possession to leasehold and to stimulate the land market.

Since the early 2000s, mining activities have increased, which can be attributed to the rise in copper prices on the global market. This has led to an increase not just in production by volume but also in the number and level of investments and, therefore, in the amount of land acquired for various mining activities. Taking advantage of this momentum, the government has targeted the production of 1 million tons of copper by 2016, which would be an all-time high. Investments, some of them domestic but mainly foreign, have been steadily flowing into the sector since the early 2000s, remaining buoyant during the 2008–09 global financial and economic crisis and doubling to US$4.6 billion in 2011 from US$2 billion reported in 2009 (ACET 2014). The recent resurgence in mining-sector investments has also led to an increase in exploration and the creation of new mines, such as Kansanshi and Lumwana in North-Western Province, which began operations after 2005. Although in most cases these investments bring the promise of improved welfare for local people (and an increased flow of revenue into the national coffers), they also bring many challenges to the local communities in which the new mining activities occur. It is not uncommon for the communities closest to mines to be among the poorest in the country.

Mining Policies

Recently, Zambia amended the Mines and Minerals Development Act, which came into effect on July 1, 2015, replacing the Mines and Minerals Development Act–2008. The amended act revised the provisions relating to exploration for mining; the processing of minerals; safety, health, and environmental protection in mining operations; the establishment of the Mining Appeals Tribunal; and matters connected with incidental issues to the foregoing. The Mines and Minerals Act 2015, Section 3 (1) also states that "All rights of ownership in, searching for, mining and disposing of, minerals wheresoever located in the Republic vest in the President on behalf of the Republic" (Mines Mineral Act 2015, 172). Prior to independence, the British South African Company (BSAC) under the colonial government controlled all mining rights in Rhodesia (now Zambia). It was only on the eve of Zambia's independence, on October 24, 1964, that the BSAC relinquished all mining rights to the incoming government, UNIP, under the leadership of former president Kenneth Kaunda (Ndulo 1986). Therefore, anyone seeking mining rights or mineral-processing licences must go through the Ministry of Mines and Minerals Development, which acts on behalf of the president. Furthermore, Section 52 (1)(c) of this act suggests that a holder of a mining right or mineral-processing licence cannot exercise any right upon land occupied by a village or under customary ownership without the consent of the chief and the local authority of the area in which the aforementioned is situated.

Land in Zambia

Zambia is a country endowed with a relatively large land mass and a relatively low population density, assessed at about 17.2 people per km^2 in 2010. The total surface area of the country is 752 615Km^2, with forest cover accounting for 9 percent, national parks for 8 percent, and game-management areas for 22 percent (Draft Land Policy 2006).

Land in Zambia is vested in the president and is held in trust on behalf of the Zambian people (per the 1995 Lands Act). Like most other parts of Africa, Zambia has a dual land-tenure system classified as state land and customary land. State land and customary land are further governed under leasehold or customary tenures, respectively (German, Schoneveld, and Mwangi 2011). At the time of independence, 94 percent of land in Zambia was believed to be under customary tenure, while 6 percent was under state ownership. Over time, these estimates have become inaccurate, particularly after the introduction of the 1995 Lands Act. Conversions of land in Zambia have increased in recent years. Currently, the ratio of customary land in Zambia is estimated at 37 percent (Committee on Agriculture and Lands 2009).

Mining on Customary Land

Current Debates

Contemporary debates suggest that the struggle for access and rights to land in Africa and in other developing countries has intensified. Hall (2011, 193) has argued that "in Southern Africa in particular, as is the case elsewhere on the continent, pressure for commercialisation of land in recent years has been accelerated by the widespread leasing or sale of public lands to foreign companies and governments." This is being done for development-oriented projects such as mineral-resource extraction, commercial agriculture, tourism, and dam development.

Zambia, like many other African countries, has been at the forefront of advocating for foreign direct investment (FDI). The need for FDI emerges from the fact that most African governments lack sufficient capacity to develop their countries, which are well endowed with mineral resources, fertile land, and climates suited to agricultural production for international markets (Borras and Franco 2010, 2). The World Bank and the International Finance Corporation (2002) have argued that most African governments need investments to be able to participate in global markets and, thus, to earn revenue through taxation. Thus, many African governments offer generous incentives to investors, often in the form of deals, to the detriment of local communities, which are normally not consulted when these deals are made. The World Bank and other international financial institutions (IFIs) have for decades strenuously promoted the transformation of the land-tenure system in Africa from communal tenure to individual, or private, tenure. The assumption has always been that Africa has a great deal of land that is just idle. Peters (2004, 269) has argued that the notion of plenty of land in Africa for whoever wants it no longer holds true for most of the continent.

Borras and Franco (2010) have also suggested that the "rich countries" (the developed countries) are using this opportunity of investing in "poor countries" (the developing countries) so that they can continue to bring wealth back to their home countries, as they did during colonisation. Such situations have, over the years, been referred to as "land grabs" or "farm races," which suggests a neocolonial push by foreign companies or governments to take possession of key resources (Hall 2011; Borras and Franco 2010). In northern Tanzania, for instance, biofuel is produced on a large scale on land acquired by land grabbing, and village communities have been displaced and their livelihoods shattered to facilitate these investments (Kamanga 2009). Another case of a land grab-related investment on the African continent is the ProCana case in Mozambique, where agrofuel production from sugarcane is taking place. Borras (2011) further argues that investors are searching not only for available land but land with available water resources. He uses the ProCana case as a typical example of land where abundant water was necessary for the cultivation of the sugar cane.

Land grabbing has many facets, and the most negative is the displacement of local people to facilitate the establishment of the plantation or whatever else will make a profit for the project's investors, and displacement is arguably always detrimental to local communities (Hall 2011). On the other hand, scholars such as Terminski (2000, 3659) argue that forced displacement results from the need to build infrastructure for new industries, irrigation, dams, new highways for transportation, schools, and so forth and, therefore, improves the lives of many people through the creation of employment and better delivery of services. Terminski calls this type of displacement "development-induced displacement."

This chapter argues that for any country's economy to develop and grow, investment projects are important. Thus, there is a need to strike a balance in mining investments between national interests and the interests of local communities where the mining activities occur, as a lack of balance can affect a country's growth. When negotiating development projects such as mining with potential investors, host governments are responsible for the needs of both the nation and local communities. The needs of local communities are not often taken into consideration; hence not only do they lose the land they have lived on for generations, but they also lose their livelihoods, which are attached to the land. This has occurred in many local communities in Zambia, as most of the communal land under customary tenure, where most locals reside, has been commercialised for projects such as mining. This is true of North-Western, Copperbelt, and Southern Provinces, for instance. The next section provides more examples of the impact of mining on customary land in Zambia.

The Impact of Large-Scale Mining Projects on Local Communities: Zambia's Experience

This section discusses implications of large-scale mining on customary land, based on Zambia's experience. The discussion draws from secondary sources and lived experiences. Based on the evidence gathered, the implications have been categorised into positive and negative implications and will be discussed further. The positive implications include the creation of employment opportunities and access to markets, infrastructure development, the development of revenue, and the performance of corporate social responsibilities. The negative implications include the loss of land, displacement and relocation, lack of employment opportunities, tension, the playing out of power dynamics, the frustration of local communities, wage-labour disputes, little or no compensation, loss of social networks, environmental and health problems, deforestation, and landscape degradation.

Positive Implications

Employment Opportunities and Market Access: Mining operations have always provided employment opportunities to skilled labour and, at times, to unskilled labour. During the colonial era in Zambia, as in other African mining countries, local or migrant black males primarily performed unskilled labour, while skilled positions were mainly reserved for expert white males. In the last fifty years, trained locals and migrants from within and outside Zambia have been employed in some management and expert positions with good salary packages and other benefits such as subsidised housing, water, electricity, transport, and education (Lungu 2009). In Mopani, Nkonkola, Lumwana, and Kansanshi, local and international employees have benefited from such opportunities. However, local residents have normally been excluded from employment due to their lack of skills in mining. Currently, at some mines such as Lumwana, the situation is slowly changing as employment priority is given to locals according to their ability and suitability (Equinox Venture Copper Limited 2005, 122).

Infrastructure and Town Development: Mining companies not only provide services for their employees but also for the surrounding communities. They maintain the roads, hospitals, and schools in their areas of operation. They also encourage economic and social growth through activities such as the construction of shops and the commercialisation of farming (Lungu 2009). Townships and mining towns have developed as a result of mining in Zambia (see also Ferguson 1999).

Revenue: Like many other mining countries, Zambia has benefited from foreign revenues and taxing exports of mined minerals since the colonial era. Currently, close to 80 percent of Zambia's foreign income derives from mining exports (see Simutanyi 2008; Mususa 2012).

Corporate Social Responsibility (CSR): According to Waldman et al. (2010, 1), CSR refers to "a management approach that takes into considera tion an integrated set of indicators that map the firm's impact and reciproca l effects within the realm of its economic, societal and environmental exist ence." Some mining companies in Zambia discharged their CSR obligatio n through projects such as women's saving programmes, education, health, sports, and agriculture (e.g., Nkonkola Copper Mine, Mopani Copper Mine, etc.). The CSR projects are one way in which the mining companies give back to the local communities in the areas in which they operate. CSR is not a substitute for mining tax but complements it.

Negative Implications

Implications for Livelihoods: When people are displaced, their livelihoods are inevitably affected. The displaced rural communities or residents usually must start life again from scratch, and this can be very difficult, especially if they have no extraneous means to sustain themselves. Often they are moved to places where they will not disturb an existing community, which means places that are more or less empty and, therefore, have poor soils and no infrastructure. The poor soils may lead to poor harvests, hunger, and famine. These effects, if not carefully resolved, can have further consequences, including loss of life. These distant areas often have poor communication networks due to poor road infrastructures and, sometimes, lack of telecommunication services. Mining investments can bring about certain benefits, but their impacts on the dislocated communities are more negative than positive.

Tensions: Over the years, many reports have surfaced, mainly in the media, of tensions and struggles over land. Long ago, such struggles were uncommon because land was abundant and the population of Zambia was quite small. Today, the issue of land is quite problematic not only in Zambia but in other African countries as well. These struggles normally cause tension, which may result in strained relations between locals and chiefs, locals and investors, chiefs and investors, or chiefs and the government. Several such cases have been reported due to activities linked to mining. Little or no research has been done regarding tensions arising from mining in Zambia. An example of where tension emerged is the case of Zambezi Resources. In 2008, a US$494 million copper mine, Zambezi Resources, belonging to an Australian company, was scheduled to operate in Lower Zambezi National Park, which is in the area of Chieftainess Chiawa. Several chiefs, including Chieftainess Chiawa, met for discussions, and all of them were opposed to the mining project (*Lusaka Times* 2014). They claimed that the project would affect the ecosystem and the seventeen chiefdoms in the area. The Zambia Wildlife Authority (ZAWA) also objected to the establishment of the mine in the national park. The Zambia Environmental Management Agency (ZEMA) also did not support the proposed mining project. This debate raged from 2008 to early 2014, when the Lands and Natural Resources Minister (as the government representative) approved the development of the mine by Zambezi Resources. The Australian company (via Zambezi Resources) was eager to start operations at whatever cost. This situation clearly shows how two opposing camps may be unwilling to consult and compromise. The situation is likely to continue to fuel strained relations among locals, chiefs, investors, and the government (in other words, the various stakeholders involved) should the mine actually be constructed. Another case includes the Maamba Collum Coal Mine in Sinazeze, where the locals and Chinese mine investors had a conflict resulting in the death of a Chinese miner (see the section below under wage-labour disputes) (Maravi 2012). There is also the Trident Mine in Solwezi in Zambia's North-Western Province, where locals were upset with the mine's management for refusing to allow them to harvest their crops, because the mine needed to start operations, and of course, the locals were not compensated (*Lusaka Times* 2011).

Power Dynamics: The case of Zambezi Resources also exemplifies issues around power dynamics, such as who has the mandate to alienate land. Is it the chiefs or is it the government? According to the Zambian Constitution, most of the land is held under customary law, according to which the chief is the custodian of the land, which he holds on behalf of his local community; at the same time, all land in Zambia is vested in the president and held in trust on behalf of the Zambian people (1995 Lands Act). These two policies are quite problematic as they seem to contradict each other and may therefore be confusing. The chiefs believe that they have the authority to allocate customary land, but according to the government the president can overrule the chiefs and give land to anyone. This indicates how insecure the customary-land tenure system in Zambia is and how problematic it can be for rural community members who believe in and derive security through communal land ownership.

The Frustration of Local Communities: In North-Western Province, where the new mines, Kansanshi and Lumwana, now operate, there are reports of poor relations between rural community members and the mine management. Rural community members have reported that they are not allowed near the mines, that the mine area has been fenced, and that they feel excluded from the mining activities in their area. They also claim that they are denied access to a nearby dam from which they need to draw water for their daily use. They believe that they do not benefit from the mine's existence, as the investors promised, and this has created poor relations between the two groups as well as frustration among the rural community members. The chiefs in the mining areas have indicated that the investors' attitude towards them was good before they obtained the mining licence (and access to land) but that their attitude changed thereafter (Ng'ombe and Keivani 2013).

Wage-Labour Disputes: The appalling treatment of workers, the poor safety environment (for instance at the BGRIMM explosives factory on the premises of the Chambishi mine, where forty-nine Zambians were killed in a blast), and the poor working conditions of certain mining companies can create poor relations. This can lead to tensions that can escalate from the local to the national and even international level if the issues are not carefully resolved. The case of Maamba Collum Coal Mine in Sinazeze, in southern Zambia, is a typical example in which wage-labour disputes were recently reported. This mine reported a wage conflict between the local mine workers and the Chinese mine management (Maravi 2012). The conflict resulted in the death of a Chinese miner, who was run down by a trolley pushed by an angry mob. After this incident, the Chinese miners and the members of the rural community hid from one another as they were living in fear and could not relate. The incident reflects the poor relations that can occur if relevant stakeholders do not engage in dialogue and certain parties feel abused or that they do not benefit. The Zambian government eventually revoked the Maamba Collum Coal Mine's licence in 2014, after investigations revealed that the mine was not complying with many regulations, including corporate social responsibilities, environmental concerns, and the payment of government royalties.

Such a situation clearly shows the deleterious effect of strained relations among the stakeholders involved. Some scholars have stressed the importance of active participation in such processes by government and other stakeholders such as the communities and investor companies, to create a trilateral dialogue (World Bank and IFC 2002). This dialogue not only improves communication but also leads to the participation of interested parties. The World Bank and IFCs also suggest that companies that plan to enter new countries need to conduct baseline studies to assess and understand local situations. The companies must obtain what are termed "social licences" to be able to operate in foreign countries productively, and attaining these would depend on their engaging in trilateral consultations and encouraging the participation of local communities. This approach can be used to avoid poor relations and conflict that may have long-term repercussions for the success of the investment.

Loss of Land, Displacement, and Relocation: Most mining operations tend to operate on communal land that is subject to customary tenure. This has often resulted in the displacement of rural residents, "a process where a group of people is forced to move from their land for purposes of planned projects" (Stanley 2004, 2; Terminski 2000, 2). The rural residents are not only displaced but lose their main source of livelihood. Once displaced, they are normally relocated to areas that are not as fertile as the land where they had previously settled. This disrupts their livelihood, as most members of rural communities rely on land as the main source of their livelihood, where they grow food for their own consumption. Living on land with poor soil basically means that displaced rural community residents cannot produce much food to sustain themselves. This may result in their further impoverishment. In some cases, rural residents are relocated to land that is not subject to customary tenure (see example on the Trident Project below), and it is often unclear whether this land has some form of title or certification. This creates more insecurities for the relocated rural residents or community members, as they usually attach the possession of land to ancestral connections, burial sites, and family inheritance. The areas to which they have been newly relocated may not provide these elements.

Recently, the Zambia Land Alliance (ZLA) reported a case of displacement in Solwezi District. Resettlement areas have been proposed, and tension has surfaced among the investors, some chiefs, rural residents, and the government because the relocation area is not on customary land (PLAAS 2014).[3] According to PLAAS, the rural communities in the Kalumbila area in Solwezi District (now known as New Copperbelt*)* are not happy with the mining company, First Quantum Minerals Ltd, which owns the local mine, the Trident Project, because the company proposes to acquire more land than is allowed (750km^2 instead of 518km^2). The company also acquired land to build a dam without consulting the chief and the local community. With the support of other agencies and after an environmental assessment, the Zambia Environmental Management Agency (ZEMA) advised the company to stop the construction of the dam, but the mining company nonetheless went ahead. This situation was reported to the government, but nothing was done. This has left the rural residents in the area discontented, untrusting, and frustrated. Other examples of similar cases of displacement include the Collum Coal Mine in Maamba and the Munali Nickel Mine in Mazabuka (Southern Province). The expansion of the Copperbelt mines over the years has meant that Chief Nkana and his people have consistently been moved since the beginning of commercial copper mining in the Copperbelt in the 1920s.

Compensation: Usually when rural community members are removed from land proposed for development, they are not adequately compensated for losing their land. Lack of compensation only worsens their poverty levels, as those displaced find it difficult to rebuild their lives. For instance, when First Quantum Minerals assumed ownership of the land in Solwezi, where the Trident mine is currently situated (in Chief Musele's area), they stopped the rural communities from harvesting their cassava fields and destroyed their crops without compensating them. This really upset the rural communities, as they were not given a chance to harvest their crops for that season. The communities voiced complaints, and the Permanent Secretary of North-Western Province was notified, but nothing was done. Questions were raised about why the investors were dealing directly with the local communities and not with community representatives such as the chiefs, elders, or government officials (*Lusaka Times* 2011). In the Lumwana Copper Mine, the rural residents who were displaced in 2009 were promised compensation of US$150 per hectare (and most of them had less than one hectare), but even this small compensation had not been paid by 2012 (see Ngo'mbe and Keivani 2013, 40). Such a situation raises questions about the extent to which mining operations disrupt the lives of rural communities. Moreover, is government ensuring that these displaced residents are adequately compensated after these investment projects take effect?

The Loss of Social Networks: Land symbolizes identity for rural communities. When a community's ties to the land are dislocated, it loses its social ties, including ties with its ancestors. Wherever the rural community is relocated, it has to create new social relations, which may take a long time to build, and this may negatively affect the life of the community as an entity. Sometimes distant relocation makes it difficult for community members to access employment, which could contribute to the locals' income and enable them to purchase farming inputs such as seeds, fertiliser, and equipment. Relocation to distant places also makes it difficult for community members to access schools, hospitals, social amenities, and markets where they can buy and sell goods.

Environment and Health: By its nature, mining usually brings environmental problems such as air and water pollution and degradation of the soil. The mining companies are responsible for ensuring that they adhere to the environmental standards by which they are allowed to operate, to reduce the risk of environmental and health problems. Yet, many incidents have been reported all over Africa of mining companies failing to assess and manage the protection of the environment. During mining, underground rocks containing metals are crushed and exposed to the air. This may result in air pollution, which has health implications such as the chest infections pneumoconiosis and silicosis, asthma, bronchitis, and coughing, and other infections such as throat irritations, skin rashes, allergies, and cancer. Polluted air may also cause acid rain, which damages trees and plants. In cases where poisonous chemicals are emitted during the processing of mineral ores, the chemicals can leak into drainage systems and contaminate water that eventually runs into lakes and rivers. Contaminated water can affect babies and sometimes cause birth defects. Furthermore, contaminated lake or river water can result in the contamination or death of fish and other water species. For instance, the Mopani Mine in Mufulira was shut down in 2012 due to its emission of acid mist from its extraction processes, which was affecting local communities and damaging the environment.[4] For example, the Kankoyo community reported that their houses were cracking (due to the explosions occurring at nearby mines) and that the vegetation in the area was dying (*Zambia Weekly* 2010, 4).

Deforestation and Landscape Reconfiguration: When a mine is set up for operations, normally land must be cleared to provide an environment that enables operational activities to take place. During the deforestation process, trees and plants are cut down and cleared. Wildlife habitats are thus destroyed, causing the animals to move elsewhere, and sometimes some die in the process. Trees and plants produce oxygen, and when they are cleared, oxygen production is reduced. Soil erosion may occur, and mining activities may cause permanent damage to the landscape. This may last for years if no controls are established to help curb the problem. Nkana Mine in Kitwe is a typical example where mining dumps have been created and left for more than two decades, and these are close to the main road and the surrounding communities. Other mines, such as Lumwana and Nchanga, are open-pit mines, and as the mining extraction progresses, the pits or hollows become deeper, leaving the land disastrously reconfigured. Because of the nature of the damage caused, these mining areas are rarely reused for any other form of development such as farming.

Approaches to Benefit Mining and Subsistence-Farming Resources/Stakeholders

Mining and local subsistence farming (agriculture) are critical sectors in any developing economy such as Zambia. Each of these resources requires adequate attention so that it can contribute to a country's growth and wealth as well as benefit the local communities. This attention should not exclude other possible ways that can enhance economic growth. In Zambia's case, the focus should be on how to manage both mining and farming (in the interest of local communities) so that all stakeholders involved benefit fully in their own respect without one sector overriding the other. Below are proposed approaches to help better manage the coexistence of mining and local subsistence farming.

Proper engagement and communication should occur between government and new investors entering a new country. Aspirant investors should conduct research so that they understand the needs of local communities, especially in relation to possible relocation. The World Bank and IFC model (2002) on trilateral dialogue (refer to the Wage-Labour Disputes section above for a model) could be adopted so that stakeholders can participate in discussions effectively and maintain good relations.

- The Zambian government should establish polices that they can implement to the benefit of all stakeholders/parties involved, i.e., investors, chiefs and their local communities, residents living on customary land intended for investment, and the nation as a whole.
- The government should take responsibility for ensuring that the local communities or residents have alternative land to which they can be relocated and are compensated adequately and on time. Thus, the government should set up a regulatory body that will ensure that the following conditions are met before the relocation process starts:
    - Assess that the relocation area is habitable, accessible, and has arable land (as most rural residents' livelihoods depend on using land for subsistence farming and grazing for their livestock).
    - Ensure that those relocated are given some form of tenure certification for the new land to which they are relocated, so that they feel secure.
    - Ensure that the new area has access to clean water.
    - Build proper houses, clinics, and schools before the relocation takes place, and provide farming implements and start-up capital as part of the compensation for the dislocation.
    - Compensation should be provided for crops they cannot harvest, or they should be allowed to harvest the crops before they are relocated.
    - Ensure that the relocation is a smooth process (e.g., counselling, transportation, etc.).
- The communities living in proximity to the mines are often neglected in terms of development. Government should invest tax resources back into the communities where mining activities occur, to develop these communities as well.
- The government should negotiate with the mining companies to

train a certain percentage of local community members interested in working for the mines in technical skills and expert programmes. They should be qualified in such fields as mining engineering, civil engineering, geology, human resources, and administration, so that local people, rather than migrant workers, are employed at these levels.
- The government should continuously support subsistence farming and commercial agriculture in mining districts as a way of diversification and to encourage locals to be entrepreneurial by providing agricultural products to local and possibly international markets.

Conclusion

In conclusion, land remains a core asset for sociocultural, economic, and political activities for local communities, chiefs, governments, and investors. When land is leased out for investments such as mining, implications come with it, and these mostly affect the livelihoods of local community members (in both positive and negative ways) in areas where mining takes place. Some of the implications also extend to government and the investors in the mines.

Mining and agriculture (subsistence or commercial) are important economic activities for Zambia, as both contribute to the country's GDP. However, mining is the main foreign-currency earner for Zambia, and how much of these earnings trickles down to local communities has never been explained clearly. To operate, mining activities often require the use of huge tracts of land. In most cases, these operations take place on customary land, and traditional leaders often fail to retain the land for their local communities, especially if the government intervenes and reserves the land for the purpose of investment. For most local communities or residents, such investment has led to the loss of land, which is their main source of livelihood. As land is lost or grabbed (through conversions), the local communities are eventually displaced. The loss of land goes beyond displacement, as livelihoods are disrupted to pave the way for investments such as mining. The plight of the local communities is hardly ever taken into account when these investments are negotiated. This has resulted in insecurities of tenure for the people living on customary land. It has also caused continuous struggles between investors and local communities, fomenting strained relations because one party has lost land with little or no compensation, while the other party gains at their expense.

In sum, there is a need for the government of Zambia to create policies that will benefit not only investors but also the local communities surrounding the mine areas and the nation as whole. As stated, there is a need to invest in both mining and agriculture without one dominating the other. Both resources are important to the country's development and growth. Government should ensure that equal attention is given to farming and mining-related investments, as farming is the main source of livelihood for rural communities. Once both mining and farming receive equal attention, then the plight of the local communities will have been addressed.

Notes

[1] The four mines are the Lumwana Copper Mine, the Kansanshi Copper Mine in North-Western Province, the Mulaishi Copper Mine in the Copperbelt Province, and the Munali Hills Nickel Mine in Southern Province.

[2] The definition of the term "privatisation" in this paper is adopted from the OECD report on "Privatisation in the 21st Century: Summary of recent experiences." According to the OECD (2010, 7), the term privatisation may refer to any material transaction by which the state's ultimate ownership of corporate entities is reduced.

[3] The information discussed here on the land-displacement situation in Solwezi District is based on a recent online report titled "Zambian villagers 'hinder development' by resisting Canadian mining?" See Miller et al. 2014.

[4] This is just one example of the cases reported by the Zambia Environmental Management Authority (ZEMA). See also the article on http://www.facing-finance.org/database/cases/severe-health-and-environmental-damages-mopani-copper-mines-plcschwere-gesundheits.

References

African Centre for Economic Transformation. 2014. *Zambia Transformation Profile*. Accessed September 3, 2014. www.acetforafrica.or.

Bostock, Mark, and Charles Harvey. 1972. *Economic Independence and Zambian Copper: A Case Study of Foreign Investments.* New York: Praeger.

Buthe, Tim, and Helen V. Milner. 2008. "The Politics of Foreign Direct Investment into Developing Countries: Increasing FDI through International Trade Agreements?" *American Journal of Political Science* 52: 4, 741–762.

Committee on Agriculture and Lands. 2009. *Second Report of the Committee on Agriculture and Lands for the Fourth Session of the Tenth National Assembly.* Presented to Parliament on September 24. Lusaka: Committee on Agriculture and Lands.

Cunningham, Simon. 1981. *The Copper Industry in Zambia: Foreign mining companies in a Developing country. Praeger Special Studies.* New York: Praeger.

Equinox Venture Copper Limited. 2005. *Lumwana Copper Project Environmental Impact Assessment Report.* http://www.eib.org/attachments/pipeline/1570_eia_en.pdf.

Ferguson, James. 1999. *Expectations of Modernity: Myths and Meanings of Urban Life on the Zambian Copperbelt.* California: University of California Press.

German, Laura, George Schoneveld, and Esther Mwangi. 2011. *Contemporary processes of large-scale land acquisition by investors: Case studies from sub-Saharan Africa*. CIFOR, Occasional Paper 68. Bogor: Centre for International Forestry Research.

Government Republic of Zambia. n.d. *Zambia: Investment Opportunities in the Mining Industry*. Lusaka: Ministry of Mines and Mineral Development.

Hall, Ruth. 2011. "Land grabbing in Southern Africa: the many faces of the investor rush." *Review of African Political Economy* 38: 128, 193–214.

Hichaambwa, Munguzwe, and T. S. Jayne. 2012. *Smallholder Commercialization Trends as Affected by Land Constraints in Zambia: What Are the Policy Implications?* Working Paper No. 61. Lusaka: IAPRI. http://fsg.afre.msu.edu/zambia/wp61.pdf .

International Monetary Fund. 2015. *Zambia: Selected Issues.* IMF Country Report No. 15/153. IMF Zambia Report.

https://www.imf.org/external/pubs/ft/scr/2015/cr15153.pdf.

Limpitlaw, Daniel. 2011. "Nationalization and Mining: Lessons from Zambia." *The Journal of The Southern African Institute of Mining and Metallurgy* 111: 737–739.

Lungu, John. 2009. "Socio-economic change and natural resource exploitation: a case study of the Zambian copper mining industry." *Development Southern Africa*. Kitwe: Copperbelt University.

Lungu, John, and Alistair Fraser. 2007. *Report on 'For whom the windfalls? Winners and losers of privatization of the Zambian copper mines.'* Lusaka: Catholic Centre for Justice, Development and Peace Zambia Episcopal Conference.

Lusaka Times. 2014. "Compensate Solwezi residents displaced by US$1 billion Trident mine project – CCZ." Accessed September 29, 2014. http://www.lusakatimes.com/2011/11/14/compensate-solwezi-residents-displaced-us1-billion-trident-project-ccz/.

Maravi. 2012. "Chinese at Maamba mine stay indoors." Accessed October 24, 2014. http://maravi.blogspot.com/2012/08/chinese-at-maamba-mine-stay-indoor.html.

Miller, Darlene, Dimuna Phiri, Caesar Katebe, Gillian Kerchhoff, Mahongo Mazeze, and Genevieve Musongole. 2014. *Zambian villagers 'hinder development' by resisting Canadian mining?* PLAAS. April 25. http://www.plaas.org.za/blog/zambian-villagers-resisting-canadian-mining-company .

Ministry of Mines, Energy and Water Development. 2013. *Ministry of Mines, Energy and Water Development Policy.* http://www.azmec.co.zm/downloads/acts/2013%20Mineral%20Resources%20Development%20Policy%20Zambia.pdf.

Mususa, Patience. 2012. "Mining, welfare and urbanisation: the wavering urban character of Zambia's Copperbelt." *Journal of Contemporary African Studies* 30: 4, 571–587.

Ndulo, Muna. 1986. "Mining Legislation and Mineral Development in Zambia." *Cornell International Law Journal* 19: 1, 1–33.

Negi, Rohit. 2011. "The Mining Boom, Capital, and Chiefs in the 'New Copperbelt'." In *Zambia, Mining and Neoliberalism: 'Boom & Bust on the Globalised Copperbelt,'* edited by A. Fraser and M. Larmer, 209–36. New York: Palgrave Macmillan.

Ng'ombe, Austin, and Ramin Keivani. 2013. "Customary Land Reform to Facilitate Private Investment in Zambia: Achievements, Potential and Limitations." *Urban Forum* 24: 33–48.

Saasa, O. 1996. Policy Reforms and Structural Adjustment in Zambia: *The Case of Agriculture and Trade.* Technical Paper No. 35. Washington:

AFRI/SD & REDSO/SA.

Saturnino, M. Borras Jr., David Fig, and Sofia Monsalve Suarez. 2011. "The Politics of agro-fuels and mega-land and water deals: Insights from the ProCana Case, Mozambique." *Review of Africa Political Economy* 38: 128, 215–234.

Simutanyi, Neo. 2008. "Copper mining in Zambia: The developmental legacy of privatization." *Institute for Security Studies*. ISS Paper 165. https://www.files.ethz.ch/isn/98950/PAPER165.pdf.

Stanley, Jason. 2004. *Development-induced displacement and resettlement*. Accessed September 25, 2014. http://www.forcedmigration.org/research-resources/expert-guides/development-induced-displacement-and-resettlement/fmo022.pdf.

Tagliarino, Nick. 2014. *Placing land rights at the heart of development: Conversion of Customary land to leasehold titling – Zambia*. Focus on Land in Africa brief.
http://www.focusonland.com/fola/en/countries/brief-conversions-of-customary-lands-to-2leasehold-titles/.

Lusaka Times. 2011. "Compensate Solwezi residents displaced by US$1 billion Trident mine project – CCZ." Accessed March 20, 2015. http://www.lusakatimes.com/2011/11/14/compensate-solwezi-residents-displaced-us1-billion-trident-project-ccz/.

—. 2014. "Injunction against Mining in Lower Zambezi successfully lodged at the High Court." Accessed March 21, 2015. http://www.lusakatimes.com/2014/02/04/injunction-mining-lower-zambezi-successfully-lodged-high-court/.

Waldman, David, Ron S. Kenett, and Tami Zilberg. 2010. *Corporate Social Responsibility: What it really is, why it's so important, and how it should be managed.* Accessed April 22, 2015. http://www.ecrc.org.eg/backend/ uploads/resourcesArticles_Corporate%20social%20Responsibility.pdf.

World Bank. 2010. *Lao PDR: Investment and Access to Land and Natural Resources: Challenges in Promoting Sustainable Development*. Washington, DC: World Bank.

—. 2011. *What would it take for Zambia's Copper Mining to achieve its full potential?* Report No. 62378-ZM. World Bank. http://documents.worldbank.org/curated/en/461971468170956129/pdf/ 623780ESW0Gray0e0only0900BOX361532B.pdf.

World Bank and International Finance Corporation. 2002. *Mining Development: Large mines and local communities: Forcing partnership, building sustainability*. Second Issue of Mining and

Development Series. Washington, DC: World Bank.

Zambia Extractive Industries Transparency Initiative. 2012. *Independent Reconciliation Report for the Year 2009.* ZEITI Secretariat. http://zambiaeiti.org/wp-content/uploads/2017/05/2009-Reconciliation-Report.pdf.

Zambia Weekly. 2010. "News." *Zambia Weekly,* December 24.

PART IV:

COMPARATIVE CASE STUDIES OF LAND-TENURE REFORMS AND LIVELIHOODS IN AFRICA

CHAPTER NINE

FORMALISATION OF LAND RIGHTS AND ITS EFFECTS ON AGRICULTURAL RESOURCE MANAGEMENT: LESSONS FROM ETHIOPIA, MALAWI, AND GHANA

BRIDGET BWALYA UMAR

Introduction

Formalisation of land rights in Africa has been in vogue since the 1980s. Since independence, almost all governments have, at one point or another, embarked upon programmes of "land-tenure reform" aimed at reworking their property-rights systems and the institutions associated with them (Bruce and Knox 2009). Proponents of land-rights formalisation have emphasised individual land titling or registration as the mechanism for creating incentives to increase farm productivity and address concerns that customary-tenure arrangements constrain agricultural development and farm productivity (Atwood 1990). The publication in 2000 of the international bestseller *The Mystery of Capital*, by the Peruvian economist Hernando de Soto, galvanised interest in and debate about the titling of land in the global South (Sjaastad and Cousins 2009). De Soto and his Institute for Liberty and Democracy (ILD) received significant support from pro-formalisation governments, international organisations such as the World Bank and the International Monetary Fund (IMF), and scholars who espoused formalisation of land rights as beneficial for the poor in developing countries. Formalisation of property rights, in de Soto's conceptualisation, involves the provision of legal representation of property in the form of title deeds, licences, permits, and contracts, all of which must receive official sanction and protection from legitimate national authorities (Benjaminsen et al. 2009).

Formalisation of land rights in sub-Saharan Africa (SSA) thus refers to the legal sanctioning of primary land claims that are already recognised informally by the local community (Atwood 1990). Meinzen-Dick and Mwangi (2009) use the term "formalisation" to refer to the processes of identifying, adjudicating, and registering interests.

Land rights can be secured at the individual level or collectively by a village or clan. Registration of land, it has been argued, stimulates more efficient land use by improving security of tenure and providing incentives to invest in the longer-term management and productivity of the land (Toulmin 2009). Without security of tenure, scholars argue, farmers are uncertain of the value of improvements made to the land, and this insecurity tends to increase as farming becomes more commercialised (Feder and Noronha 1987). Scholars also argue that land-rights formalisation provides farmers with a title that can be offered as collateral to banks, thereby improving farmers' access to credit (Benjaminsen and Sjaastad 2002; de Soto 2000). In principle, land-rights formalisation can also increase productivity by providing more privatised and secure land rights in situations where their absence is a deterrent to land-intensification decisions made by farmers and lenders (Place and Hazell 1993). Such formalisation can also reduce poverty and encourage natural-resource management (Toulmin 2009).

This chapter reviews the performance of initiatives aimed at formalising land rights and the effects of such initiatives on agricultural-resource management in selected countries in sub-Saharan Africa (SSA). Some observers have argued that without well-established property rights, incentives to preserve agricultural resources (e.g., soil, water, trees) and other land improvements are thwarted simply because the future benefits will not accrue to those who are currently managing the resources (Feder and Noronha 1987). Governments in SSA have thus been increasingly called on to institute land-formalisation programmes because in this region, most land rights are in the form of customary tenure. SSA is also a region where a large proportion of its people depend on natural resources, and the region suffers from low agricultural productivity and minimal use of capital resources. Pursuing land-formalisation initiatives, some scholars have claimed, will lead to productivity improvements relating to land and other natural resources. Such formalisation of land, through land registration and titling, can promote investment, reduce poverty, and encourage better agricultural-resource management (de Soto 2000; Toulmin 2009). Several countries in SSA have implemented a wide range of land-formalisation initiatives, with mixed results. The results have shown that land-formalisation programmes are not a panacea for the productivity challenges that millions of smallholder farmers in SSA encounter. Thus, the rationale behind this review is to share the experiences of three countries in different regions of Africa, to draw potentially useful lessons for other countries (such as Zambia) that are undergoing conversion of customary land. The chapter argues that land-rights formalisation does not always result in increased access to credit and land investment or improved productivity. Nor does it necessarily determine how agricultural resources are managed. Factors other than (in)security of tenure may, in fact, be more important for securing improvements in land productivity and access to credit. Land reforms that do not address the insecurity of tenure suffered by tenant farmers are unlikely to affect this large group of land users, a group whose members typically operate in diverse environments but who share the phenomenon of insecure tenure. It is important, therefore, to avoid a one-size-fits-all approach to land-rights formalisation; rather, such approaches should be tailored to local contexts and have the full participation of all relevant stakeholders.

The next two sections briefly review the main arguments for and criticisms of land-rights formalisation in SSA. A presentation of three case studies follows, covering Ethiopia, Malawi, and Ghana, countries that have implemented wide-ranging land-formalisation programmes. A dedicated section immediately following the case studies presents the main lessons learned from the studies, and the overall conclusion follows.

The Arguments for Land-Rights Formalisation

A land-tenure system and its associated tenure relationships are interwoven with and related to other societal structures and institutions, including family structures and marriage and inheritance systems (Lastarria-Cornhiel 1997; see also chapter 2 in this volume). A lack of formalised land tenure is thus seen as leading to inefficient resource allocation. Scholars believe that inefficiencies arise because indigenous land rights are ambiguous, communal, and insufficiently protected by law, resulting in tenure insecurity, which in turn leads to inferior investment incentives, undersupply of credit, and constraints on efficiency-enhancing market exchanges (Sjaastad and Bromley 1997). The World Bank (2003) reports that more than 50 percent of the peri-urban population in Africa lives under customary tenure and, therefore, has highly insecure land rights. Toulmin (2009) notes that in many areas in SSA, insecure rights to land in part stem from the high proportion of land for which no written paperwork exists to document the rights held or the terms on which these rights can be exercised. In many situations, rights to land involve a series of overlapping claims dependent on customary use, season, and negotiation. This "web of interest," as Meinzen-Dick and Mwangi (2008) call it, allows individuals, households, and communities to access (and even control) different ecological niches that correspond to different tenure niches. But these overlapping interests are variously affected when land-tenure regimes are formalised.

Holden and Otsuka (2014) observe that the establishment of land-rights formalisation policies in areas of high tenure insecurity may potentially improve land-tenure security. The World Bank (2003) asserts that where effective demand for credit exists, giving formal titles to land can help producers gain access to credit and improve the functioning of financial markets. Smith (2004) found that title holders in southern Zambia had greater fixed investment and credit usage and that the association of title holding with fixed investment was independent of an array of socioeconomic variables.

The arguments in favour of land-rights formalisation build on neoclassical economic theories of property rights suggesting that privatisation raises the incentives for long-term investment in land, thereby increasing the productivity and sustainability of land use and encouraging accumulation of land by entrepreneurial and economically successful farmers. In turn, this process facilitates the outward migration of labour (economically less successful farmers) to other economic sectors located in urban centres (Crewett and Korf 2008). The pro-formalisation analysts argue that ill-defined property rights inevitably lead to natural-resource mismanagement. This especially applies to the resource of land, which, as the foundation of many livelihoods, is possibly the most significant natural resource available to the rural population. Insecure property rights diminish farmers' incentive to invest in the land they hold because of the uncertainty they feel about whether they can fully capture their return on investment (Omura 2008). Defining such property rights through formalisation is envisioned to remove this uncertainty and bring multiple benefits.

The Arguments Against Land-Rights Formalisation

Various initiatives aimed at formalisation of land rights have been attempted in SSA, with mixed results. Empirical evidence suggests that many of the benefits assumed to stem from formalisation are not automatic, and in some circumstances formalisation may have the opposite effects of those expected (Toulmin 2009). Benjaminsen et al. (2004) warn that formalisation may inherently cement existing inequalities since those without possessions, such as the landless, women, and orphans, may not only be unable to take advantage of formal rights to assets, but they may also find access effectively closed by the price increases that invariably result from formalisation. In a similar vein, Tsikata (2004) argues that women's rights are often weakened during the course of economic and political transformations because women are systematically disadvantaged within both the market- and the state-backed systems of property rights. Other observers have noted that the introduction of title deeds has (1) caused opportunistic behaviour among elites at the expense of poorer groups, through opportunistic land-acquisition activities that may precede formalisation; and (2) erased important secondary rights through the simplification of complex tenure relations, resulting in more exclusive forms of resource ownership (Benjaminsen et al. 2008; Meinzen-Dick and Mwangi 2008; Sjaastad and Cousins 2008). Place and Hazell (1993) report that with few exceptions, land rights were not a significant factor in determining whether farmers made land-improving investments or used yield-enhancing inputs. Where resource-access rights are multiple and overlapping, as in much of rural Africa, registering individual property rights raises important technical and political challenges and risks unregistered rights-holders losing access to vital resources (Cotula et al. 2007). Several chapters in this volume that have discussed the conversion of customary land in Zambia have highlighted this point.

Empirical evidence concerning the impact of land reforms is mixed. Most studies have focused on investment impacts (Deininger 2005; Feder 2002) and whether land reforms can contribute to allocative efficiency, thereby improving the productivity and poverty-reduction effects of land (Holden et al. 2011).

Customary-Tenure Regimes in sub-Saharan Africa

Customary-tenure systems are administered by traditional authorities (Hansen et al. 2005). Under customary-land tenure systems, claims to land-based resources are asserted primarily through kinship links (Biru 1998). Customary social systems are the central components of resource tenure and resource management since they provide the basis on which individuals claim land and the vegetation on it (Nankumba and Machika 1988). The content of customary law in SSA is extremely diverse and varies among communities. In addition, customary rules are not static but evolve continually in response to diverse factors, including cultural interaction, population pressure, socioeconomic change, and political processes (Arko-Adjei 2011; Cotula 2007).

What is known as "customary" regulation does not necessarily consist of indigenous rules only; it often results from "institutional *bricolage*," or borrowing and adaptation, between the formal and the informal, the traditional and the non-traditional (Cleaver 2002). While the label "customary" may suggest homogeneity, its meaning may differ from place to place, and interpretations of what constitutes a "custom" in one setting may differ markedly and be contested in another (van Leeuwen 2014). Customary institutions may discriminate against women and youth, they may marginalise non-indigenous community members and nonresidential user groups such as pastoralists (Meynen and Doornbos 2004), and they often benefit local elites. Although customary institutions in the past were often characterised by flexibility, negotiability, and adaptation, intensifying competition for land under customary arrangements seems, instead, to have contributed to increased levels of exclusion and deepening social divisions (Peters 2004, cited in van Leeuwen 2014).

Since land is central to the social and economic development of most people living in SSA, the link between customary-tenure arrangements and productivity-enhancing investments has attracted the attention of both researchers and policymakers (Abdulai et al. 2011). Customary tenure has been invariably blamed for most rural households' inability to access credit from formal financial institutions, the low levels of investment in agriculture, and the concomitant low agricultural productivity. The premise has been that customary-land tenure confers insecure land rights on the rights-holder, rights that preclude land investment and long-term agricultural-resource management. This chapter argues that customary tenure is not synonymous with insecure tenure and that formalisation of customary tenure does not guarantee increased land and agricultural investment.

Customary-tenure systems have developed in diverse local systems. They reflect the history, socioeconomic and political institutions, and biophysical factors of the environments under which they have developed. Blanket attribution of tenure insecurity and lack of agricultural investment to customary-tenure systems misses the complex interaction of such systems with other factors. Customary-tenure systems may promote and yet also hinder soil and water conservation and tree-planting, depending on the land users' perceptions of the security of their land rights and their experiences of past land-tenure reforms. It is thus important to design locally relevant land reforms that account for local norms and practices as well as to introduce piecemeal measures to tackle the most pressing land challenges, rather than institute radical reforms.

The remainder of this chapter presents and discusses three case studies showcasing attempts at land formalisation and their effects on the management of agricultural resources relating to the use of farmlands. The three case studies, Ethiopia in east Africa, Malawi in southern Africa, and Ghana in west Africa, were selected because they had all implemented land-formalisation programmes in the recent past but in very different contexts.

Land-Rights Formalisation Initiatives in SSA: Three Case Studies

Ethiopia

Ethiopia has undertaken one of the largest and least expensive land-rights formalisation programmes in SSA (Deininger et al. 2008). This was achieved through a two-stage approach. The broad-scale first-stage land registration and certification involved the registration and demarcation of land plots, using simple local technologies that required little training. The main sources for guiding the determination of plot boundaries were field markings in conjunction with the memories of neighbours whose farm plots bordered those owned by the households in question. The initial cost of this registration was low, approximately US$1 per farm plot, or US$3.50 per household (Deininger et al. 2008). For individual households, certificates are not issued when their land is registered but, rather, when all village land has been registered and verified (Bezu and Holden 2014). The registration programme began in Tigray in 1998, followed by another in Amhara in 2002. Oromia and the Southern Nations Nationalities and Peoples (SNNP) initiated registration in 2004. Approximately 6 million households and 20 million plots were registered and certified within a few years (Bezu and Holden 2014). The second stage is being piloted in selected districts in the highland regions. This stage involves registering the precise geographic locations and sizes of individual farm plots, using technologies such as GPS and satellite imagery. Farmers receive plot-level certificates with maps, rather than a household-level certificate as during the first-stage registration process (Bezu and Holden 2014).

Ethiopia's current land-rights formalisation programme partly confirmed and repealed the radical land-reform programme introduced by the socialist military (Derg) regime in 1975. The Derg regime had decreed that all rural lands were state property, and abolished all forms of customary tenure (Baye 2013). A major land-redistribution period followed, with land redistributed to tillers every year, primarily based on family size and land quality, as part of an attempt to create equity and fairness in land acquisition (Ahmed et al. 2002). All kinds of land transactions were banned, resulting in farmers not being able to sell, mortgage, lease out, and transfer land allocated to them. Prohibitions against using hired labour to cultivate holdings were introduced. The only formal way of obtaining access to land was through the periodic redistribution of existing crop and pasture lands among households (Ahmed et al. 2002; Baye 2013). After the fall of the Derg regime in 1991, the new government reaffirmed state ownership of all rural land. The constitution adopted in 1994 allows temporary leases and guarantees peasants and pastoralists the right of free access to land, the right to use the land indefinitely, to lease it out temporarily to other farmers, and to transfer it to their children but not to permanently sell or mortgage it (Ahmed et al. 2002).

Several studies have investigated the impacts in Ethiopia of this low-cost land-registration and -certification process. Deininger et al. (2008) report significantly improved tenure security, as evidenced by increased levels of investment, productivity, and land-rental markets. Holden et al. (2009) found that in Tigray, in the northern region, land certification enhanced efforts to improve or maintain existing soil-conservation structures, stimulated tree-planting on arable land, and enhanced land productivity. Similarly, Gebremedhin and Swinton (2003) reported results from Tigray confirming that farmers who had long tenure security were more likely to invest in costly (but more durable) stone terraces, while farmers who had only short-term tenure security were more likely to invest in cheaper, less durable soil bunds. The main reason given for these positive impacts is that certification reduced the insecure tenure that had once been common as a result of frequent land distributions and restricted land-use rights. Such insecurity had undermined investment incentives (Deininger and Jin 2006).

Conversely, 73 percent of respondents in Bewket's (2007) study from the northwestern highlands of Ethiopia said that periodic land redistribution had discouraged them from adopting soil- and water-conservation measures, while 58 percent expected further land redistribution in the future. The study concluded that insecure tenure was an important factor in discouraging most farmers from attempting to adopt soil- and water-conservation measures. This is consistent with Besley's (1995) and Otsuka and Place's (2001) assertions that lack of secure rights over land decreases farmers' incentives to invest in land improvement. The differences between the study results on soil conservation and other long-term investments (such as the planting of perennials) from the Amhara region in the north and the results in southern Ethiopia may be explained by differences in the two regions' land-redistribution experiences (Teshome 2014). Expectations of further land redistribution in the future eroded a sense of tenure security to such an extent that farmers did not undertake land-improving investments on the grounds that they might be unable to benefit fully from such investments

(Teshome 2014). Bewket (2007) notes that Ethiopia is among the most agrarian countries in the world and that soil erosion is a major constraint to agricultural production and food security. This challenge, explains Teshome (2014), has led to the implementation of massive soil- and water-conservation programmes since 1975. Given the extent of the erosion problem, it is not surprising that soil- and water-conservation measures remain important; in fact, they are more likely to be implemented immediately following improvements in tenure security, especially among farming households in highland areas that are most prone to erosion.

Holden and colleagues' (2009) findings lend support to the low-cost and highly participatory, coordinated approach to the land-certification process. They concluded that Ethiopia's first-stage land-rights formalisation initiative appeared not to be anti-poor, unlike the more conventional high-tech demand-based approaches that have dominated policy efforts and have tended to exclude the poor as a result of their high costs. However, the first-stage certification has limitations on the maintenance and updating of land-registration records and information access for the purposes of land administration. This has made policy analysis difficult since data registration is paper-based and not easily available. Second-stage land registration and certification will likely be substantially costlier than the first-stage certification and will take much longer to complete (Bezu and Holden 2014).

Ethiopia's land-reform programme is unique and instructive in many ways. Unlike other countries in SSA, Ethiopia was never colonised and thus does not have a legacy of colonial land policies. Yet, it does have a history of highly unequal land distribution that developed during the imperial regime. Before 1975, the country operated under a feudal system that was characterised, in the southern part of the country, by absentee landlords and poor tenants (Holden and Otsuka 2014). In the north, a communal rist system was operated. The frequent evictions of tenant farmers and high levels of tenure insecurity led to the overthrow of the imperial regime in 1975.

After the radical land-tenure reform process of 1975, all land was declared state-owned, and a land-redistribution programme was implemented. This redistribution programme led to a perception of land insecurity among rural populations and concomitantly reduced incentives to implement long-term conservation measures on what were becoming increasingly fragmented and small-sized farm plots (Holden and Yohannes 2002). It is imperative to note here that tenure insecurity was associated with *state* land. Land-tenure studies are replete with reviews of tenure insecurity associated with *customary*-tenure systems. The Ethiopian case demonstrates that it is not, a priori, the tenure system that engenders tenure insecurity; rather, it is the specific experiences that land-rights holders have with that system. It was not the reform of customary tenure that led to increased tenure security and the subsequent adoption of soil- and water-conservation and tree-planting programmes in northern Ethiopia; it was the reform of state-owned land. In the words of Alemu (1999), in a country with high and increasing levels of land scarcity and a land policy that historically promoted insecurity of tenure, the issuing of land certificates represented a substantial improvement. History matters.

Malawi

Following political independence in 1964, there was a surge in efforts to change the land-tenure system of Malawi on the assumption that customary tenure, the predominant system in the country, did not provide the security needed to ensure agricultural investment and a productive use of land. The titling of land, it was felt, was necessary to ensure clearly defined and enforceable property rights (Peters 2009). Land is transferred through allocations by village headmen and women and predominantly through inheritance (Lovo 2013). Customary-tenure systems, which vary among villages and are based on a mixture of marriage and residency cultural practices, govern transfers via inheritance. The inheritance system provides differing tenure security to individuals in the houschold, depending on the amount of land they bring into the marriage and into their residential area (Lunduka 2009). The two common marriage and residency practices are matrilineal-matrilocal and patrilineal-patrilocal (see Figure 9.1).

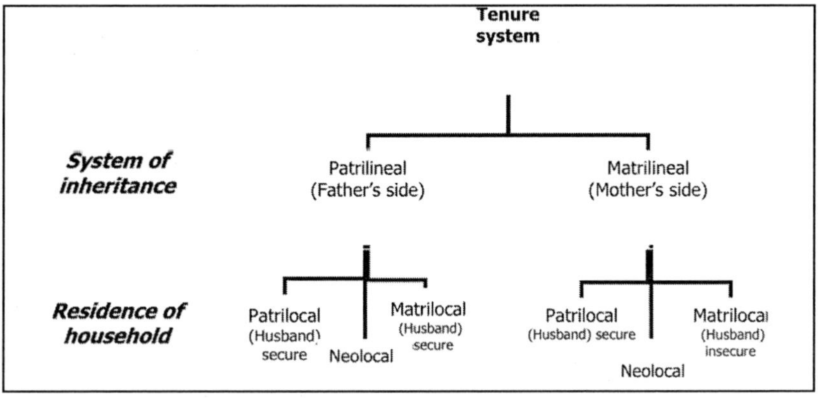

Figure 9.1: Common inheritance and residence systems in Malawi

In the matrilineal-matrilocal system, land is bequeathed from uncle to nephew, and the couple resides in the wife's village. This system is common among the Chewa, Lomwe, and Yao, the most populous ethnic groups in Malawi, who are mainly located in the south of the country. In the patrilineal-patrilocal system, land is passed on to male heirs, and the couple lives in the husband's village (Lovo 2013). A third residency option is where both the husband and the wife leave their respective homes and settle in a neutral village, where land is either bought or given to them by the resident chief (Figure 9.1). Land ownership is mostly awarded to the head of the household: the man (Lunduka 2009).

In essence, these differing patterns may be interpreted as representing variations in the transferability of property rights upon dissolution of marriage and/or death and have been hypothesised to have important effects on investment behaviour (Hansen et al. 2005).

Efforts to reform the customary-land system date back to the late 1960s and early 1970s, when the government of Malawi implemented the Lilongwe Land Development Programme (LLDP), supported by the World Bank. The aim of this programme was, among other things, to change the organisation of land-tenure systems from usufruct to one of consolidated holdings held under a deed of freehold title. This was seen as necessary to make land preservation and improvement worthwhile for individuals (Mbalanje 1982). A review of the LLDP concluded that although privatisation through tenure conversion had been carried out, none of the benefits predicted by the policy planners, such as greater ownership security, the negotiability of title, and the creation of a robust land market, actually materialised. Instead, the LLDP tended to erode customary social values and institutions, especially in matrilineal societies, and was a fundamental source of insecurity over customary landholdings throughout Malawi (CoILPR 1998). By 1997, less than 10 percent of customary land had been converted to leasehold (Lunduka 2009). Peters (2009) noted that most of the land-policy reforms and titling programmes that were actually implemented failed to achieve their stated aims, and a large body of social research demonstrated that these reforms and programmes were based on faulty premises.

In response to these developments, a new land policy was promulgated in 2002. Its stated purposes included the clarification and strengthening of customary-land rights and the formalisation of traditional authorities' role in the administration of customary land. Such land covers about 70 percent of the country's entire land mass (Peters 2009). The land policy allows customary landholders to (1) register their land as "customary estates"; (2) have private usufructuary rights in perpetuity; and (3) once registered, the owner's title will have full legal status and can be leased or used as security for a mortgage (Peters 2009). While usage rights are well articulated, there is no formal market for land since traditionally it cannot be alienated by way of sale (Berge et al. 2014). Given the increasing demand for allocatable land, an informal rental market has emerged and is expanding. What initially started as a form of land-borrowing between relatives has evolved over the past twenty years into a system of one-season-long informal rental agreements, mostly between non-relatives (Peters 2009). The dominance of short-term contracts in informal land markets introduces uncertainty about future renewals and can prevent the adoption of soil-conservation measures, because of fears that landlords will expropriate investment and maintenance efforts (Lovo 2013).

Empirical analyses of the effects of the land reforms (in a Malawian context) on two dominant marriage and residency systems have produced mixed results. Lunduka (2009) found that secure male household heads in patrilocal residential systems had high incentives to invest in tree-planting. Since primarily men inherit land in patrilocal residence systems, a man can ensure his security and therefore make long-term investment decisions. Lunduka concluded that these tenure-secure men were likely to plant both agroforestry and non-agroforestry trees, since the men are assured of reaping the benefits of their investments. Conversely, the probability of investing in trees was low in matrilocal residences, where matrilocal marriage patterns might deter tree-planting by men (Hansen et al. 2005). Although the husband is usually the family's key decision-maker concerning farm management, he possesses weak land rights under the matrilineal-matrilocal system (Place and Otsuka 2001).

Similarly, Place and Otsuka (2001) found, after controlling for other factors, that farmers operating land under the relatively weak security of matrilineal-matrilocal systems (compared to those acquiring land through patrilocal means) invested less in the planting of poles used in the tobacco-drying process. However, they found no differences in the efficiency of plot-level crop production under the different tenure arrangements, implying that short-term inputs that yield short-term benefits appear to drive maize- and tobacco-production systems, and tenure does not play a major role (Place and Otsuka 2001). In a similar vein, Lovo (2013) observed that tenure insecurity did not affect the adoption of hybrid seed and positively correlated with household wealth. He further noted that tenure insecurity posed disincentives to the adoption of soil-conservation measures, which were discouraged by gender-biased inheritance systems that rendered male decision-makers insecure and, therefore, less likely to invest in trees.

Lunduka (2009) found that neolocal residence households had more plots planted with trees. This was attributed to their being insecure, and investing in trees would increase their tenure-security status (in neolocal residences a tree planted by a parent or grandparent is undisputed evidence of ownership). Thus, when a household is tenure-insecure, the probability of investing in trees is high if such action is perceived to increase tenure security and low if tenure insecurity cannot be changed (Lunduka 2009). These results reveal that customary-use rights are well established in Malawi and that land titles will not necessarily increase security (Lovo 2013). Lunduka (2009) notes that a registration title held by a man in a matrilocal situation may not guarantee the security of his tenure under existing cultural practices, because members of his wife's lineage may resort to behaviour that compels him to leave. Thus, argues Matchaya (2009), registration of a piece of land may not necessarily confer greater security; rather, context-specific traditions may actually help to predict whether a household feels that their land tenure is insecure.

The Malawi National Land Policy of 2002 protects the right of inheritance for children and the surviving spouse, without discrimination on the basis of gender. Paradoxically, if actually implemented, this policy would greatly reduce women's current rights in matrilineal-matrilocal areas since it provides for sons as *equal* heirs. However, the policy provides more rights for some women in patrilineal-patrilocal areas. Strict application of these principles would require changes to customary inheritance and marriage/divorce practices (Hansen et al. 2005; Peters 2009). However, Place and Otsuka (2001) warn that direct interventions aimed at customary-tenure systems would prove difficult and risky and may not be worth pursuing. They further caution that customary-land tenure systems are so complex, diverse, and elusive that devising an appropriate intervention scheme might not be possible.

Peters (2009) is of a similar opinion, noting that the current policy seeks to effect a far more radical change to existing patterns of land rights and usage than seems necessary or wise. She advised that a far less radical step than titling and registering would support some of the ongoing changes. A particular need is some form of legal recognition of the renting out of land so that those who rent out a field, for example, will not fear—as many do now—that the tenants might claim the protracted use of such land as "evidence" of ownership. It is undoubtedly a challenge to introduce land reforms that replace customary law and provide tenure justice and security in a country such as Malawi, where two markedly different land-tenure and inheritance systems exist (Berge et al. 2014; Lunduka 2009). The differential effects of the two main variants of customary-land tenure systems, and land-rights formalisation in Malawi more generally, underscore the dangers of one-size-fits-all recommendations and reiterate the need for locally tailored and context-specific reforms. The Malawian case also shows that formalisation of land-tenure rights does not always lead to the development of a formal and robust land market.

Ghana

Ghana depends heavily on its rich natural-resource base for economic growth and development. Land plays a significant role in the country's development aspirations, but tenure-security issues are claimed to have hampered investment and slowed the pace of growth (Government of Ghana 2011). Landholdings in Ghana can be broadly classified into two types: customary and state lands. Customary lands are further categorised into stool/skin, family/clan, and private individual lands. Stool/skin land refers to allodial title, the highest interest in land. This right is acquired either by being the first to cultivate the land or via succession from the first owning group, and the members of a community hold the land in common. Family/clan and private lands have the highest interest vested in families or clans and private individuals, respectively. Private land is given or sold as freehold by stools, skins, and families to individuals, corporations, and institutions, and applies only to cases in which the freehold ownership was obtained prior to the enactment of the 1992 Constitution. State lands comprise lands compulsorily acquired by the state using the right of eminent domain, and lands vested in the president of Ghana or the Lands Commission are held in trust on behalf of the people of Ghana (Government of Ghana 2011; Kwasi et al. 2013; World Bank 2003). Estimates put customary landholdings at 80 percent, compared to 20 percent for state landholdings (Government of Ghana 1999).

In Ghana, tenure security is not universally attributable to an individual but, rather, to that individual's position within their local social and political hierarchy and to the manner in which the plot was obtained. Individuals who are not central to the village networks of social and political power are much more likely to have their land expropriated when the land is fallow; a cultivator's rights over growing crops are more secure. This induces individuals to leave their land unsown less often than would technically be optimal (Goldstein and Udry 2008). For such individuals, greater land-security tenure is associated with greatly reduced investment in land fertility.

Ghana's recent land-rights formalisation efforts started with the enactment of the Land Title Registration Act in 1986 as the official system for registering property (Government of Ghana 1986). This has been weakly implemented. In 1999, Ghana adopted a national land policy that aimed to strengthen land-administration institutions and increase the security of land tenure on both state and customary land (Government of Ghana 1999). This policy has been implemented through the Land Administration Project (LAP). This drive towards formalisation of land rights, via registration, is based on the assumption that increased formalisation will improve tenure security, increase investment in land, and lead to economic growth (Spichiger and Stacey 2014). The government also sought to divest responsibility for the management of stool lands to Customary Land Secretariats (CLS). According to Kanji et al. (2005), chiefs originally developed CLSs to keep track of land transactions by recording the land allocations they made. The LAP sought to streamline this system into a formal land-administration system.

Both successes and challenges have characterised Ghana's experience with land-rights formalisation. Kwasi et al. (2013) report that the rate of title formalisation is low, estimated at 8 percent, despite the compulsory deeds-registration legislation. The authors attribute this in part to the high cost of land-title formalisation and observe that approximately 95 percent of title-formalisation costs came in the form of costs other than official fees. Similarly, Jones-Casey and Knox (2011) noted the cost of the registration process for both landholders and land administrators and warned that persistent challenges in this regard risk jeopardising the massive investment in reforming the registration systems. Among the successes of the LAP, the government of Ghana cites the establishment of thirty-seven CLSs to facilitate traditional authorities' management and record-keeping of land allocations and transactions as well as the testing of title registration and the demarcation of customary-land boundaries via private surveyors (Spichiger and Stacey 2014). Nonetheless, studies show that mostly urban elites undertake land-title registration in peri-urban areas, while mostly mining, forestry, and agribusiness owners undertake deed registration in rural areas, i.e., not to the benefit of smallholders (Spichiger and Stacey 2014).

In numerous locations, disputes over the legitimacy of customary authorities and debates about customary law, both between and within ethnic groups, have revealed disagreements over the legitimacy of traditional institutions (as recognised by the government) (Spichiger and Stacey 2014).

Studies of land-tenure and natural-resource management show that current formalisation efforts have failed to increase incentives to invest in the land. Insecure land and tree tenure have been identified as a cause of deforestation in Ghana (Hatcher 2009). Tenant farmers who are required to give part of their cultivated food crop to landowners over-exploit the land to minimise losses incurred under tenancy arrangements and continuously intensify their farming of rented lands (Gyasi 1997, cited in Damnyag et al. 2012). In essence, tenancy arrangements discourage the planting of trees. Tenant farmers generally farm under conditions of high tenure insecurity, having obtained land from landholding families on short-term sharecropping arrangements or in exchange for services. They thus lack incentives to plant and protect trees, and landowners would discourage such activities as an attempt to stake long-term claims over land (Leach and Fairhead 2000). Landowners issue restrictions to their tenants on the types of plants they may grow on their allotments, because allowing the planting of trees with long gestation periods may enable the tenant farmer to lay claim to the land (Damnyag et al. 2012). This demonstrates that land-tenure insecurity does not result from customary tenure per se; rather, it emerges from short-term arrangements between land-rights holders who have parcels of land to rent out and a "supply" of farmers wanting to rent such land. As Berge et al. (2014) observe, formalisation in which Malawian land-rental arrangements consisted of simple, locally designed measures would help to minimise the mistrust that characterises current land-rental arrangements—arrangements under which both land-rights holders *and* tenants feel insecure.

Lessons Learned from the Case Studies

These case studies of land formalisation provide insights that are potentially useful to other countries pursuing or contemplating land reforms in SSA. These insights are presented below.

Ethiopia's low-cost first-stage registration saw over 20 million plots registered within just a few years (Deininger et al. 2008), whereas Ghana's relatively more expensive land-formalisation process has engendered a low rate of formalisation. An effective, efficient land-rights formalisation regime that reduces time and monetary cost is fundamental to developing countries' efforts; hence, efforts should be made to reduce the time and costs of title formalisation (Kwasi et al. 2013).

Improved land-tenure security has resulted in increased investments, increased land productivity, and more vibrant land-rental markets in Ethiopia (Deininger et al. 2008). In Malawi, however, although the legislation has resulted in increased land investments, it has not led to the introduction of *formal* rental markets since the legislation did not provide for this. Instead, an *informal* rental market has developed, characterised by short-term leases and concomitant insecurity of tenure (Peters 2009). In northern Ethiopia, land certification has promoted more sustainable natural-resource management through activities such as improvement and maintenance of existing soil-conservation structures. It has also stimulated tree-planting on arable land. In southern Ethiopia, a history of periodic land redistribution has discouraged farmers from adopting soil- and water-conservation measures (Bewket 2007; Holden et al. 2009). One system of land-rights inheritance has discouraged the adoption of soil-conservation measures, given that insecure male decision-makers are less likely to invest in trees in the matrilineal-matrilocal areas of Malawi (Lunduka 2009).

It is imperative to understand how any proposed land-rights formalisation programme will affect land-tenure security and other associated benefits. Moreover, communities are not homogeneous. Groups and individuals within groups have differentiated and multiple rights to land-resource bundles, and the introduction of formalisation programmes may result in both winners and losers. Intra- and inter-group differences may lead to situations whereby some groups are worse off than they were pre-formalisation. History also plays an important role and affects current perceptions of land-tenure (in)security. Land-reform programmes must factor this historical perspective into the equation; current *ahistorical* proposals usually result in contestation from some stakeholders.

Land-rights formalisation measures that do not change perceptions of tenure insecurity (or indeed improved tenure security) are unlikely to be widely adopted; neither are those that entail radical change to deeply entrenched customary practices. For instance, implementation of the Malawi National Land Policy of 2002 requires changes to customary inheritance and marriage/divorce practices among the matrilineal-matrilocal tribes. Such changes are likely to meet strong resistance from affected tribal members. As Peters (2009) advises, small and gradual change is better than a radical shift. Cotula et al. (2004) express similar sentiments, arguing that legislation must aim to secure resource claims based on locally recognised tenure systems rather than aiming to overhaul such systems. In many cases, the less-is-more approach will be the most effective way to secure access to natural resources.

To prevent (or minimise) the prospect of urban and business elites capturing all the benefits of land reform, information about proposed land reforms must be disseminated to rural residents. This will prevent the kind of information asymmetry that allows better-informed urban residents to buy up land from their rural counterparts at low prices, in anticipation of future increases in land values that are expected to result from the land-rights formalisation process.

Conclusion

This chapter has reviewed the formalisation of land rights and its effects on natural-resource management. It concludes that land-rights formalisation in SSA has led to mixed results concerning access to credit, land productivity, and the adoption and maintenance of soil- and water-conservation measures that will enhance sound agricultural-resource management. Formalisation does not always result in increased access to credit or to increased land investments, improved land productivity, or better agricultural-resource management. Factors others than (in)security of tenure may be more important for securing improvements to land productivity and access to credit. Land productivity depends on factors other than property rights, primarily natural fertility and climatic conditions (Ouedraogó et al. 1996). Land reforms that fail to address the tenure insecurity of tenant farmers are unlikely to affect this large group of land users who operate in diverse environments yet share insecurity of tenure. It is important to avoid one-size-fits-all approaches to land-rights formalisation; rather, such processes should be tailored to local contexts to attract the full participation of all relevant stakeholders. Efforts to improve land investments and agricultural-resource management must be holistic and not limited to security of tenure. Customary tenure does not always entail insecure land rights, and land-formalisation programmes must not assume this to be the case.

References

Abdulai, A., V. Owusu, and R. Goetz. 2011. "Land tenure differences and investment in land improvement measures: Theoretical and empirical analyses." *Journal of Development Economics* 96: 1, 66–78. doi: http://dx.doi.org/10.1016/j.jdeveco.2010.08.002.

Ahmed, M. M., S. K. Ehui, B. Gebremedhin, S. Benin, and A. Teklu. 2002. *Evolution and Technical Efficiency of Land Tenure Systems in Ethiopia*. Socioeconomics and Policy Research Working Paper No. 39. Nairobi: International Livestock Research Institute.

Alemu, T. 1999. Land tenure and soil conservation: Evidence from Ethiopia. PhD diss., Goteborg University, Goteborg.

Arko-Adjei, A. 2011. *Adapting Land Administration to the Institutional Framework of Customary Tenure: The Case of Peri-Urban Ghana.* Amsterdam: ISO Press, Inc.

Atwood, D. A. 1990. “Land registration in Africa: The impact on agricultural production.” *World Development* 18: 5, 659–71. doi: http://dx.doi.org/10.1016/0305-750X(90)90016-Q.

Awuah, K. G. B., F. N. Hammond, and J. E. Lamond. 2013. “The cost of land title formalisation in Ghana.” *Property Management* 31: 5, 389–403. doi: doi:10.1108/PM-01-2013-0004.

Baye, T. G. 2013. “Peasants, land reform and property rights in Ethiopia: The experience of Gojjam province, 1974 to 1997.” *Journal of African Studies and Development* 5: 6, 145–56.

Benjaminsen, T. A., and E. Sjaastad. 2002. “Race for the prize: Land transactions and rent appropriation in the Malian cotton zone.” *European Journal of Development Research* 14: 2, 129–52.

Benjaminsen, T. A., S. Holden, C. Lund, and E. Sjaastad. 2009. “Formalisation of land rights: Some empirical evidence from Mali, Niger and South Africa.” *Land Use Policy* 26: 1, 28–35. doi: http://dx.doi.org/10.1016/j.landusepol.2008.07.003.

Berge, E., D. Kambewa, A. Munthali, and H. Wiig. 2014. “Lineage and land reforms in Malawi: Do matrilineal and patrilineal landholding systems represent a problem for land reforms in Malawi?” *Land Use Policy* 41: 61–9. doi: http://dx.doi.org/10.1016/j.landusepol.2014.05.003.

Besley, T. 1995. “Property rights and investment incentives: Theory and evidence from Ghana.” *Journal of Political Economy* 103: 5, 903–37. doi: 10.2307/2138750.

Bewket, Wo. 2007. “Soil and water conservation intervention with conventional technologies in northwestern highlands of Ethiopia: Acceptance and adoption by farmers.” *Land Use Policy* 24: 2, 404–16. doi: http://dx.doi.org/10.1016/j.landusepol.2006.05.004.

Bezu, S., and S. Holden. 2014. “Demand for second-stage land certification in Ethiopia: Evidence from household panel data.” *Land Use Policy* 41: 193–205. doi: http://dx.doi.org/10.1016/j.landusepol.2014.05.013.

Biru, U. 1998. *Land tenure, resource management and food security in sub-Saharan Africa: Implications for rural sustainability, land and agricultural policy analysis: A case of Malawi*. PhD diss., University of Guelph, Guelph, Canada.

Bruce, J. W., and A. Knox. 2009. “Structures and stratagems: Making decentralization of authority over land in Africa cost-effective.” *World Development* 37: 8, 1360–69. doi: http://dx.doi.org/10.1016/j.worlddev.2008.08.011.

Cleaver, F. 2002. "Reinventing institutions: *Bricolage* and the social embeddedness of natural resource management." *European Journal of Development Research* 14: 2, 11–30.

Commission of Inquiry on Land Policy Reform. 1998. *Preliminary Report of the Presidential Commission of Inquiry on Land Policy Reform*. Lilongwe: Commission of Inquiry on Land Policy Reform.

Cotula, L. 2007. *Changes in 'Customary' Tenure Systems in Africa*. Hertfordshire: International Institute for Environment and Development and Food and Agricultural Organisation.

Cotula, L., C. Toulmin, and C. Hesse. 2004. *Land tenure and administration in Africa: Lessons of experience and emerging issues*. London: International Institute for Environment and Development.

Crewett, W., and B. Korf. 2008. "Ethiopia: Reforming land tenure." *Review of African Political Economy* 35: 116, 203–20. doi: 10.1080/03056240802193911.

Damnyag, L., O. Saastamoinen, M. Appiah, and A. Pappinen. 2012. "The role of tenure insecurity in deforestation in Ghana's high forest zone." *Forest Policy and Economics* 14: 1, 90–98. doi: http://dx.doi.org/10.1016/j.forpol.2011.08.006.

de Soto, H. 2000. *The Mystery of Capital. Why Capitalism Triumphs in the West and Fails Everywhere Else*. New York: Basic Books.

Deininger, K. 2005. *Land Policies for Growth and Poverty Reduction: Key Issues and Challenges Ahead*. Washington DC: World Bank.

Deininger, K., and J. Songqing. 2006. "Tenure security and land-related investment: Evidence from Ethiopia." *European Economic Review* 50: 5, 1245–77.

Deininger, K., D. Ayalew Ali, S. Holden, and J. Zevenbergen. 2008. "Rural land certification in Ethiopia: Process, initial impact, and implications for other African countries." *World Development* 36: 10, 1786–1812. doi: http://dx.doi.org/10.1016/j.worlddev.2007.09.012.

Feder, G. 2002. "The intricacies of land markets—why the World Bank succeeds in economic reform through land registration and tenure security." Conference of the International Federation of Surveyors, April 19–26, Washington DC.

Feder, G., and R. Noronha. 1987. "Land rights systems and agricultural development in sub-Saharan Africa." *The World Bank Research Observer* 2: 2, 143–69.

Gebremedhin, B., and S. M. Swinton. 2003. "Investment in soil conservation in northern Ethiopia: The role of land tenure security and public programs." *Agricultural Economics* 29: 1, 69–84. doi: http://dx.doi.org/10.1016/S0169-5150(03)00022-7.

Goldstein, M., and C. Udry. 2008. "The profits of power: Land rights and agricultural investment in Ghana." *Journal of Political Economy* 116: 6, 981–1022. doi: 10.1086/595561.

Government of Ghana. 1986. *The Land Title Registration Law* (PNDCL 152). Accra: Ghana Publishing Corporation (Assembly Press).

—. 1999. *National Land Policy Document*. Accra: Ghana Publishing Corporation (Assembly Press).

—. 2011. *Land Administration Project. Phase Two*. Accra: Ministry of Lands and Natural Resources.

Hansen, J. D., M. K. Luckert, S. Minae, and F. Place. 2005. "Tree planting under customary tenure systems in Malawi: Impacts of marriage and inheritance patterns." *Agricultural Systems* 84: 1, 99–118. doi: http://dx.doi.org/10.1016/j.agsy.2004.05.003.

Hatcher, J. 2009. *Securing Tenure Rights and Reducing Emissions from Deforestation and Degradation (REDD). Costs and Lessons Learned.* Social Development Working Paper No. 120. Washington DC: The World Bank.

Holden, S. T., K. Deininger, and H. Ghebru. 2009. "Impacts of low-cost land certification on investment and productivity." *American Journal of Agricultural Economics* 91: 2, 359–73. doi: 10.1111/j.1467-8276.2008.01241.x.

—. 2011. "Tenure insecurity, gender, low-cost land certification and land rental market participation in Ethiopia." *Journal of Development Studies* 47: 1, 31–47. doi: 10.1080/00220381003706460.

Holden, S. T., and K. Otsuka. 2014. "The roles of land tenure reforms and land markets in the context of population growth and land use intensification in Africa." *Food Policy* 48: 88–97. doi: http://dx.doi.org/10.1016/j.foodpol.2014.03.005.

Holden, S. T., and H. Yohannes. 2002. "Land redistribution, tenure insecurity, and intensity of production: A study of farm households in southern Ethiopia." *Land Economics* 78: 4, 573–90.

Jones-Casey, K., and A. Knox. 2011. "Ghana's land administration at a crossroads." Focus on Land in Africa. https://agriknowledge.org/downloads/0r9673801.

Kanji, N., L. Cotula, T. Hilhorst, C. Toulmin, and W. Witten. 2005. *Can Land Registration Serve Poor and Marginalised Groups? Summary Report*. Research Report 1, Securing Land Rights in Africa. London: International Institute for Environment and Development.

Kwasi, G. B., F. Awuah, N. Hammond, and J. E. Lamond. 2013. "The cost of land title formalisation in Ghana." *Property Management* 31: 5, 389–403. doi: 10.1108/PM-01-2013-0004.

Lastarria-Cornhiel, S. 1997. "Impact of privatization on gender and property rights in Africa." *World Development* 25: 8, 1317–33. doi: http://dx.doi.org/10.1016/S0305-750X(97)00030-2.

Leach, M., and J. Fairhead. 2000. "Challenging neo-Malthusian deforestation analyses in West Africa's dynamic forest landscapes." *Population and Development Review* 26: 1, 17–43. doi: 10.2307/172451.

Lovo, S. 2013. *Tenure Insecurity and Investment in Soil Conservation: Evidence from Malawi*. Working Paper No. 114. London: Grantham Research Institute on Climate Change and the Environment.

Lunduka, R. W. 2009. *Land Rental Markets, Investment and Productivity Under Customary Land Tenure Systems in Malawi*. Department of Economics and Resource Management. As: Norwegian University of Life Sciences.

Matchaya, G. 2009. "Land ownership security in Malawi." *African Journal of Agricultural Research* 4: 1, 1–13.

Mbalanje, A. B. T. 1982. "Land law and land policy in Malawi." In *Land Policy and Agriculture in Eastern and Southern Africa*, edited by L. D. Ngcongco, J. W. Arntzen, and S. D. Turner. New York: United Nations University.

Meinzen-Dick, Ruth, and Esther Mwangi. 2008. "Cutting the web of interests: Pitfalls of formalizing property rights." *Land Use Policy* 26: 1, 36–43. doi: http://dx.doi.org/10.1016/j.landusepol.2007.06.003.

Meynen, W., and M. Doornbos. 2004. "Decentralising natural resource management: A recipe for sustainability and equity." *European Journal of Development Research* 16: 1, 235–54.

Nankumba, J., and M. Machika. 1988. *Dynamics of land tenure and agrarian systems in Africa: The case of Malawi*. Research report to the food and agricultural organisation. Lilongwe.

Omura, M. 2008. "Property rights and natural resource management incentives: Do transferability and formality matter?" *American Journal of Agricultural Economics* 90: 4, 1143–55. doi: 10.1111/j.1467-8276.2008.01151.x.

Otsuka, K., and F. Place. 2001. *Land Tenure and Natural Resource Management: A Comparative Study of Agrarian Communities in Asia and Africa*. Washington DC: International Food Policy Research Institute.

Ouedraogó, R. S., J. P. Sawadogo, Volker Stamm, and Taladia Thiombiano. 1996. "Tenure, agricultural practices and land productivity in Burkina Faso: Some recent empirical results." *Land Use Policy* 13: 3, 229–32. doi: http://dx.doi.org/10.1016/0264-8377(96)84061-0.

Peters, P. E. 2009. "Challenges in land tenure and land reform in Africa: Anthropological contributions." *World Development* 37: 8, 1317–25. doi: http://dx.doi.org/10.1016/j.worlddev.2008.08.021.
Place, F., and P. Hazell. 1993. "Productivity effects of indigenous land tenure systems in sub-Saharan Africa." *American Journal of Agricultural Economics* 75: 1, 10–19. doi: 10.2307/1242949.
Sjaastad, E., and D. W. Bromley. 1997. "Indigenous land rights in sub-Saharan Africa: Appropriation, security and investment demand." *World Development* 25: 4, 549–62. doi: http://dx.doi.org/10.1016/S0305-750X(96)00120-9.
Sjaastad, E., and B. Cousins. 2008. "Formalisation of land rights in the South: An overview." *Land Use Policy* 26: 1, 1–9. doi: http://dx.doi.org/10.1016/j.landusepol.2008.05.004.
Smith, R. E. 2004. "Land tenure, fixed investment, and farm productivity: Evidence from Zambia's Southern province." *World Development* 32: 10, 1641–61.
Spichiger, R., and P. Stacey. 2014. *Ghana's Land Reform and Gender Equality*. DIIS Working Paper 2014:01. Copenhagen: Danish Institute for International Studies.
Teshome, A. 2014. "Tenure security and soil conservation investment decisions: Empirical evidence from East Gojam, Ethiopia." *Journal of Development and Agricultural Economics* 6: 1, 22–32.
Toulmin, C. 2009. "Securing land and property rights in sub-Saharan Africa: The role of local institutions." *Land Use Policy* 26: 1, 10–19. doi: http://dx.doi.org/10.1016/j.landusepol.2008.07.006.
Tsikata, D. 2004. *Gender, Land Rights and Inheritance. Securing Women's Land Rights: Approaches, Prospects and Challenges*. Paper presented at the Land in Africa Conference, November 8–9. London: Natural Resources Institute and Royal Africa Society.
van Leeuwen, M. 2014. "Renegotiating customary tenure reform – Land governance reform and tenure security in Uganda." *Land Use Policy* 39: 292–300. doi: http://dx.doi.org/10.1016/j.landusepol.2014.02.007.
World Bank. 2003. Land Policies for Growth and Poverty Reduction, A World Bank Policy Research Report. London: Oxford University Press.

CHAPTER TEN

LAND USE AND LIVELIHOODS ON CUSTOMARY LAND: A COMPARATIVE ANALYSIS OF CASE STUDIES FROM SOUTH AFRICA AND ZAMBIA

HORMAN CHITONGE

Introduction

This chapter presents a comparative analysis of land-use forms and livelihood strategies of households living in customary areas in South Africa and Zambia. The Zambian and South African case studies discussed in this chapter highlight the differences and similarities regarding land-use and livelihood strategies in the case-study areas. Research for the Zambian case study was conducted in 2014 under the Land Use and Rural Livelihood in Africa Project (LURLAP), and research for the South African case study was conducted between 2010 and 2011.[1] Details about the case studies are provided later in the chapter. Land use and rural livelihoods are discussed in the broader context of current debates on the role and future of customary land, focusing on the former homelands (reserves) in South Africa and rural areas (under traditional authorities) in Zambia.

Using survey data in both cases, this comparative analysis shows that despite obvious differences between the two countries, there are surprising similarities, especially in terms of wage employment as a source of livelihood, the means of accessing land, and the size of land owned or cultivated. Thus, while the socioeconomic, historical, and political contexts of land may differ in the two countries, people living on customary land in rural areas have comparable forms of land-use and livelihood strategies and face similar constraints. Although the livelihood portfolios of households discussed in this chapter are quite diversified and complex, access to land, especially in the Zambian context, plays a strategic role for most households. The data analysis also reveals that land access and use influence other livelihood strategies that households pursue.

The Role of Land in Rural Livelihoods

The role of access to land in rural livelihoods has been a contested topic over the last two-and-a-half decades, especially in the global South. Since the late 1980s, scholars in the agrarian-transformation literature have claimed that land is becoming less important, globally, in the livelihoods of rural residents, as rural households diversify away from land-based strategies (see Bryceson 2002; López and Valdés 2000; Rigg 2006). These claims have also emerged in the case of sub-Saharan Africa (SSA) (see Bryceson 2009; Ellis 2005). However, evidence on the ground suggests that access to land, particularly in rural Africa, remains a critical source of income, from which most rural households launch their various livelihood strategies (Baiphethi and Jacobs 2009; Chimhowu 2006; Chitonge and Ntsebeza 2012; Cotula et al. 2009; Ellis and Mode 2003). Although some studies suggest that land-based livelihood strategies are contributing relatively less to total household income in rural areas (see Brycesson 2002; Rigg 2006), other studies show that access to land, particularly in Africa, is still the most (in some cases the only) vital pillar of rural livelihoods (AGRA 2013; AU/AfDB/ECA 2010), such that many households would struggle to survive without it (Ellis and Bahiigwa 2003; Ellis and Mode 2003; Sheckleton et al. 2001). As a respondent interviewed in the Zambian case study observes, "without land there will be no survival, no life" (LURLAP Interviews 2014). A recent report on the status of agriculture in Africa acknowledges that land is a critical resource for rural dwellers, arguing, "there is no doubt that land is a key asset for rural poverty alleviation" (AGRA 2013).

The debate over the role of land in rural livelihoods has taken centre stage in Africa because most African economies have grown more than 5 percent annually for the past decade-and-a-half but have not generated enough real jobs to provide alternative sources of livelihood, especially for people in rural areas and the urban informal sector (See Jayne et al. 2010; UNDP 2014). This failure to create employment opportunities to absorb the growing labour force leaves land as the major resource for survival, especially for households in rural areas. In this context, it is important to understand how people use land and what types of livelihood they generate from and around land. It is also important to examine some of the key constraints hindering households that do have access to land from using it more productively to improve their well-being.

Access to land is critically important in Africa for many related reasons, even after we account for the alleged trend towards diversification of rural livelihoods. First, Africa has the largest proportion of people deriving their livelihoods directly from land (AGRA 2013; Akuffo 2009; Chitonge 2012a; Cotula et al. 2009; UNDP 2014). Although the rural population of sub-Saharan Africa was only the second largest (at 64 percent) in 2013 (after South Asia at 67 percent; see UNDP 2014, 219), low levels of off-farm employment and livelihood opportunities in Africa leave the majority of households directly dependent on land for survival.

Second, and related to this fact, the majority (more than 90 percent) of people in rural SSA have no access to any form of social protection or any form of social assistance from the state (Chitonge 2012b; ILO 2010), leaving access to land as the main safety net available, even among those who have diversified livelihood portfolios. This fact is well known to many, including senior politicians such as the former US secretary of state Hillary Clinton, who in 2011 acknowledged that for millions of Africans, farming is a lifeline, the only source of income and food (Leahy 2011). For this reason, access to land in Africa has always been considered "a birth right of every community member" (Mafeje 2003), such that a person acquires the right to access land by virtue of being a community member, not by contract, title, or any other contractual arrangements (Akuffo 2009; Shipton and Goheen 1992).

Third, land in Africa holds unique religious and spiritual significance (Makunike 2009). Because of the intricate web of relations concerning land, it touches the entire human existence, such that you can take the oil, copper, platinum, gold, diamonds, tin, and uranium from the soil without any serious backlash, but the moment land itself is taken, the stakes become inestimably high (Chachage 2011). Land in the African context, therefore, is not just a source of livelihood or a mere factor of production (see also chapter 2 above). As Makunike (2009, 86) has observed, in Africa

> so many livelihoods, and entire cultural and economic experiences, are directly tied to the land – more so perhaps than on any other continent. Such strong ties engender a strong sensibility about land that is poorly understood by many non-Africans, and particularly Westerners.

Perspectives on the Role of Land in Rural Livelihoods

As noted, while there is wide acknowledgement that access to land is important for rural livelihoods, especially in Africa, different views and approaches on this exist. These views can be grouped into three broad categories: the *minimalist*, *distributionist,* and *instrumentalist* perspectives.

The Minimalist Perspective

The minimalist perspective on land and livelihood is that land access provides a limited contribution to improving the well-being of poor rural residents engaged in subsistence farming. An extreme form of this view is generally referred to as "agro-pessimism," which essentially argues that there is no future for subsistence farming; land should be allocated to large-scale farmers who have the capacity to utilise it more efficiently. For instance, Paul Collier, a proponent of this view, argues that "contrary to the romantics, the world needs more commercial agriculture, not less. The Brazilian model of high-productivity large farms could readily be extended to areas where land is underused" (Collier 2008, 68).

A moderate minimalist perspective acknowledges that land plays a role in rural livelihoods, but asserts that its contribution to livelihoods and poverty reduction is small and dwindling. Evidence often cited for this includes an empirical study based on survey data from six Latin American countries[2] conducted by López and Valdés (2000). The authors argue that a key reason for the limited impact of land access on the well-being of the poor is that the poor often fail to convert the land asset into a viable income and livelihood source. Bryceson (2002) and Rigg (2006) express a similar view, arguing that the significance of land and farm-related activities as an income and livelihood source for the rural poor is dwindling. The reason given is that the livelihoods of the poor are becoming delinked from land and farming (Rigg 2006), giving rise to a phenomenon referred to as "deagrarianisation" and, more specifically, "depeasantisation" (Bryceson 1999).

The Distributionist Perspective

The second perspective on the role of land in rural livelihoods is the distributionist view, which acknowledges the significant role of land in reducing rural poverty in low-income countries where most people have predominantly land-based livelihoods. According to this view, making land available to the majority of the rural poor resolves the problem (de Janvry and Sadoulet 2002; Griffin et al. 2002; WDR 2001). On this basis, the distributionists support policies that promote access to land for small-scale farmers, not large-scale (commercial) farmers, arguing that small-scale farmers are more efficient than their commercial counterparts. This view is often supported by the *inverse-farm size-productivity* argument, which asserts that small-scale farmers use land more efficiently and produce more per unit of land (Deininger 2003; van den Brink et al. 2009).

The distributionists further argue that the creation of small-scale farms achieves the dual objective of equity and efficiency, thereby reducing rural poverty and promoting economic growth (de Janvry and Sadoulet 2002; Griffin et al. 2002).

However, although this view acknowledges that the state should play a role in making land available to small-scale land users, it emphasises a market-driven process that is alleged to promote efficient land use and allocation among small-scale farmers (see de Janvry and Sadoulet 2002; Griffin et al. 2002).[3] Factors considered crucial for the success of this strategy include secure tenure rights and well-functioning land and capital markets. Deininger (2003, xix) makes a strong case for this approach, arguing that

> secure property rights will increase the incentives of households and individuals to invest, and often will also provide them with better credit access, something that will not only help them make such investments, but will also provide an insurance substitute in the event of shocks.

In this approach, the state's role is confined to creating an atmosphere that promotes the efficient functioning of markets.

There are two major contentious ideas in the two perspectives discussed above. The first is the implicit assumption that simply making land available to the poor is enough to generate viable livelihoods in rural areas. For land to have a noticeable impact on poverty and well-being, enabling or complementary services that help the poor to convert land into a sustainable livelihood source must also be present (Hichambwa and Jayne 2014; Neves and du Toit 2013). The second is that reducing the state's role to merely creating a market-friendly environment overlooks the complexity of rural livelihoods and poverty.

For these reasons, the minimalist and distributionist approaches are unlikely to have a significant impact on the livelihoods of poor rural households in developing countries where market failure is rampant and the poor need different forms of support to enable them to convert various assets, including land, into viable livelihood sources. For countries such as South Africa, where land distribution has been influenced by systematic exclusion of most people from accessing land and other opportunities for centuries, the government needs to play a more proactive role, beyond merely consolidating land markets and securing tenure rights. In other countries such as Zambia, where the rural poor have access to some pockets of land, the state needs to provide support to enable them to use land more productively. As some respondents in both the South African and Zambian case studies argue, lack of support and access to markets makes it difficult for them to increase production and create sustainable livelihoods.

The Instrumentalist Perspective

The third approach, referred to here as the instrumentalist perspective, sees access to land as a first step towards improving the livelihoods of the rural poor. In this perspective, provision of enablers such as on- and off-farm support services, infrastructure, input support, access to credit, human and skills development, access to water, and viable technology are indispensable for land to serve as a poverty-alleviation instrument (Cox et al. 2003; DfID 2002). In this framework, making a piece of land available to a poor household is not an end in itself. Proponents of this approach argue that the effectiveness of using land as a poverty-reducing tool lies fundamentally in providing context-specific support such as the building of roads, irrigation schemes, schools, primary healthcare, skills development, and extension services (Cox et al. 2003; FAO 2006; Finan et al. 2005).

Thus, while the instrumentalist perspective acknowledges diversification of livelihoods and sees rural residents as "people with multiple livelihood strategies that may or may not be linked to farming at all times," it acknowledges that land access is critical for providing the poor "with a base from which to launch other livelihood ventures. It may provide chronically poor households with a key commodity [land], but one that needs to be turned into a livelihood through other complementary activities" (Chimhowu 2006, 7). Thus, an instrumentalist perspective views access to land as a necessary but not wholly sufficient condition for reducing poverty; and to play an important role in reducing poverty, land reform must be conceptualised as "a long-term process that requires sustained support" (DfID 2002, iv).

The Livelihood Approach

The livelihood approach was first proposed by Robert Chambers and Gordon Conway in the early 1990s (see Chambers and Conway 1991). This approach became popular as a result of growing criticism of income-based conceptualisations of poverty. A fundamental contribution of the livelihood approach is the realisation that poverty is "not just a question of low income, but also includes other dimensions such as bad health, illiteracy, lack of services, etc., as well as a state of vulnerability and feelings of powerlessness in general" (Krantz 2001, 2). With this broader conceptualisation of poverty, it becomes apparent that people construct livelihoods from complex processes that combine different forms of assets or resources. Understanding the complex livelihood portfolios that the poor create and manage requires a more holistic approach. For this reason, a serious livelihood analysis must account for the different assets and resources that a household combines to generate its sustenance (Scoones 1998).

To capture the complex set of factors that influence how people put together a means of living, a livelihood is understood to comprise four key components: (1) *people* with the ability to adopt and successfully negotiate at least one livelihood strategy; (2) *assets* that enable a household to successfully pursue and accomplish a specific livelihood outcome; (3) a set of *activities* through which livelihoods are generated and sustained; and (4) viable *outcomes* (a means of living) from the strategies adopted (Chambers and Conway 1991, 7). To analyse people's livelihoods, proponents of the livelihood approach suggest taking seriously the broader context in which the strategies are pursued, including the policy context, local politics, macroeconomic conditions, and historical, demographic, climatic, agroecological, and social factors (Scoones 1998).

The livelihood analysis conceptualises livelihood resources (capital) in broad terms to include physical (such as plough, hoe, axe, bicycle, etc.), financial (cash, loans, savings, etc.), human (healthy, skilled, working-age members of a household), social (networks, claims, access to private and public services), and natural (land, water, vegetation, etc.) resources. In general, a household combines all these different forms of capital to create a livelihood portfolio (Carney et al. 1999). As might be expected, such portfolios are not static; they change according to the nature and types of capital available.

Because of its overreaching scope, the livelihood approach's inherent weakness is its subjective notion of poverty, which makes an objective analysis and assessment of poverty difficult. Critics have also noted that the livelihood approach is difficult to implement on a large scale since one must consider different portfolios for different groups of people (Krantz 2001). However, the strength of this approach is that it allows one to account for the complex dynamics that people negotiate to construct viable livelihoods.

Background to the Two Case Studies

Before presenting the two case studies, we briefly discuss the background to land and livelihoods and how the case studies were conducted.

The South African Land Context

The South African case study, which was conducted in 2010 and 2011, examined land use in the context of the land-redistribution programme. The main objective of the South African case study was to investigate whether the land-reform programme has helped to improve the livelihoods of its intended beneficiaries. This question is essential given the various reports from media, government officials, and analysts that most of the land transferred through land reform has not been productive (see, for instance, CDE 2008; Nkwinti 2010).[4] In view of such reports, the case study sought to systematically examine the contribution of land reform to the livelihoods of the beneficiaries. The contributions were conceived in broad terms to include non-material benefits such as restoring a sense of justice, self-confidence, and social stability.

Colonial and apartheid policies created highly skewed land distribution along racial lines, such that while Africans have always constituted the overwhelming majority, they have held a significantly lower share of the country's land resources (7 percent in 1913, which was later expanded to 13 percent in 1936; see Ntsebeza 1998; Walker and Cousins 2014). Because many indigenous Africans were confined to areas called *Bantustan*, or *homelands*, land access in these communities has been severely constrained (as evident in the case study below), making it difficult for them to engage in meaningful agricultural activities (see Butler et al. 1978, 181).

To address the unequal distribution and ownership of land as a result of the prolonged period of land dispossession and alienation from indigenous African people during colonial and apartheid rule, the African National Congress (ANC)-led government began to formulate and implement land reforms immediately after coming to power in 1994. This reform has been implemented through three principal programmes: *land redistribution,* which focuses on redressing inequalities in land ownership by transferring white-owned land to black South Africans; *land restitution*, which seeks to compensate people who were forcibly dispossessed from their land between 1913–90; and *land-tenure reform*, which addresses the tenure rights and land administration of marginalised groups, particularly farm workers and farm dwellers.

Although the ANC-led government has been implementing land reform since 1994, various studies and official reports acknowledge that very little has been achieved in addressing unequal land access and ownership. According to official agricultural statistics, in 2010 approximately 82 percent (86 million hectares) of the total area was owned by 40,000 commercial farmers, most of them white, while only 11.8 percent (14 million hectares) is shared by the 2.2 million smallholder and semisubsistence farmers in the former homeland areas (DAFF 2010).[5] In terms of land redistribution achieved so far, less than 10 percent of the targeted 25 million hectares has been redistributed (see Chitonge and Ntsebeza 2012, 89; Walker and Cousins 2014, 4).

Analysts have observed that the legacy of apartheid in terms of asset ownership and distribution patterns remains largely unchanged, with landlessness and overcrowding persisting in many former Bantustan areas (May 2000, 21). Unequal land access and ownership is an enduring reminder of the racial disparities and social-segregation policies pursued by the apartheid regime (Walker and Cousins 2014, 1). Walker and Cousins further observe that, "[L]and looms large as a powerful symbol of enduring racial inequalities and social exclusion in post-apartheid society" (2014, 1).

With reference to the redistribution programme (on which our case study focused), the Land Reform Policy describes its objective as providing "the poor with access to land for residential and productive uses, in order to improve their income and quality of life" (DLA 1997, Section 4.3). Subsequent Land Reform Policy documents have restated this vision. For example, the Land Reform for Agrarian Development (Department of Land Affairs 2001) asserts that one of the strategic objectives of land redistribution is to improve the livelihoods of poor people, especially in rural areas. But the land-redistribution programme has recently shifted focus—away from helping the poor access land, towards developing an emerging pool of black commercial farmers (see, for example, the RECAP Programme, DRDLR 2013).

The Zambian Land Context

The land context in Zambia is quite different from the South African case in several respects, including the size and type of land and the historical dynamics surrounding it. Unlike South Africa, which follows a three-tenure system (freehold, leasehold, and customary tenure), Zambia has followed a dual-tenure system (leasehold or state land and customary land; see chapter 1 for more details) since 1975, when freehold titles were abolished. Customary land constitutes the largest share, although it has diminished because of various factors, including the policy of converting customary land into leasehold (Chitonge 2015; PCLET 2013).[6]

The other difference between Zambia and South Africa is historical: because Zambia had a smaller proportion of European settlers, land dispossession of indigenous people occurred on a much smaller scale compared to South Africa. For instance, in Zambia only 6 percent of the land (compared to South Africa's 87 percent) was reserved for white settlers and urban development, although this did constitute the most fertile land (Adams 2003). Furthermore, while black South Africans have constrained access to land, rural areas in Zambia are perceived to have plenty of land, although some studies indicate that shortages have emerged in many areas (including in the area where the LURLAP study was conducted), especially among semisubsistence farmers (Hichaambwa and Jayne 2014).

Despite differences between the two countries, similarities also exist in terms of land dynamics. Of particular relevance to this volume is that both countries have maintained the institution of traditional authorities responsible for the administration of customary land (see Ntsebeza 1998; and Claassens 2014 for South Africa).

As noted, this chapter is based on two case studies: the Zambian study was conducted in Chongwe and Chibombo Districts, and the South African case study was conducted in Chris Hani District.

Access to Land in South Africa

South Africa is one of the five large countries in Africa, with a total land mass of 1.2 million km^2, or 122.3 million hectares (Table 10.1). Of this, more than 82 percent (100 million hectares) is classified as farmland, while only 13 percent (16.7 million hectares) is arable land.

Province	Total area (km^2)	Farmland (km^2)	Farm-land (%)	Arable land (km^2)	Arable land (%)	HL total area (km^2)	HL % of total area
Eastern Cape	170,616	148,177.2	86.8	11,729.01	6.9	51,754	30.3
Free State	129,439	117,601.0	90.9	42,214.23	32.6	2,322	1.8
Gauteng	18,760	8,286.23	44.2	4,386.23	23.4	0	0.0
Kwa-Zulu Natal	91,481	65,293.1	71.4	11,996.75	13.1	36,074	39.4
Limpopo	119,606	105,482.90	88.2	17,004.42	14.2	36,124	30.2
Mpuma-langa	81,816	49,788.27	60.9	17,348.96	21.2	6,775	8.3
North West	118,710	100,984.73	85.1	33,604.59	28.3	38,079	32.1
Northern Cape	363,389	295,438.32	81.3	4,544.65	1.3	0	0.0
Western Cape	129,386	115,606.09	89.3	24,547.88	19.0	0	0.0
RSA (total)	**1,223,201**	**1,006,657.92**	**82.3**	**167,376.72**	**13.7**	**171,128.0**	**14.0**

Table 10.1. South African land use profile

Source: Author, based on data from Department of Agriculture, Forestry and Fisheries (2010).

HL = former homelands.
Note: there were no homelands or *Bantustans* in what is now Western Cape and Northern Cape provinces.

As noted above, colonial and apartheid policies created highly skewed land distribution along racial lines (see Ntsebeza 1998). Following the racial-segregation policy, ten separate territories, called "homelands" (Bantustans or reserves), were created for Africans (see Butler et al. 1978).

As Table 10.1 shows, land reserved for Africans since 1936 accounted for only 14 percent of the total land mass, and most of this was of poor quality (Hendricks 1990; Ntsebeza 1998), leading not only to constrained access to land but also overcrowding and soil degradation (Ntsebeza 1998). Agricultural activities in the former homelands have always been limited to a "family plot and a few head of livestock grazing on common land" (Butler et al. 1978, 181).

Province	Total area (mha)	State land (mha)	State land (%)	Private land (mha)	Private land (%)	HL total area (mha)	HL % of total area
Eastern Cape	16.89	4.73	28.0	12.16	72.0	51,754	30.3
Free State	12.98	1.42	11.0	11.55	89.0	23,22	1.8
Gauteng	1.65	0.91	55.0	0.74	45.0	0	0.0
KwaZulu-Natal	9.43	3.86	41.0	5.56	59.0	36,074	39.4
Limpopo	12.57	3.39	27.0	9.18	73.0	36,124	30.2
Mpumalanga	7.64	1.83	24.0	5.81	76.0	6,775	8.3
North West	10.65	4.47	42.0	6.17	58.0	38,079	32.1
N. Cape	37.28	2.98	8.0	34.30	92.0	0	0.0
W. Cape	12.94	7.12	55.0	5.82	45.0	0	0.0
RSA	122.08	30.74	25.2	91.33	74.8	17.1	14.0

Table 10.2. Proportion of private and state land, and land ownership by racial group (millions of hectares)
Source: South African Institute of Race Relations (SAIRR 2012: 612–13).
Note: The total surface area here is slightly different from what is reported in Stats SA, as well as the FAO database.

HL = former homelands.
mha = millions of hectares.

Table 10.2 shows the current distribution of land in South Africa, highlighting the three-tenure system: freehold tenure (private land), state land (leasehold), and customary tenure (mostly in the former homelands). This table also highlights the concentration of land ownership within the commercial agricultural sector, which accounts for more than 86 percent of farmland.

	Total	Eastern Cape	Free State	KZN	Mpumalanga	N. West	Northern province
Less than 1 ha	50%	30.9%	77%	47.9%	75.6%	52.3%	65%
1–2 ha	22.1%	26.8%	5.3%	30.7%	8.4%	13.9%	18.1%
2–3 ha	12%	18.1%	5.7%	10.6%	4.3%	7.5%	8.5%
3–5 ha	10.2%	16.7%	1.1%	6.3%	6.4%	12.4%	5.6%
5–10 ha	4.7%	7%	8.7%	3.2%	2.3%	8.5%	2.4%
10+ ha	0.5%	2.2%	2.2%	1.2%	3%	5.4%	0.5%
Households (n)	1,448,628	534,441	23,459	200,546	77,996	89,443	521,743
Main reason for accessing land							
Grow food for household	92.6%	95.4%	77%	89.4%	93.5%	84.3%	93.8%
Produce for sale	5.4%	2.8%	20.3%	7.6%	6.1%	11.4%	4.5%
Other	2.1%	1.9%	2.7%	3%	0.4%	4.3%	1.7%
Households (n)	1,654,299	587,656	33,345	226,897	88,766	150,882	566,753

Table 10.3. Size of land accessed by households, 1999
Source: *Former Homelands Survey*, Stats SA (1999).

The constraint of land access is evident when one considers the average size of land to which people in the former homelands have access. Although some claim that large tracts of land in the former homelands are either not used at all or are underutilised (NPC 2011, 197), analysts have argued that these constraints have stifled development of viable farming for most households (Jacobs et al. 2008, 10; Mecarini 2000). According to a survey conducted by Statistics South Africa (1999), half of the population in the former homelands has access to less than one hectare (see Table 10.3).

In the semiarid agroecological conditions of parts of the Eastern Cape and Free State, a single hectare is not much for farming. While not everyone in the former homelands has aspirations to farm, especially production for market, many household heads interviewed indicated that they would like to grow crops primarily for home consumption but that lack of access to land discouraged them. As the bottom part of Table 10.3 illustrates, more than 90 percent of those with access to land indicated that they were only producing food for their families. It is also noteworthy that while nearly three-quarters of the population in the former homelands reported having access to some land for farming, almost 95 percent had access to communal land for livestock farming, common grazing land (see Table 10.4).

This is the context in which land access as a means of livelihood in South Africa should be situated. In view of the livelihood approach, which looks at different activities and resources used to construct a livelihood, it is important to bear in mind that constrained access to land inevitably limits the available strategies that people can pursue.

	Total	Eastern Cape	Free State	KZN	Mpumalanga	N. West	Northern province
Have access to land?							
Yes	71.3%	83.5%	48.8%	90.09%	47.8%	44.6%	74.1%
No	28.7%	16.5%	51.2%	9.91%	52.2%	55.4%	25.9%
Households (n)	2,355,916	711,682	68,496	252,996	199,362	354,125	769,254
Have access to land for livestock?							
Yes	56.1%	75.7%	43%	73.9%	25.9%	45.4%	37%
No	43.9%	24.3%	57%	26.1%	74.1%	54.6%	63%
Type of land accessed?							
Communal	97.3%	99.7%	95.1%	96.1%	95.2%	94.7%	94.6%
Individual	1.6%	0.1%	4.9%	2.3%	1.9%	4.2%	3%

Table 10.4. Households with access to land for farming purposes in the former Homelands

Source: Author, based on data from *Former Homelands Survey* (Stats SA 1999).

Access to Land in Zambia

Zambia has a total land mass of 752,600km^2, or 75.2 million hectares. Since the introduction of colonial rule, the country has followed a dual-tenure system whereby statutory law administers state land, while customary law administers customary land. Customary land constitutes the largest share, although it has been diminishing for several reasons, including the policy of converting it to leasehold (PCLET 2013; Chitonge 2015; see also chapters 1 and 2 in this volume).

Unlike South Africa, Zambia abolished freehold titles in 1975 and replaced them with leasehold titles of up to ninety-nine years, following the nationalisation of land. Like South Africa, Zambia has maintained the institution of traditional authorities' responsibility for the administration of customary land.

A perennial land-reform concern in Zambia is the issue of tenure reform, which includes finding ways to protect the land rights of people who have access to customary land. Tenure reform now features more prominently in public debates and policy discussions because the practice of converting customary land into leasehold poses a significant challenge to the future of customary land (PCLET 2013).

Agrarian Structure in Zambia

A trimodal structure featuring a small number of commercial farmers (less than 0.1 percent of all farmers), a relatively small number of emerging and medium-sized farming enterprises, and a large number of smallholder farmers characterises the Zambian agrarian structure (see Table 10.5). Most of the smallholder farmers (largely subsistence growers) access and use land under customary tenure.

All farmers (2005)			Average for smallholders only (2005-10)		
	Land size (ha)	**% of total land cultivated**	**Land size (ha)**	**No. of farms**	**%**
Smallholders	0.5–9	75	0.5–1.9	1,106,804	75.2
Emerging farmers	10–20	20	2–4.9	315,459	21.4
Medium-scale	20–60	4	5–9.9	42,332	2.9
Large-scale	60+	0.1	10–20	6,626	0.05
Total				1,471,221	

Table 10.5. The agrarian structure in Zambia
Sources: Author, based on data from Diaz-Chavez et al. 2010: 94 (for 2005 figures) and Jayne et al. 2011: 18 (for 2005–10 figures).

The majority (three-quarters) of these are smallholder farmers using less than two hectares. However, although large in number, smallholders account for only 30 percent of all cultivated land. Data from Chongwe and Chibombo Districts confirm the dominance of this group of land users (see Table 10.7). While Zambia is well known as a land-surplus country, the plot sizes of subsistence farmers have declined over the years (Jayne et al. 2010; Sitko and Jayne 2014). Cases of local people failing to find land are becoming common, especially in areas with good infrastructure such as roads, access to markets, healthcare, education, and water (FSRP 2010; Hichaambwa and Jayne 2014).

Study Sites

Chris Hani District Municipality, South Africa

As mentioned, the South African case study was conducted in the Chris Hani District municipality (CHDM), one of the six district municipalities that make up the Eastern Cape Province. The municipality included portions of the former homelands of Transkei and Ciskei as well as portions of formerly white South Africa. The district is largely rural, dotted with many urban centres and towns that constitute the administrative centres for the eight local municipalities. The larger section of the district lies in the Karoo, which falls within the semiarid agroecological zone, with annual rainfall below 600 mm. Because of these climatic conditions, the main agricultural activity in the district is livestock, although rain-fed crops are grown, especially among small-scale farmers who do not have irrigation facilities.

Chongwe and Chibombo: Zambia

In Zambia, research was conducted in Chongwe and Chibombo Districts, bordering the city of Lusaka on the eastern and northern sides, respectively. Despite being close to the city of Lusaka, these two districts are predominantly rural, with most people (95 percent for Chibombo and 94 percent for Chongwe) living in rural areas under customary land (Table 10.6). The majority of people in both districts are smallholder farmers relying largely on subsistence crop farming, although a small percentage o f households engages in livestock farming.

Chongwe						
	De facto		De jure			
	Population	(%)	Population	(%)	Area (km^2)	Households (number)
Rural	169,973	93.5	180,143	93.7		
Urban	11,843	6.5	12,160	6.3		
Total	181,816		192,303		8,669	3, 319
Household size (average)	5.0		5.29			
Population density/ km^2	20.9		22.2			
Chibombo						
Rural	277,781	95.6	290,115	95.6		
Urban	12,775	4.4	13,404	4.4		
Total	290,556		303,519		13,423	53,179
Household size	5.46		5.70			
Population density/ km^2	21.6		22.6			
Zambia						
Rural	7,505,292	59.9	7,919,216	60.5		
Urban	5,021,022	40.1	5,173,450	39.5		
Total	12,526,314		13,092,666		75, 612	2,513,768
Household size	4.98		5.20			
Population density/ km^2	16.6		17.4			

Table 10.6. Demographic profile in Chongwe, Chibombo and Zambia, 2010

Source: Central Statistics Office (CSO 2012), 2010 Population Census.

Methodology and Data Collection

The Chris Hani case study was conducted primarily through a household survey administered in 2010 and 2011. Data were collected on a wide range of issues, including land ownership, public and private remittances, non-agricultural activities, household income and expenditure, agricultural production, and assets profiles. Data were also collected through participatory poverty assessment (PPA) techniques on several selected land-reform beneficiary groups. A total of 255 households consisting of land-reform beneficiaries and non-beneficiaries were interviewed for the study.

Data for Chongwe and Chibombo were collected using three main methods: in-depth interviews, focus-group discussions, and a short survey. In total, about 129 residents were interviewed and participated in focus-group discussions. A total of eighty-five household heads were interviewed through a short survey questionnaire.[7]

Land Use and Livelihood in Chongwe, Chibombo, and Chris Hani Districts

Landholding

This section presents the data and the findings of the two case studies. Although these cases studies were conducted at different times (South Africa in 2010 and 2011 and the Zambian study in 2014), it is possible to compare the households' forms of land-use and livelihood strategies in the study areas. In terms of land access and use, almost half the households in the Chris Hani case study have access to less than 0.5 hectares, while most of the households (75.3 percent) in Chongwe and Chibombo have access to between 0.5 and one hectare.[8] However, a lower ratio of households accesses between two and five hectares of land in Zambia compared to South Africa (see Table 10.7). For instance, only 1 percent of households in the Chongwe and Chibombo case study accessed between five and nineteen hectares of land, while in the Chris Hani study this was 9 percent of households.

Two points emerge from the comparison of landholdings in Chris Hani and in Chongwe and Chibombo Districts. First, in both cases, there is differentiation among households regarding the size of land held or accessed. While most households in both cases access fewer than two hectares, some households have access to much larger pieces of land, especially in the Chris Hani case. Differences in the size of land accessed often translate into differences in terms of income (Hichaambwa and Jayne 2014), wealth, other assets, and types of livelihood that a household can pursue.

	Chongwe and Chibombo				Chris Hani			
	Mode of accessing land							
	Inherited	Bought	Chiefs	Total	Inherited	Bought	Chiefs	Total
(n)	23	9	53	85	29	10	49	88
Land size (ha)								
< 0.5	4.3	11.1	3.8	4.7	31	20	57.2	45.5
0.5–1	73.9	55.6	79.3	75.3	24.1	0	8.2	12.5
1–2	17.4	33.3	9.4	14.1	6.9	0	4.1	4.5
2–5	4.4	0	5.5	5.3	13.8	0	20.4	15.9
5–10	0	0	1.9	1.1	7	30	6.1	9
10–20	0	0	0	0	3.4	10	2	3.4
20+	0	0	0	0	14	40	0	9

Table 10.7. Land size by mode of land access in customary areas
Source: Author, based on data from LURLAP Survey (2014) and Land and Poverty Study (2011).

The visible differentiation in land ownership challenges the widely held view that customary tenure promotes equality of access to land (see Bruce 1986; Platteau 1996). However, differences in land size accessed in Chongwe and Chibombo and in Chris Hani can also be accounted for by the difference in ecological conditions. While Chongwe and Chibombo Districts are both located in an ecological zone with adequate annual rainfall averaging between 1000 and 1200 mm, most of Chris Hani District is located in the semiarid area, with an annual average rainfall between 300 to 600 mm. Thus, in comparisons of landholding and land use in the case-study areas, it is important to bear in mind the different climatic conditions that influence the size of land owned and the nature of land use. As Lipton argues, "Half a hectare of reliably watered peri-urban land … is a bigger farm than 250 hectares of low quality grazing land in the karoo" (Lipton 1996, viii).

In the Chongwe and Chibombo case, respondents indicated that the size of one's land depends on whether the person was born in the area and when the person settled in the area (see also chapter 2). However, this does not validate the claim that customary-land tenure tends to promote equal land access. There are cases of land concentration reported in many customary areas, even in places where monetary transactions for land are not dominant (Bassett 1993). In the Chris Hani case study, the exposure to marketable farming in the homelands may have induced a tendency to accumulate land, especially among those with resources (Hendricks 1990).

The other important point emerging from this is that the widely held perception of Zambia as a land-surplus country needs to be reassessed on the basis of new evidence. While Chongwe and Chibombo may not perfectly represent the experience of other parts of Zambia, in many parts of the country village heads have reportedly run out of land to allocate to newcomers or those who need more (FSRP 2010; USAID 2010). A recent analysis of a nationally representative sample of landholdings in Zambia concludes, "In many areas … unallocated land appears to be unavailable… Many small farming areas have become enclaves that cannot expand because of claims and titles on adjacent land" (Hichaambwa and Jayne 2014, v). During interviews, one of the village heads confirmed this, saying, "now the situation is different because the land is limited, even the village headmen do not have extra land. Land is already allocated to people. Land only becomes available when someone leaves the community to settle in another area" (LURLAP Interviews 2014).

Forms of Land Use

There are differences in land use between Chris Hani and Chongwe and Chibombo. In the Chris Hani area, where the agroecological conditions are drier, indeed almost semiarid, the main form of land use is livestock rearing, although rain-fed crops are also grown on a much smaller scale. In Chongwe and Chibombo, the area is an agroecological zone favourable for production of various rain-fed crops.

Although more than half of the households in Chongwe and Chibombo (more than 60 percent if we include those reporting livestock farming and crop and livestock farming) reported their main source of livelihood as crop farming, only 10 percent reported farming as their main livelihood source in Chris Hani District (see Table 10.8, end of chapter). The higher proportion of respondents identifying farming as their main source of livelihood in Chongwe and Chibombo, compared to Chris Hani District, may reflect a stronger dependence on land as a main source of livelihood.

Chibombo & Chongwe Districts					Chris Hani District				
Source	Inherited	Bought	Chiefs	Total	Source	Inherited	Bought	Chiefs	Total
(n)	23	9	53	**85**	(n)	29	10	49	**88**
Main sources of Livelihood									
Crop Farming	43.5	33.3	58.5	51.8	Formal job	6.90	0.00	2.04	**3.41**
Livestock	0	0	3.8	**2.4**	Farming	13.8	20	6.1	**10.2**
Trading	21.7	55.6	13.2	**20**	Business	3.5	10	6.1	**5.7**
Crop & Livestock	17.4	0	3.8	**7.1**	Remittances	6.9	10	22.4	**15.9**
Brickmaking	0	11.1	3.8	**3.5**	Social Grant	37.9	20	36.7	35.2
Wage Employment	4.4	0	3.5	**3.5**	Casual Work	6.9	0	4.1	**4.5**
Beer Brewing & Selling	8.7	0	7.6	**7.1**	Farm Work	10.3	30	10.2	**13.6**
Other	4.3	0	5.7	**4.7**	Social Grant + Farming	6.9	0	8.2	**6.8**

Table 10.8. Households' Main Source of Livelihood (%)
Source: Author based on data from LURLAP and Land and Poverty Surveys

Several factors account for this difference, including the fact that rural livelihoods in South Africa tend to be more diversified, with a wide range of non-farm activities backed by a broad-based state-funded social-assistance programme in the form of social grants (see Neves and du Toit 2013; Walker and Cousins 2014). As mentioned above, there was also more extensive dispossession of indigenous people from their land in South Africa; consequently, more widespread disruption of land-based subsistence activities occurred in South Africa than in Zambia. As the data on landholding show, while almost everyone in Chongwe and Chibombo has access to at least *some* land for farming, a much higher proportion of people in Chris Hani (26 percent) has no access at all to land for farming (see Table 10.4), and most of those with access to land for farming (65 percent) have less than half a hectare (see Table 10.7).

Social Grants

A main factor accounting for the difference in primary sources of livelihood between Chris Hani and the Zambian case study is the presence of social grants in South Africa, which are largely absent in Zambia apart from a few donor-supported cash-transfer pilot projects (see Chitonge 2012b). Widespread access to social grants in South Africa constitutes a crucial (although not the only) source of income for the poorest in most former homeland areas. It has been suggested that increased access to social grants provides poor households with alternative income, which in turn reduces the pressure to embark on subsistence agriculture (see NPC 2011, 198). Yet, evidence that social grants create a disincentive to engage in subsistence agriculture has not been examined carefully (Baiphethi and Jacobs 2009). Numerous studies have reported that most rural households, including land-reform beneficiaries, are increasingly relying on social grants (Anseeeuw and Mathebula 2008; Mencarini 2000) or that social grants constitute the largest source of income and livelihood, especially for poorer households (Bradstock 2006; Carter and May 1997). A study comm issioned by the Development Bank Southern Africa (DBSA) reported that among smallholder households, social grants accounted for 50 percent of t otal household income, followed by wages at 22.9 percent, private remitta nces at 18.6 percent, and income from agriculture accounting for only 3.7 percent (Vink and van Rooyen 2009, 14).[9]

While social grants contribute significantly to the livelihoods of poor households in rural South Africa, the role of social grants in rural livelihoods tends to be exaggerated because household production for self-consumption is excluded. In a study that accounted for estimated production for self-consumption, the contribution from social grants to overall household income was much lower among households that had access to land for farming purposes (see Chitonge and Ntsebeza 2012, 98). However, this is not to deny that social grants play an important role in rural livelihoods in South Africa.

In the case of Zambia, none of the respondents interviewed via the short survey or in-depth interviews reported receiving any form of state social assistance except for the farm-input support that is given once a year to a small number of smallholder farmers. When we asked participants in focus-group discussions in Chongwe and Chibombo whether they received social assistance from the government, the response was, "We do not have such assistance; we actually do not know of such services in this area" (LURLAP FGD 2014). In contrast to Chongwe and Chibombo, more than half of households in Chris Hani District reported public and private remittances as their main source of income and livelihood (see Table 10.8).

In Chongwe and Chibombo, trading is the second major source of livelihood after crop farming. Trading in rural areas in Zambia can range from selling a bunch of sweet bananas to owning a small grocery shop or selling dry fish or vegetables and other farm produce. But trading is usually a coping strategy, often undertaken to complement other strategies such as farming, especially during the dry season, when opportunities for crop production are limited. In this sense, the prominence of trading as a livelihood source also indicates a lack of other viable sources of income, especially wage employment.

Interestingly, wage employment or formal jobs as sources of livelihood are equally rare in both case studies. This contradicts claims that in rural South Africa, "the sources of most people's livelihoods now lie in wages" (Walker and Cousins 2014, 4). The number of households reporting wage employment as their main source of income is surprisingly low, at only 3 percent. In this context, even in the case of Chris Hani, where public and private remittances constitute the largest source of income for many households, "land remains a significant resource for the rural poor," not just for generating income but also for consolidating rural-urban linkages among families (Neves and du Toit 2013, 102).

The broader picture that emerges from this livelihood profile for Chris Hani and for Chongwe and Chibombo is that different households have different sources of income; in most cases, while households have one main source of livelihood, they complement the main source with other sources such as harvesting natural resources (mainly grass, mushrooms, etc.). For example, one woman in the Mungule area (Chibombo District) reported that in addition to growing crops, mainly maize and sweet potato, she also cuts grass for roof thatching, which she sells, and she works for other people by weeding their fields. In some households, the harvesting of natural resources supplements crop and livestock production. In the case of the rural Eastern Cape, scholars have reported that harvesting natural products forms an important livelihood source (Shackleton et al. 2001).

In all of this, land is reported to be a key asset on which poorer households rely, contrary to the minimalist claim that the role of land in rural livelihoods is actually diminishing. Many studies that identify land as a critical asset in rural Africa, even in a context where livelihoods are significantly diversified (AGRA 2013), have confirmed this finding. For example, a study of rural livelihoods in one district in Tanzania concludes that land is a key asset that enables rural residents to successfully construct viable livelihoods (Ellis and Mode 2003). The study found that although the local residents had different assets and livelihood strategies, "the poorest … are distinguished by lack of livestock and land … while exhibiting similar mean levels of education, tools and household labour as the other income tercile" (Ellis and Mode 2003, 1372).

Crop Production

As noted above, crop production is a major form of land use, especially in Chongwe and Chibombo. Households in the case-study areas produce a wide range of crops, as Table 10.9 indicates.[10]

Chibombo & Chongwe Districts					Chris Hani District				
	Inherited	Bought	Chiefs	Total		Inherited	Bought	Chiefs	Total
(n)	23	9	53	**85**	(n)	29	10	49	**88**
Crops Gown and Quantities Produced									
HH growing Maize (%)	60.9	44.4	73.6	**67.1**	HH growing Maize (%)	66	60	49	**58.3**
50Kg Maize Bags	45.6	23.7	28.6	**32.4**	50Kg Maize bags	13.2	15.8	8.75	**12.6**
HH growing Cotton (%)	0	0	96.2	**52.1**	HH Growing Potatoes (%)	48	60	55	**54.3**
Cotton (50Kg)	0	0	5.9	**5.9**	10kg Potato bags	15.2	24.8	20.2	**20.1**
Groundnuts HH(%)	78.3	0.0	83.0	**62**	HH growing Cabbage (%)	31	30	51	**37.3**
Groundnut (50kg)	0.3	0	2.4	**1.6**	Cabbage(Kg)	120.8	541.7	269.3	**310.6**
					HH growing Onion (%)	34	70	45	**49.7**
HH growing sunflower (%)	0	0	94.3	**50**	10kg Onion Pockets	15.3	24.8	20.2	**20.1**
Sunflower (50kg)	0	0	1.6	**1.6**	HH Producing Wool (%)	86.7	40	45	**57.2**
					Wool Bales	2.9	0.8	4.2	**2.6**
HH growing Potato (%)	78.3	100.0	79.2	**69**	HH growing Fodder (%)	17	50	22	**29.7**
10kg Potato bags	0.8	1.7	4.5	**81.2**	Fodder Bales	0.4	1	1.3	**0.9**

Table 10.9. Household Crop Production Profile
Source: Author Based on Data form LURLAP and Land and Poverty Surveys
Note: HH= household

In both case studies, maize is the most popular crop, although the proportion of households growing maize in Chongwe and Chibombo Districts is much higher than in Chris Hani. Other major crops in Chongwe and Chibombo include cotton, groundnuts, and sweet potatoes; while in Chris Hani, potato, onion, wool, cabbage, and fodder are among the major products. Despite different ecological conditions in the two case-study areas, maize is still the most widely grown crop. The main reason is that in both cases, maize is one of the major staple foods. Most poor households grow maize for home consumption and not for the market (see McAllister 1999). A study in South Africa reviewing patterns of household food-supply sources confirms that maize grain and its associated products are the staple food for most people living in rural areas (see D'Haese and Huylenbroek 2005). In Zambia, although a study conducted in 2007–08 on staple-food consumption patterns suggested that maize is no longer the most important staple food among urban households (except among the poorest households) (Mason and Jayne 2009), it remains the most important staple food for rural households, including in Chongwe and Chibombo.

Also important is that the average amount of maize produced in the Zambian case-study areas is almost three times more than that produced in Chris Hani. Several factors could account for this, including ecological differences. However, the average figures presented for maize output can be misleading since both cases reflect great variation among households regarding the amount of maize produced, as Table 10.10 indicates.[11]

	Chongwe & Chibombo					Chris Hani			
	inherited	**bought**	**Chief**	**Total**		**inherited**	**bought**	**Chief**	**Total**
(n)	**23**	**9**	**53**	**85**		**29**	**10**	**49**	**88**
Quantities of Maize Produced									
50kg Bags	**Percentage of households**				**50kg Bags**	**Percentage of households**			
0	17.4	0	15.1	**14.1**	-	-	-	-	-
1-5	0	11.1	7.6	**5.8**	1-2	21.1	16.7	20.8	**20.4**
5-10	4.4	0	13.2	**9.4**	2-4	10.5	0	33.3	**20.4**
10-20	21.7	0	16.9	**16.5**	4-10	36.8	50	16.7	**32**
20-50	8.7	33.3	11.3	**12.9**	10-20	5.3	0	20.8	**14.3**
50-100	4.35	0	7.5	**5.9**	20-40	21.1	33.3	4.2	**16.3**
More Than 100	43.5	55.6	28.3	**35.3**	More than 40	5.3	0	4.2	**6.1**

Table 10.10. Maize production by Type of land Acquisition (% of HH)

Source: Author Based on Data form LURLAP and Land and Poverty Surveys

In both cases, some households produce large amounts of maize, while others produce very small amounts. In the case of Chongwe and Chibombo, a high concentration of households produces a large volume of maize, while in Chris Hani close to three-quarters of households produce less than ten 50-kg bags. This difference can also be explained by the fact that livestock farming dominates agricultural activities in the Eastern Cape, where Chris Hani District is located (Chitonge and Ntsebeza 2012), while maize farming dominates agricultural activities in Chongwe and Chibombo.

In Chongwe and Chibombo, if we look at maize production by chiefdom, Mungule chiefdom produces more maize when compared to the other two chiefdoms, as Table 10.11 suggests.

The higher maize volume produced in Mungule is confirmed by agriculture-survey data showing that maize production is, on average, higher in Chibombo District where Mungule chiefdom is located, compared to Chongwe District where the other two chiefdoms are situated (see CSO 2003, 25).

	Mungule	Nkomesha	Bunda Bunda	Total
n (50kg bags)	42	23	20	85
(No. of 50kg bags)	**Percentage of households**			
0	14.3	17.4	10	14.1
1–5	7.1	8.7	0	5.9
5–10	7.1	8.7	15	9.4
10–20	4.7	17.4	40	16.5
20–50	11.9	13	15	12.9
50–100	2.4	13	5	5.8
100+	52.4	21.7	15	35.3

Table 10.11. Maize production by chiefdom (% of HH)
Source: Author, based on data from LURLAP Survey (2014).

Livestock

The other form of land use common in the two case-study areas is livestock, mainly cattle, goats, pigs, and sheep in the case of Chris Hani. The most popular livestock owned by households in Chongwe and Chibombo are poultry (chickens), goats, and cattle, in that order, while for Chris Hani it is cattle followed by sheep, horses, and goats (see Table 10.12, end of chapter).

In terms of cattle, while only 15 percent of households in Chongwe and Chibombo reported owning cattle, the ratio was more than two-thirds of households for Chris Hani District. Similarly, while almost half the households in Chris Hani own sheep, in Chongwe and Chibombo only 1 percent of households reported owning sheep. We also found huge differences in the average number of livestock owned by households in the study areas. For instance, while cattle-owning households in Chongwe and Chibombo own about eight cattle on average, the average in Chris Hani is eighteen. Households in Chris Hani own a higher average number of livestock, except for pigs, compared to Chongwe and Chibombo.

Chibombo & Chongwe Districts					Chris Hani District				
	Inherited	Bought	Chiefs	Total		Inherited	Bought	Chiefs	Total
(n)	23	9	53	**85**	(n)	29	10	49	**88**
Livestock Owned									
HH owning Cattle (%)		33.3	11.3	**15.3**	HH owning Cattle (%)	82.8	60.0	56.0	**66.3**
Cattle (No.)	8	8	8.5	**8.2**	Cattle (No.)	16.6	24.5	13.3	**18.1**
HH owning Goat (%)		33	17	**22.4**	HH owning Sheep (%)	51.7	50	40.8	**47.5**
Goat (No.)	6.7	5	7.2	**6.8**	Sheep (No.)	59.8	65.4	57	**60.7**
HH owning Sheep (%)	0	0	1.9	**1.2**	HH owning Goat (%)	41.4	40	32.7	**38.0**
Sheep (No.)	0	0	8	**8**	Goats (No.)	19.9	34.3	13.6	**22.6**
HH owning Pigs (%)	0	11.1	11.3	**8.2**	HH owning Pigs (%)	13.8	20	16.3	**16.7**
Pig (No.)	0	2	12	**11.3**	Pig (No.)	1.2	3	6	**3.4**
HH owning Poultry (%)	39.2	77.8	62.3	**57.6**	HH owning Horse (%)	24.1	20	16.3	**20.1**
Poultry (No.)					Horse (No.)	1.4	3	4.5	**3.0**
					HH owning Donkey (%)	6.9	0	6.1	**4.3**

Table 10.12. Household Owning Livestock by Mode of Land Access (%)
Source: Author Based on Data form LURLAP and Land and Poverty Surveys.
Note: HH= household

One possible explanation for this difference might, again, be the difference in ecological conditions, with the semiarid conditions in the Eastern Cape being more conducive to livestock farming, compared to conditions in Chongwe and Chibombo. While in both cases local people are traditionally known to practise mixed farming, livestock farming is traditionally more dominant in the Eastern Cape. A national survey conducted by Statistics South Africa found that the Eastern Cape accounted for 43 percent of all the livestock farming units in South Africa, with 55 percent of dairy cattle units, 46 percent of beef cattle, and 48 percent of goat units located in the province (Stats SA 2002, 32–34).

However, like crop production, livestock ownership in both case studies varies greatly among households in both composition and numbers. For instance, in the Chongwe and Chibombo case study, only two households reported owning twenty cattle or more, while in the Chris Hani study several households reported owning more than 100 cattle. Since cattle are an important asset in terms of their contribution to rural livelihoods, differences in the numbers owned can lead to significant differences in income, wealth, and most important, the livelihood strategies that a household pursues.

Earlier studies on livestock production in smallholder and communal areas suggested a very limited use of livestock, mainly for use in boosting status and *lobola*, and little economic value. For instance, a study of Nkandla in KwaZulu-Natal (KZN) reported that the "wide incidence of cattle ownership and the importance attached to stockholding should not be seen as a reflection of their economic value to the community – something which often did not extend beyond their value as draught animals" (Ardington 1986, 50). Delali et al. (2006) make a similar observation, stating that in the past, livestock in communal areas was given symbolic value, mainly that of enhancing social status. Yet, some studies have acknowledged the value and multiple benefits of owning livestock (see Scoones 1992), with several analysts arguing that subsistence-livestock production provides multiple, complex benefits—more than conventional economic models of livestock valuation often assume (Stroebel et al. 2008). For instance, scholars have argued that livestock "ownership and production in communal areas is multipurpose in character, with both cattle and goats serving a greater diversity of functions than in a typical commercial production system" (Shackleton et al. 2001, 586).

The literature on livestock production in communal and smallholder farms establishes a strong relationship between livestock ownership and other agricultural activities such as crop production (Barrett 1992; McAllister 1999). Other studies have reported a similar view suggesting that livestock ownership (especially cattle) is associated with higher crop production (mainly maize, cabbage, and potatoes) (see Makhura et al. 1998). Many factors explain this relationship, including the ploughing power provided by large livestock such as bulls and donkeys and the manure produced from livestock. Additionally, the income generated from livestock is often used to invest in crop production (Scoones 1992). Some studies have observed that income from livestock, crop production, and off-farm activities is used interchangeably, such that income from livestock is invested in crop production, and vice versa (Shackleton et al. 2001, 586). In this sense, cattle and other large livestock constitute a highly strategic asset that influences the type of livelihoods a household constructs.

Physical Household Assets

As noted, a pool of physical assets influences the livelihood strategies that a household pursues. Often, households with more assets, such as land, livestock, skills, political connections, and education, are more likely to construct viable and sustainable livelihoods than are those with a small pool of assets (Chambers and Conway 1991). Although the two case studies profiled different types of assets, households in the Chris Hani area generally tend to hold more assets than do those in Chongwe and Chibombo. For instance, while only about 6 percent reported owning vehicles in the Chongwe and Chibombo area, the ratio in Chris Hani was four times higher (Table 10.13).

However, a higher proportion of households own bicycles in Chongwe and Chibombo, compared to Chris Hani. This may indicate the importance of bicycles in the respective study areas. A bicycle in the Chongwe and Chibombo area was reported to be an important means of transport, particularly for carrying farm produce to the nearby markets and for transporting farm inputs and other household goods. Respondents in the area noted that life is very difficult without a bicycle. Households with bicycles were reported to engage in various kinds of activities, including trading and charcoal production. In the Chris Hani area, on the other hand, a bicycle did not have the same currency since the district is largely accessible by public transport, mainly minibuses (taxis) and open vans.

It is also apparent that households in Chris Hani have more assets, especially in the electronic household-goods category: washing machines, refrigerators, electric stoves, and microwaves. The prevalence of electronic goods in Chris Hani District could be explained by the more common rural electricity supply in South Africa than in Zambia.

Chibombo and Chongwe districts (%)				
	Inherited	**Bought**	**Chiefs**	**Total**
Tractor	0.0	0	3.8	2.4
Plough	21.7	44.4	19	22.3
Irrigation equip.	17.4	22.2	9.3	12.9
Vehicle	9.1	0	5.7	5.9
Bicycle	21.7	88.9	55.7	49.9
Other assets	26.2	1.1	15.1	17.7
(n)	**23**	**9**	**53**	85
Chris Hani district (%)				
Vehicle	24.1	20	24.5	22.9
Washing machine	6.9	30	18.4	18.4
Microwave	27.6	50	30.6	36.1

Radio	89.7	90	85.7	88.5
Water tank	31.0	20	30.6	27.2
Generator	10.3	10	4.1	8.1
Cell phone	93.1	90	81.6	88.2
Electric stove	79.3	80	75.5	78.3
Fridge	58.6	60	57.4	58.7
Furniture	89.7	100	93.9	94.5
Bicycle	10.3	1	12.2	7.8
(n)	29	10	49	88

Table 10.13. Household asset profile
Source: Author, based on data from LURLAP Survey (2014) and Land and Poverty Study (2011

Land and Livelihoods Perspectives

The above analysis reveals that the instrumentalist view is plausible, namely, that mere access to land is not sufficient to improve the livelihoods of the rural poor unless some form of support enables them to convert land into a viable livelihood asset. In both Chongwe and Chibombo and in Chris Hani, many respondents indicated that they have been unable to use their land effectively because they lack resources such as seed, fertiliser, and dipping tanks, all of which can help them produce more from their land. Access to markets was also mentioned as a major problem, especially among households growing crops for sale. In the Chongwe and Chibombo study area in particular, respondents indicated that even when they grow crops, they often find it difficult to access markets, resulting in some crops going to waste or being sold at very low prices. In this context, while people may have access to land and be able to use it, they may not be able to generate a viable livelihood from it. The assumption of the distributionists and the minimalists that mere access to land should be sufficient to reduce poverty is therefore simplistic and less helpful for understanding complex livelihood dynamics in rural areas.

Conclusion

This chapter has examined forms of land use and the accompanying livelihoods of people in the Chongwe and Chibombo areas in Zambia and in Chris Hani District in South Africa. Although these case studies seem incomparable due to the differences in the historical, socioeconomic, and ecological conditions of their areas, analysis of land-use and livelihood strategies reveal numerous interesting similarities as well as differences. This exercise is important for trying to understand the forms of land use and livelihoods across different contexts in Africa in order to comprehend changing land-tenure and livelihood dynamics in rural areas. In both cases, the study focused on households with land under customary tenure.

In terms of land ownership, the study found that the three most common forms of access to land in these areas are inheritance, "buying," and allocation from traditional authorities, mainly village heads and chiefs. In all three study areas, almost half the households received the land they use directly from chiefs, followed by households that inherited land from relatives. Only a small percentage of households, in both case studies, reported "buying" the land they use. A cautionary note must accompany the notion of buying, since land in customary areas is not bought in the same way that it is under a leasehold or freehold arrangement (see chapter 2 above). The buying reported in these cases does not involve the issue of a title deed or any form of documentation, but it is interesting that in all the study areas, "buying" land appears to be one way that people access it.

The other interesting finding in this study is that the size and patterns of land access are similar to cases reported in many parts of Africa where people access customary land (see Ellis 2005; Ellis and Bahiigwa 2003; Ellis and Mode 2003), with the majority of households having access to fewer than two hectares. We also found that in both cases, the most common forms of land use are crop and livestock farming, with crop farming dominating in Chongwe and Chibombo and livestock farming more dominant in Chris Hani. One factor accounting for this difference in land use is the different ecological conditions in the study areas.

It is interesting that lack of inputs hinder productive land use in both study areas. Respondents in all three cases cited the lack of inputs and general support as a major barrier to improving land production and productivity. In addition, most respondents in all the case studies indicated that even if they manage to grow crops and have a good yield, it is always difficult to find a market for their produce, such that some of the produce goes to waste during harvest season. In this regard, the distributionist and the minimalist approaches to the issue of land appear to be inadequate responses to the challenges of rural livelihoods in Africa today. The act of simply giving someone a piece of land does not solve the problem of constructing a viable livelihood in rural areas.

The other interesting finding of this study is the low level of wage employment in both case studies, with only about 3 percent of households reporting employment as their main source of livelihood. This is contrary to claims that rural households predominantly rely on wage employment.

While we found several similarities regarding land use and livelihoods, the study also revealed differences, including the nature of livelihood strategies pursued by different households. One possible factor that accounts for this difference is the presence of a wide-reaching state social-assistance programme in the form of social grants, which provide a significant proportion of rural household income in South Africa but are almost nonexistent in Zambia. The absence of such a programme in Zambia means that rural households have no support and must construct livelihoods using their own capital. However, even in South Africa, which has a massive social-assistance programme for poor households, recipients of these grants still engage in land-based livelihood strategies such as crop and livestock farming to supplement their social-assistance payments. Some even invest the money they receive from social grants in crop and livestock farming.

Thus, while households in the study areas combine several livelihood strategies, including both farm and non-farm activities, the role of land in these households is still central. This role is especially important in the current context, in which the economies of most African countries cannot create real employment opportunities that provide viable alternatives to a growing labour force in both urban and rural areas.

Notes

[1] The LURLAP research study was conducted in 2014 in Zambia. The Zambian case study was conducted in two districts (Chongwe and Chibombo) involving three chiefdoms (Chieftainess Mungule, Chieftainess Nkomesha, and Chief Bunda-Bunda). The project was partially supported by a grant from the Programme for the Enhancement of Research Capacity (PERC) and by a Harry Oppenheimer Institute (HOI) grant from the University of Cape Town. The South African case study was conducted in 2010 and 2011 in the Chris Hani District municipality in the Eastern Cape and was supported by the National Research Foundation (NRF) Chair in Land Reform and Democracy in South Africa, at the University of Cape Town.

[2] The countries include Chile, El Salvador, Colombia, Peru, Paraguay, and Honduras. For Honduras and Paraguay, household panel data were used, while for the rest of the countries cross-sectional household data were used.

[3] Frequently cited examples of successful land reforms include the post-World War II Japanese, and later, the Chinese, South Korean, Taiwanese, and Vietnamese agrarian reforms (Deininger 2003).

[4]According to a CDE report (2005, 14), "In many cases, productive land has stayed unoccupied for a year or more after DLA acquisition. As a result, formerly high-quality land loses much of its value and productive potential."
[5] The total land mass area of South Africa is about 122 million hectares, and of this, 75 percent is suitable only for livestock production. Approximately 12 percent of the total is categorised as arable land, and only 2 percent is classified as prime agricultural land (DAFF 2010).
[6] Officials at the Ministry of Lands maintain that the size of customary land has not changed because even after customary land is converted into leasehold, the category does not change; it still remains customary land. However, no policy document states this, and some lawyers argue that this is merely a technical tactic designed to pacify chiefs who are agitating that customary land is being depleted.
[7] The details of the methods for the Zambian case studies are provided in chapter one.
[8] In a national sample by the Ministry of Agriculture and Cooperative (MACO)/Central Statistics Office (CSO), a post-harvest survey conducted in 2011 shows similar patterns of landholding among smallholder and semi-subsistence farmers (MACO/CSO 2011).
[9] The estimated contribution of agriculture in this case included only sales of farm produce, which may have the effect of significantly underestimating the actual value obtained from agriculture in cases where more of the farm's produce is consumed at home.
[10] The data for Chris Hani were collected using a full multitopic household survey, which collected detailed information on various aspects of livelihoods, including income and expenditure. In contrast, the survey for Chongwe and Chibombo was short and focused mainly on data on customary land conversion.
[11] Unfortunately, there are no accurate data to estimate the production per hectare in Chongwe, Chibombo, and Chris Hani.

References

Adams, M. 2003. *Land Tenure Policy and Practice in Zambia: Issues Relating to the Development of the Agricultural Sector.* Zambia: Mokoro Ltd. (for DfID).

African Union, African Development Bank, Economic Commission for Africa. 2010. *Framework and Guidelines on Land Policy in Africa.* Addis Ababa: AU-AfDB-ECA.

Akuffo, K. 2009. "The conception of land ownership in African customary law and its implications for development." RADIC 17 (2009). DOI: 10.3366/E0954889009000280.

Alliance for a Green Revolution in Africa. 2013. *Africa Agriculture Status Report: Focusing on Staple Crops.* Nairobi: AGRA.

Anseeuw, W., and N. Mathebula. 2008. "Evaluating land reform's contribution to South Africa's pro-poor growth pattern." Paper presented at the TIPS Annual Forum, n.d. Accessed September 18, 2012. www.tips.org.za/publication/evaluating-land-reforms-contribution-south-africas-pro-poor-growth-pattern.

Ardington, E. 1986. Nkandla Revisited: A Longitudinal Study of the Strategies Adopted to Alleviate Poverty in a Rural Community. Centre for Social and Development Studies, Rural-Urban Studies Working Paper No. 16, University of Natal.

Baiphethi, N., and P. Jacobs. 2009. "The contribution of subsistence farming to food security in South Africa." *Agrekon* 48: 4, 459–82.

Barrett, J. C. 1992. The Economic Role of Cattle in Communal Farming Systems in Zimbabwe. Overseas Development Institute (ODI) Pastoral Development Network, Working Paper No. 32b. London: ODI.

Bassett, T. 1993. "Introduction: The land question and agricultural transformation in sub-Saharan Africa." In *Land in African Agrarian Systems,* edited by T. Bassett and T. J. Crummey, 5–18. Madison: University of Wisconsin Press.

Bradstock, A. 2006. "Land reform and livelihoods in South Africa's Northern Cape province." *Land Use Policy* 23: 247–59.

Bruce, J. W. 1986. Land Tenure Issues in Project Design and Strategies for Agricultural Development in Sub-Saharan Africa. Madison: Land Tenure Centre, University of Wisconsin.

Bryceson, D. F. 1999. "African rural labour, income diversification and livelihood approaches: A long-term development perspective." *Review of African Political Economy* 26: 80, 171–89.

—. 2002. "The scramble in Africa: Reorienting rural livelihoods." *World Development* 30: 5, 725–39.

—. 2009. "Sub-Saharan Africa's vanishing peasantry and the spectre of global food crisis." Accessed September 12, 2012. http://monthlyreview.org/2009/07/01/sub-saharan-africas-vanishing-peasantries-and-the-specter-of-a-global-food-crisis.

Butler, J., R. Rotberg, and J. Adams. 1978. *The Black Homelands of South Africa: The Political and Economic Development of Boputhaswana and KwaZulu.* Berkeley: University of California Press.

Carney, D., M. Drinkwater, T. Rusinow, K. Neefjes, S. Wanmali, and N. Singh. 1999. "Livelihood approaches compared." London: Department for International Development.

Carter, Mi., and J. D. May. 1999. "Poverty, Livelihood and Class in Rural South Africa." *World Development* 1: 1–20.

Central Statistical Office. 2003. 2000 Population Census: Agriculture Analytical Report. Lusaka: CSO.

—. 2012. 2010 Census of Population and Housing: National Descriptive Tables. Lusaka: CSO.

Chachage, Chambi. 2011. "Why land matters to Africans regardless of agriculture." Accessed August 12, 2014. http://udadisi.blogspot.com/2011/01/why-land-matters-to-africans-regardless.html.

Chambers, R., and G. Conway. 1991. Sustainable Rural Livelihoods: Practical Concepts for the 21st Century. Institute of Development Studies (IDS) Working Paper No. 296. Brighton: University of Sussex.

Chimhowu, A. 2006. Tinkering on the Fringes? Redistributive Land Reforms and Chronic Poverty in Southern Africa. Chronic Poverty Research Centre Working Paper No. 58. Manchester: Chronic Poverty Research Centre.

Chitonge, H. 2012a. "Land resource ownership and use in Africa of the Labour Reserves (Southern African Development Community)." In *Land Relations Policy in African Development Community,* edited by Ben Chigara, 57–88. London: Routledge.

—. 2012b. "Social protection challenges in sub-Saharan Africa: Rethinking regimes and commitments." *African Studies* 17: 3, 1–23.

—. 2013. "Land use and rural livelihood in South Africa: Emerging evidence from the eastern Cape." *Agrarian South: Journal of Political Economy* 2: 1, 1–40.

—. 2015. "Customary land in Zambia at cross-roads: Two decades of contested land reform." *SADC Law Journal* 4: 1, 45–67.

Chitonge, H., and L. Ntsebeza. 2012. "Land reform and rural livelihood in South Africa: Does access to land matter?" *Review of Agrarian Studies* 2: 1, 87–112.

Claassens, A. 2014. “Law, land and custom, 1913–2014. What is at stake today?” In *Land Divided, Land Restored: Land Reform in South Africa for the 21st Century,* edited by S. Walker and B. Cousins, 68–84. Johannesburg: Jacana Media.

Collier, P. 2008. “The politics of hunger: How illusion and greed fan the food crisis.” *Foreign Affairs* 87: 6, 67–79.

Cotula, L., S. Vermeulen, R. Leonard, and J. Keeley. 2009. *Land Grab or Development Opportunity? Agricultural Investment and International Land Deals in Africa.* London/Rome: IIED/FAO/IFAD.

Cox, M., M. Paul, A. Harrera, P. Mathieu, D. Paulmer, and P. Groppo. 2003. *Land Reform, Land Settlement and Cooperatives.* Rome: FAO. Accessed September 4, 2008.
www.fao.org/docrep/006/y5026e/y5026e00.htm.

Deininger, K. 2003. *Land Policies for Growth and Poverty Reduction.* New York: Oxford University Press.

de Janvry, A., and E. Sadoulet. 2002. “Access to land and land policy reforms: Policy brief.” Helsinki: United Nations University/ Institute for Development Economics Research.

Delali, B., K. Dovie, C. M. Shackleton, and E. T. F Witkowski. 2006. “Valuation of communal area livestock benefits, rural livelihoods and related policy issues.” *Land Use Policy* 23: 260–71.

Department for International Development. 2002. *Better Livelihoods for the Poor People: The Role of Land Policy.* London: DfID.

Department of Agriculture, Food, and Fisheries. 2010. Abstract of Agricultural Statistics. Pretoria: DAFF.

Department of Rural Development and Land Reform. 2013. “Policy Framework for the Recapitalisation and Development Programme (RECAP) of the Department of Rural Development and Land Reform.”
http://www.ruraldevelopment.gov.za/legislation-and-policies/file/2053.

D’Haese, M., and Guido Van Huylenbroeck. 2005. “The rise of supermarkets and changing expenditure patterns of poor rural households. Case study in Transkei area, South Africa.” *Food Policy* 30: 97–113.

Diaz-Chavez, R., S. Mutimba, S. Rodriguez-Sanchez, and M. Nguer. 2010. Mapping Bioenergy in Africa: A Report Prepared on Behalf of the Forum for Agricultural Research in Africa (FARA). Ghana: FARA.

Ellis, F. 2005. “Small-farms, livelihood diversification and rural-urban transformation: Strategic issues in sub-Saharan Africa.” Paper prepared for the research workshop on The Future of Small Farms, organised by the International Food Policy Research Institute (IFRI), Overseas Development Institute (ODI), June 26–29, Kent, United Kingdom.

Ellis, F., and G. Bahiigwa. 2003. "Livelihoods and rural poverty reduction in Uganda." *World Development* 31: 6, 997–1013.

Ellis, F., and N. Mode. 2003. "Livelihoods and rural poverty reduction in Tanzania." *World Development* 31: 8, 1367–84.

Finan, F., E. Sadoulet, and A. de Janvry. 2005. "Measuring the poverty reduction potential of land in rural Mexico." *Journal of Development Economics* 77: 27–51.

Food and Agriculture Organisation. 2006. "Agrarian reforms, social justice and sustainable development." Paper presented at the International Conference of Agrarian Reforms and Rural Development, March 7–10, Porto Alegere, Brazil.

Food Security Research Project. 2010. The Status of Customary Land and How it Affects the Rights of Indigenous Local Communities. Submission to the Committee on Agriculture and Land Study. Lusaka: FSRP.

Griffin, K., A. R. Khan, and A. Ickowitz. 2002. "Poverty and the distribution of land." *Journal of Agrarian Change* 2: 3, 297–330.

Hendricks, F. 1990. *The Pillars of Apartheid: Land Tenure, Rural Planning and Chieftaincy.* Uppsala: Studia Sociologica Upsaliensa.

Hichaambwa, M., and S. T. Jayne. 2014. Poverty Reduction Potential of Increasing Smallholder Access to Land. Indaba Agricultural Policy Research Institute (IAPRI) Working Paper No. 83. Lusaka: IAPRI.

International Labour Organisation. 2010. *Extending Social Security to All: A Guide Through Challenges and Options.* Geneva: International Labour Office.

Jacobs, P., M. Aliber, T. Hart, and M. O'Donovan. 2008. Review of Rural Development: 15 Year Review of Economic and Social Sector Programme. Human Science Research Council Research Paper. Accessed March 12, 2011. http://www.hsrc.ac.za/Document-3218.phtml.

Jayne, T. S., N. Mason, W. Blake, A. Shipekesa, A. Chapota, and C. Kabaghe. 2011. "Mountains of maize, persistent poverty." Food Security Research Project (FSRP), Zambia, Policy Synthesis, no. 48. Accessed May 29, 2013. http://fsg.afre.msu.edu/zambia/ps_48.pdf.

Jayne, T. S., D. Mather, and E. Mghenyi. 2010. "Principal challenges confronting smallholder agriculture in sub-Saharan Africa." *World Development* 38: 10, 1384–98.

Krantz, L. 2001. "The sustainable livelihood approach to poverty reduction: An introduction." Upsala: Division for Policy and Social Economic Analysis, Swedish International Development Agency (SIDA).

Land Use and Rural Livelihood in Africa Project. 2014. Interview transcripts.

Land Use and Rural Livelihood in Africa Project (LURLAP, Focus Group Discussions). 2014. Focus Group Discussion transcripts.

Land Use and Rural Livelihood in Africa Project (LURLAP). 2014. Survey data.

Land and Poverty Study. 2011. Survey data.

Leahy, S. 2011. "Corrupt global food system, farmland is the new gold." *All Africa Global Media,* January 13. Accessed April 13, 2011. www.ipsnews.net/2011/01/in-corrupt-global-food-system-farmland-is-the-new-gold.

Lipton, M. 1996. "Introduction." In *Land, Labour and Livelihoods in Rural South Africa,* edited by M. Lipton, M. de Klerk, and M. Lipton, v–xxi. Durban: Indicator Press.

López, R., and A. Valdés. 2000. "Fighting rural poverty in Latin America: New evidence of the effects of education, demographics and access to land." *Journal of Agrarian Change* 2: 3, 279–330.

Mafeje, A. 2003. The Agrarian Question: Access to Land and Peasant Response in Sub-Saharan Africa. Civil Society and Social Movement Programme, Paper No. 6, United Nations Research Institute for Social Development. Geneva: UNRISD.

Makhura, M., F. Goode, and G. K. Cotzee. 1998. "A cluster analysis of commercialisation of farmers in developing rural areas of South Africa." *Development Southern Africa* 15: 3, 429–48.

Makunike, C. 2009. "Large-scale agricultural investment in Africa: Points to ponder." In *Land Grab: The Race for The World's Farmland,* edited by M. Kugelma and S. Levenstein, 85–93. Washington DC: Woodrow Wilson International Centre for Scholars.

Mason, N. M., and T. S. Jayne. 2009. Staple Food Consumption Patterns in Urban Zambia: Results from the 2007/08 Urban Consumption Survey. Lusaka: Food Security Research Project/Ministry of Agriculture and Cooperative.

May, J. 2000. "The structure and composition of rural poverty and livelihoods in South Africa." In *At the Crossroads: Land and Agrarian Reform in South Africa into the 20th Century,* edited by B. Cousins, 21–34. Cape Town: Programme for Land and Agrarian Studies.

McAllister, P. 1999. Agriculture and Cooperative Labour in Shixini, Transkei, South Africa. ASC Working Paper No. 33. Grahamston.

Mecarini, L. 2000. "A note on landholding and fertility in rural South Africa." *Genus* 56: 3/4, 109–19.

Ministry of Agriculture and Cooperatives and Central Statistical Office. 2011. 2010/2011 Crop Forecast Survey Report. Lusaka: MACO/CSO.

Mudenda M. M. 2006. "The challenges of customary land tenure in Zambia." Paper presented at the XXIII FIG Congress, October 8–13, Munich, Germany.

National Planning Commission. 2011. National Development Plan: Vision 2030. Accessed October 17, 2012. www.npconline.co.za/medialib/downloads/home/NPC%20National%20Development%20Plan%20Vision%202030%20-lo-res.pdf.

Neves, D., and A. du Toit. 2013. "Rural livelihoods in South Africa: Complexity, vulnerability and differentiation." *Journal of Agrarian Change* 13: 1, 93–115.

Ntsebeza, L. 1998. Land Tenure Reform, Traditional Authorities and Rural Local Government in Post-Apartheid South Africa: Case Studies from the Eastern Cape. Programme for Land and Agrarian Studies (PLAS), Research Report No. 3. Cape Town: University of the Western Cape.

—. 2006. *Democracy Compromised: Chiefs and the Politics of Land in South Africa.* Pretoria: HSRC Press.

Parliamentary Committee on Lands, Environment and Tourism. 2013. Report of the Committee on Lands, Environment and Tourism for the Second Session of the Eleventh National Assembly. Appointed September 27, 2012. Lusaka: Zambia National Assembly.

Platteau, J. P. 1996. "The evolutionary theory of land rights as applied to sub-Saharan Africa: A critical assessment." *Development and Change* 27: 1, 29–86.

Republic of Zambia. 2006. Draft Land Administration and Management Policy. Lusaka: Ministry of Lands.

Rigg, J. 2006. "Land, farming, livelihoods, and poverty: Rethinking the links in the rural South." *World Development* 34: 1, 180–202.

Scoones, I. 1992. "The economic value of livestock in communal areas of southern Zimbabwe." *Agricultural Systems* 39: 339–59.

—. 1998. Sustainable Rural Livelihoods: A Framework for Analysis. Institute of Development Studies (IDS) Working Paper No. 72. Brighton: University of Sussex.

Shackleton, C., S. Shackleton, and B. Cousins. 2001. "The role of land-based strategies in rural livelihoods: The contribution of arable production, animal husbandry and natural resource harvesting in communal areas in South Africa." *Development Southern Africa* 18: 5, 581–602.

Shipton, P., and M. Goheen. 1992. "Understanding African land-holding: Power and meaning." *Journal of International African Institute* 62: 3, 307–25.

Sitko, N., and T. S. Jayne. 2014. "Structural dynamism or elite land capture? A case study of emergent farm growth in Zambia." *Food Policy* 48: 194–202.

South African Institute of Race Relations. 2012. South Africa Survey 2010–11. Accessed June 12, 2012. www.sairr.org.za/services/publications/south-africa-survey.

Statistics South Africa. 1999. Rural Survey. Statistical Release P0360. Pretoria: Stats SA. www.statssa.org.

—. 2002. Report on the Survey of Large and Small Scale Agriculture. Pretoria: Stats SA.

Stroebel, A., F. J. Swanepoel, N. D. Nthakheni, A. E. Nesamvuni, and G. Taylor. 2008. "Benefits obtained from cattle by smallholder farmers: A case study of Limpopo province, South Africa." *Australian Journal of Experimental Agriculture* 48: 7, 825–28.

United Nations Development Programme. 2014. *Sustaining Human Progress: Reducing Vulnerability and Building Resilience.* New York: UNDP.

USAID. 2010. "Property rights and resource governance: Zambia country profile." Accessed August 11, 2011. www.usaid.org.

van den Brink, R., G. S. Thomas, and H. Binswanger-Mkhize. 2009. "Land reform in South Africa: Additional data and comments." In *Agricultural Land Redistribution: Towards a Greater Consensus,* edited by H. Binswanger-Mkhize, C. Bourguignon, and R. van den Brink. Washington DC: World Bank, 201–14.

Vink, N., and J. van Rooyen. 2009. The Economic Performance of Agriculture in South Africa Since 1994: Implications for Food Security. Development Bank of Southern Africa, Development Planning Division Working Paper No. 17. Johannesburg: DBSA.

Walker, S., and B. Cousins. 2014. "Introduction." In *Land Divided, Land Restored: Land Reform in South Africa for the 21st Century,* edited by S. Walker and B. Cousins, 1–26. Johannesburg: Jacana Media.

World Development Report. 2001. *World Development Report 2000/01: Attacking Poverty.* New York: Oxford University Press for the World Bank.

INDEX